FRANCO

Books by Alan Lloyd

FRANCO

Alan Lloyd

Doubleday & Company, Inc., Garden City, New York, 1969

Grateful acknowledgment is made to the following for permission to reprint material copyrighted or controlled by them:

Curtis Brown, Ltd., London, for excerpts from *Ambassador on a Special Mission* by Viscount Templewood.

Mrs. Carlton Hayes, for excerpts from *Wartime Mission In Spain* by Carlton Hayes.

To Spanish "moderates" everywhere

Contents

1. The Fateful Rendezvous

On the evening of July 5, 1936, a journalist named Luis Bolin, London correspondent of Madrid's Monarchist newspaper *ABC*, received an extraordinary phone call from Biarritz. The caller, the Marqués de Luca de Tena, the paper's publisher and an active conspirator against his country's Republican government, was brisk with instructions.

From a Spaniard who worked at Kleinwort's, the City bankers, Bolin was to draw £2000 with which he was to charter a British aircraft for a flight to Casablanca, with a view to a further trip between Africa and the Canary Islands. In the event of the pilot reaching the Canaries, a certain Dr. Gabarda was to be contacted, given the unlikely message: *"Galicia saluda a Francia"* ("Galicia salutes France") and told that the plane had arrived.

Two aspects of the assignment were impressed upon the journalist: on no account should the Spanish authorities have reason to connect the flight with antigovernment activity, nor was there any time to be wasted. "Act quickly," ordered the Marqués. "Good luck!"

Bolin concluded, in his astonishment, that he would need it.

Knowing little about aircraft, or how to hire them, his first move was to seek the advice of a friend, Juan de la Cierva, who had rooms in London's Half Moon Street. Cierva, inventor of the autogiro and the godfather of Bolin's young daughter, provided the name of a charter company at Croydon and the suggestion that the plane should carry a couple of blondes and an Englishman to give the enterprise the appearance of a holiday escapade.

From an English publisher and writer, Douglas Jerrold, Bolin next sought help in recruiting such passengers.

"I'm in a fix," he confided over a luncheon of roast lamb and claret at Simpson's. "I need two blondes and a trustworthy fellow to fly with me next Friday to an unknown destination on the west coast of Africa . . . can't say more."

Jerrold left the table, made a phone call, returned. A man named Hugh Pollard would see them that afternoon. His qualifications—Jerrold described him as a retired Army major, a hunting man, an expert on fire arms and "a regular contributor to *Country Life*"—struck Bolin as about right. Moreover, Pollard's daughter Diana, and a friend, Dorothy Watson, might be persuaded to make up the party.

By nightfall, all three had agreed. If the Misses Pollard and Watson, wholesomely English county in type, were not exactly the blonde adventuresses Cierva had envisaged, both were fair and freshly attractive. For them, a free air flight to Casablanca and beyond was an exciting offer. "I did not know what was happening when we set out," the major's daughter said later.

Pollard was not inclined, it seems, to ask questions. A tweedy, thickset man of heavy Anglo-Saxon imperturbability, he poured drinks in the paneled room of his country house in Sussex, a deal was discussed and he told Bolin, "I'm on."

On the morning of July 11, as a sporty conglomeration of cars and motorcycles converged on the north-of-London airport at Hatfield for the start of the King's Cup Air Race, a small group of people crossed the less festive airfield of Croydon, south of the capital, and clambered aboard a twin-engined de Havilland Rapide seven-seater. The flight of the Rapide was to beat all entries in the King's Cup for incident.

After a brief stop at Bordeaux, where the radio operator quickly revealed a strong taste for liquor, the small passenger biplane crossed the north coast of Spain flying so high, on Bolin's instructions, that the wings took on ice and the pilot had trouble maintaining speed. When he dived the machine through the clouds into warmer air, it was to discover himself lost over the sprawling plains of Castile.

With the radio operator of dubious assistance, and the female passengers miserably airsick, the Rapide buzzed vainly over the mesa in search of some identifiable feature, eventually returning to France, where it landed at Biarritz. Chastened, the travelers refreshed themselves and started again.

This time, the plane ran short of fuel over Portugal and they were forced to land at a military airfield where the Rapide was promptly impounded and its occupants placed in arrest. After an unsuccessful attempt to bribe his way out of difficulty, Bolin was able to appeal to the sympathy of a Portuguese lieutenant, and having twice come near to disaster, the expedition proceeded, via Lisbon, to Casablanca.

Here, Pollard, who had taken objection to the radio operator's behavior, recommended that they should "pack him home" on a tramp steamer. "Bebb [the pilot] will find the islands all right without that bastard's help," said the major.

At this stage, Bolin, mindful of his chief's warning and fearful lest his own presence on the plane might arouse the suspicions of the Canary authorities, decided that the Rapide should continue with only the Britons aboard. Accordingly, on July 15, the machine took off for Las Palmas, Grand Canary, the single town in the archipelago with a suitable airport, carrying one retired English Army officer, two young ladies from rural Sussex, and a freckle-faced bachelor, Cecil Bebb, their pilot.

Pollard, who had the address of Dr. Gabarda in his notebook, together with a phonetic spelling of the words "*Galicia saluda a Francia,*" prepared to carry out his promise to Bolín that he would pass on the mysterious message.

At seven-thirty next morning, the major presented himself at Gabarda's office, announcing that he wished to consult the doctor about his daughter's health. When a somewhat sleepy-eyed physician appeared, Pollard straightened his back, carefully pronounced "Galeethea salootha ah Franthea" and confided earnestly that the airplane was at Las Palmas.

The response took him aback.

"If your daughter is ill," snapped the doctor testily, "tell me the symptoms. Otherwise, kindly leave me to my work."

With some dignity, Pollard replied that while he might be at a loss to explain the message, he was not of the impression that it was unimportant. If anyone wished to see him, he would be at his hotel. Meanwhile, Bebb, who had even less idea what was going on than the major, had been approached and questioned by a number of suspicious-looking Spaniards. On the afternoon of the seventeenth, another man paid him a visit.

"After greeting me in a friendly manner," recalled the pilot afterward, "he begged me to follow him out to the terrace, where, making sure that no one was in the vicinity, he read to me from a slip of paper which carried the following order, 'Lead him to a certain person.'" At the same time, the stranger gave Bebb the torn half of a Spanish playing card. The certain person, it seemed, would identify himself by the other half of the playing card.

At four next morning, Bebb was awakened, told to dress and ushered to a different room. There he waited until 11:55, when he was warned to be ready to go. At midday, he was hurried to a car and whisked at top speed toward the airport through streets dominated by clusters of armed policemen and soldiers. He found the plane fueled and ready for take-off.

"And the passengers?" Bebb asked.

His attention was directed to a stocky figure in a dark suit and felt hat, approaching on foot across the airfield. The man had a bouncy stride, a swarthy complexion and wore the brim of his hat well forward on a round, not unbenign-looking face. In his left hand was a small valise.

"Here comes your passenger," someone exclaimed.

There was no further mention of playing cards. The man with the valise paused a moment to take in the flat expanse of the runway, the sea beyond and the clear sky, then extended to the pilot a well-manicured right hand. A plain gold ring flashed on the third finger.

"*Soy el General Franco,*" the man said. ("I am General Franco.")

That year of evil portents, 1936, had opened forebodingly. In January, two months before Adolf Hitler seized the Rhineland for Europe's "New Order," the old heads of state congregated in London for a fittingly somber requiem. On the twenty-eighth of the month, six reigning monarchs, including Carol of Rumania and Boris of Bulgaria, together with Prince Paul, the senior regent of Yugoslavia, Prince Starhemberg, vice-chancellor of Austria, and the Prince of Piedmont, heir to the throne of Italy, followed the coffin of Britain's King George V to its resting place. Symbolically, the sky was overcast. Among the unprecedented crowds assembled for the occasion, there were many who sensed the impending turbulence.

In Germany, Hitler's blackshirts were goose-stepping with mounting arrogance. Mussolini's legions were marching. Stalin nurtured his growing power to the east. Everywhere, it seemed, democratic government was threatened. Where next, people wondered, would dictatorship show its face.

One at least who appeared blandly unworried was Don Francisco Franco y Bahamonde, the army member of the Spanish mission to the royal funeral. "A little smiling man with a good-humored mouth and a dreamer's eyes," a newspaperman described him later. At the time, he passed without description. Five feet three inches tall, and dwarfed by most of the officers in the procession—especially the brawny Marshal Mikhail Tukhachevski of the Soviet Union, who walked directly ahead of him—Franco could scarcely have attracted less attention.

As a fellow-countryman observed drily afterward: for a man renowned among his colleagues for both ambition and reticence, Franquito (Little Franco) had pulled off the ultimate "double." In a single historic occasion, he had appeared before the largest audience of his career—and emerged anonymous.

For Franco, the chance to see something of England, expenses paid, with the promise of a stop at Paris on the way back, provided a pleasant break from his normal duties, and a relief from the tortured themes of the coming Spanish elections. Though one of an army traditionally involved in politics, Franco was cannily withdrawn on the subject. At forty-three, he did not own his promotion among numerous generals—he was presently Chief of Staff at the Spanish War Office—to the indiscreet parading of politics in public.

Spain, that bleak day in Great Britain, occupied few thoughts, her wrangling leaders outshone by the great names of Europe, her sunshine a mere legend in the drizzle now tarnishing the boots of crown princes and moistening the tall collar of President Albert Lebrun of France. Of all nations, it hardly seemed possible that one rid a mere five years of a disastrous history of despots could be ripe for the power of yet another dictator.

Certainly her Secretary for Foreign Affairs, Joaquin Urzaiz, shuffling uncomfortably behind the British gun carriage, did not visualize any member of his mission as a budding Primo de Rivera. Was not the Catholic Party Leader, Gil Robles, dominating the election campaigning at home? Were not the pundits tipping a conservative alliance to form the next government? With the army behind it, would not the extremists of both sides be brought to order and Spain's youthful democracy steered to calmer waters?

Time, above all things, was what the system needed, and if anything could have pleaded the case for patience, it was perhaps the quiet solidarity of the great crowds now spontaneously gathered around the shrine of a democratic government in Westminster. To a professional soldier and a Spaniard, their unity and orderliness could only be envied. "I liked England," said Franco later. "I wanted to stay longer to learn the language and play golf."

At the Spanish Embassy in Paris, an eminent Republican, Dr. Gregorio Marañón, met the general on his way home from the funeral. Physician, intellectual and ardent democrat, Marañón was well aware that many of Spain's army officers could prove untrustworthy in a crisis, and that some were actually plotting revolution. He did not, however, count Franco among them, and the two strolled affably together by the Seine.

Franco, Marañón discerned, was an unusual type of soldier, combining many of the traditional prejudices of the officer caste with the independent mind of one who had risen to high rank very quickly. On his record, he was primarily a professional and careerist. Manuel Azaña, the Republican leader whose army reforms on the fall of the monarchy and the dictatorship had infuriated military circles in Spain, had not classified the little general as a candidate for sacking. "Franco," Azaña had said, "is above all a soldier. We can count on his integrity."

Since then, that opinion had been questioned, especially from the Left. But Marañón found his fellow visitor to Paris sincere. When Franco denied any ties with conspiracy, the doctor believed him. Three weeks later, loyalties were put to the crucial test.

Instead of the electoral triumph expected by the Right, the vote as a whole proved almost equally divided, the system

producing a parliamentary majority for the Left—the so-called
Popular Front, an uneasy alliance of Republicans, Socialists,
Catalan Separatists and others, together with the relatively
small party of Spanish Communists.

If a right-of-Center Republic had offended traditionalists, a
Leftist Republic seemed doubly odious, and many officers now
openly talked of insurrection. In Lisbon, the exiled leader of
an earlier and unsuccessful rising, General José Sanjurjo,
known as "The Lion of the Rif" for his popular exploits in
Morocco, counted the days when he might return to head a
triumphant revolution.

Excitement in the army was high. In Alicante, one impatient
captain ordered his men straight into the streets and was shot
by a corporal for his temerity. Franco, by contrast, maintained
his composure. Even when the inevitable reshuffle at the War
Office resulted in his rustication to Tenerife to command the
army in the Canary Islands, his tranquillity did little to inspire
the conspirators.

Before leaving to take up the appointment, he called to pay
his respects to Alcalá Zamora, the President, and Azaña, now
back as Prime Minister in a still moderate cabinet. They found
the general's tone patriotic. Might he not be "of greater service
to the army and the peace of the country" in Madrid, asked
Franco, than sampling the delights of the Canaries? Could
they be sure that the War Office, as reconstituted, was com-
petent to deal with disturbances, particularly of the extreme
Left?

"Don't worry, General. Don't worry," said the President.
After all, as Azaña commented pointedly, recent rebellions
had brought nothing but disaster to their participants.

"I have no fear of insurrections," declared the Prime Minister.

Late that February, the Franco ménage departed for Tenerife where it quickly became evident to island society that the
general's wife, Carmen, a handsome dark-haired woman with

the physical grandeur lacking in her husband, was by temperament and breeding well-suited to mistress their gracious official
residence between the Teide and the warm sea. Their daughter, aged nine, was lively and charming.

As for the former Chief of Staff, an officer whose past might
have overawed a small community, Tenerife discovered him
by no means obtrusive.

Temperate by habit—he neither smoked nor drank—and
socially retiring, the general confined himself mostly to the
company of a few select aides, appearing concerned, as much
as with anything, over his golfing handicap. He also took up
English, another impulse dating from his visit to London.

His tutor, a Mrs. Dora Leonard de Alonso, was enchanted
by his diligence.

"Franco earned my wholehearted admiration and affection,"
she said. "He used to take his lessons three times a week, nine-
thirty to ten-thirty. He wrote two exercises for 'homework'
three times a week. Five out of six of his exercises were about
golf . . ."

While Franco brushed up his driving and putting, an uglier
pastime was engaged between extremists of the Right and Left
in Spain. Impatient with the Parliamentary impasse, hotheads
of both wings were resorting to violence. On April 14, the anniversary of the Republic, a bomb was thrown during a parade
in Madrid, and a lieutenant of the Civil Guard shot dead in
the ensuing confusion by an officer of the Guardia de Assalto,
the storm police of the government.

The funeral of the dead man, attended by excited crowds,
provided a marked contrast in public behavior to that in London earlier. As the cortège passed through the city, a running
battle broke out between Fascist demonstrators and their Left-
wing enemies. Bullets sprayed the streets. Guards charged
into the crowds. The day produced many more bodies than
expected.

Rumors of revolution now abounded, Bolsheviks, Fascists, Socialists, Monarchists, and Militarists being variously cited as the plotters. Street fights, assassinations, and arson became regular, strikes were called to intimidate Parliament and the Assembly itself was a tumult of passions.

While the moderate and broadly liberal clique which formed the government clung fondly to its faith in the efficacy of reason, the surrounding benches gave way to uncontrolled emotion. Right charged Left with betraying the nation to Moscow; Left denounced Right for conspiring, it was alleged, with the bosses of Rome and Berlin. Threats, abuse, and even blows in the corridors, added to the general disrepute of the Cortes.

"Let us not deceive ourselves," declared Gil Robles in a notable speech of June 16; "a country can live as a Monarchy or as a Republic, with a Parliamentary or a Presidential system, under Communism or Fascism. It cannot live in anarchy! Alas, Spain is today in such a condition. We are present at the funeral of democracy."

But if Señor Gil Robles caused a flurry in the Cortes, he raised few eyebrows outside Spain. While the leader of the Catholic Party spoke of 269 political murders since the Spanish elections of February, London turned unconcernedly to the first day of Ascot, where Lord Astor's colt Rhodes Scholar trounced the Derby winner, Mahmoud, by five lengths in the St. James's Palace Stakes.

While the Cortes was reminded of 113 major strikes in four months, Paris buzzed with gossip of its popular department stores and single-price bazaars, whose counter girls were campaigning for bigger pay packets. While Gil Robles called the government of Spain to account for 160 church burnings and the widespread persecution and molestation of clerics, Berlin discussed the nice point of whether or not Herr Hitler, just back from a cruise in northern waters, had in fact reviewed the German fleet off Skagen, Denmark.

United States news editors, it was true, had run some disturbing stories from Madrid, but Washington had been advised to discount them by its ambassador in Spain, Claude G. Bowers. "You are all wrong," Bowers wrote his cousin, Mrs. Alice Wolverton of New York, regarding the Spanish situation that month. "In the three years I have been here there has not been anything in all Spain as serious as the elevator strike in New York City.

"I have entire faith in Spain's future. Reports of conditions in Spain are misrepresentations, and mostly pure propaganda inspired by the old regime that hates democracies and republics."

Azaña dismissed the disorders with greater realism. "Violence," he told an American reporter with a shrug, "is deeply enshrined in the Spanish people. It is too soon to expect Spaniards to stop shooting each other."

Clearly, the military plotters thought similarly. As "Director" of the officers' conspiracy in Spain itself, General Emilio Mola, a man of strong totalitarian leanings, had already issued instructions concerning the initial rising, upon which Sanjurjo, the Lion of the Rif, was to fly in from Lisbon to head a military junta. To succeed quickly, the movement would have to be, as Mola put it, "very violent," administering "exemplary punishments" to those of unsympathetic persuasion.

Sanjurjo, returning earlier from the Winter Olympics in Germany with the tacit blessing of the regime there, had been told that the majority of Spain's officer cadre was for the rebellion. The chief government "trusties" were well known and marked. The one outstanding problem of individual loyalty centered on the enigmatic General Franco. Franco, warned the cynics, was a devoted supporter of Franco. Sanjurjo affected complacency. "With or without Franquito, we shall save Spain," he predicted.

In the Canaries, "Franquito" kept his own counsel, infuriatingly remote, as it seemed, from the passions and fears of lesser mortals. Spies and informers of all shades of political opinion were said to be watching for a hint of his intentions. If so, the news they gleaned was meager. The Commandante-General went swimming with his daughter, Maria del Carmen. The Commandante-General attended the flower festival in the Orotava Valley. The Commandante-General went to his office, and later played eighteen holes of golf. At the War Office, they spoke of "Franco's holiday" and wondered if the little general had not succumbed to the lassitude of island life.

Toward the height of summer, a letter arrived for the *Exelentisimo Señor War Minister* expressing, among other things, loyal greetings from Franco in Tenerife and dwelling affectionately on the good faith of his fellow officers.

"Those who paint the army as hostile to the Republic," wrote Franco reproachfully, "are not telling the truth; those who accuse the army of conspiracies are, in their turbid passions, deceiving you; those who misrepresent the uneasiness, the dignity and the patriotism of the army, making it appear the symbol of conspiracy and dissatisfaction, are rendering a miserable service to their country." The letter was signed *Your devoted subordinate.*

On July 16, the Ministry was alerted by a phone call from the Canaries. It turned out to be a request that General Franco might travel from Tenerife to Las Palmas, in the neighboring island of Grand Canary, to attend the funeral of its late commander, General Balmes. Balmes, seemingly more agitated than Franco by the dangers of the moment, had gone out to practice with a revolver and had accidentally shot himself. The Under Secretary for War authorized Franco's movement.

At twelve-thirty that tranquil, starlit night, the Commandante-General, clutching a small valise containing a black suit, embarked with his wife, daughter, and a guard of four officers on the interisland steamer *Viera y Clavijo*. In Santa Cruz de Tenerife, a few of the island's livelier visitors were still sipping highballs. The lights of fishing boats shone on the water.

On the pier, a group of friends had assembled to see the Francos off. To an observant spectator, their earnest farewells might have seemed disproportionate to a short stay in Las Palmas. Colonel Peral, the general's chief of staff, embraced his superior with exceptional fortitude. It was almost as if the Commandante were not expected back.

Franco's arrival at Las Palmas on the morning of the seventeenth was the signal for unusual military activity. "At first," said one resident, "I thought it was to do with the funeral of Balmes, which was planned for noon the same day But news of fighting between troops and police soon invalidated the theory. Word passed that martial law had been proclaimed throughout the islands. Franco was taking over the archipelago."

Indeed, Tenerife, which had offered no resistance, was already in the hands of his lieutenants. Grand Canary presented opposition. In Las Palmas, the civil governor called out a company of storm police to resist the army, and there was shooting in parts of the town. The government's supporters, however, were surprised and underarmed, and by evening the coup in the islands was largely effective.

Amidst the excitement, Franco remained quiet and evasive. Having attended the funeral, he returned to the hotel rooms reserved for his suite, where, surrounded by his guard of officers, he busied himself on the telephone. One caller who managed to speak to the general that Friday was the British Consul, a man on friendly terms with Franco as a golfing acquaintance. It was understood, said the Consul, that a British aircraft under charter to a Major Pollard was being held at the airport by the Las Palmas authorities. Would the Commandante be able to arrange its release? Franco replied that he would be happy to do so, once he had checked with his "legal advisers."

His lieutenants had had trouble with the aircraft from the

start. The one element in his scheme unanswerable to Franco's native caution, it had not checked with the description received in advance; its pilot had not known the passwords; Gabarda had failed to communicate.

For some time, Gabarda, a man of little political bias, had been used on the basis of personal friendship to pass on ciphers whose meaning and import eluded him. Tiring of the game at length, he seems to have regarded Pollard as part of a none-too-amusing hoax. It had taken the general's "legal advisers" some time to discover the major, and the truth.

At three o'clock on Saturday morning, a fiscal judge named Martínez Fusset, himself in Las Palmas on Franco's behalf, hastened to the general's suite in high excitement. "The army in Africa has risen!" cried Fusset. "The military holds Melilla, Tetuán, and Ceuta."

He found the Commandante-General dressed and about to leave for the staff offices. Fusset had plainly brought stale information.

For the next hour or more Franco worked at headquarters on the draft of a public declaration. He was thus occupied when a phone call was received from Madrid. The Prime Minister wished to know General Franco's whereabouts. Told that the general was inspecting island garrisons, the Prime Minister was able to report to the President concerning the Moroccan crisis that Franco was safely under observation in the Canaries.

At 5:15 A.M., July 18, before either Sanjurjo or Mola had uttered a single public statement, Francisco Franco issued his own manifesto from the Canaries to the Spanish nation. Immediately transmitted by rebel radio stations in the islands and Morocco, it called on the Spanish armed forces, together with "whoever feels a holy love of Spain," to rise in "defense" of the country against "anarchy," "revolutionary hordes obedient to foreign directives," and "the malice and negligence of the authorities." Couched in emotional nonspecifics, its promises were vague. From the "disaster" of past legislation, the rebels would "know how to save what is compatible with internal peace and Spain's desired grandeur."

The manifesto left no doubts about Franco's position. The cautious conspirator had launched the rebellion in his own name.

As the morning matured, a screen of troops and Civil Guards appeared along the road from the command offices to Las Palmas airport. They saw Bebb's car speed through, with an armed motorcycle escort. They waited to salute the Commandante. With characteristic prudence, Franco ignored the prepared route, slipping down to a deserted beach where he took a boat to the seaside airfield. He wore his "funeral" suit, a dark hat with a snap brim and had donned spectacles to confuse the casual observer. This time, the valise in his hand contained his army uniform. It was almost two o'clock when he disembarked at the edge of the airport and, accompanied by two men in mufti, strode purposefully toward the British aircraft.

Had the pilot been rash enough not to fall in with their plans, the general was ready. One of his companions, his cousin Colonel Salgado, late of the Foreign Legion, carried a loaded pistol. The other, an officer named Villalobos, was an experienced flier. Bebb concluded that their trip was all part of the charter.

At five minutes past two, the Rapide took off from Las Palmas on an uneventful flight to Agadir, French Morocco, where it landed to refuel some three hours later. As the machine touched down, Villalobos identified three military aircraft from Cape Juby, Spanish Sahara, on the field, and Bebb was ordered to give them a wide berth.

For two hours, Bebb waited for service from the languid airport authorities while his passengers kept an anxious lookout for the crews of the Spanish government airplanes. At 6:55, having avoided the scrutiny of the Republican fliers, the

Rapide climbed once more to safer regions, following the coast northeast to Casablanca.

It was dark as the biplane dipped toward the city and, for a moment, an unexpected hazard faced the travelers. Bolin, waiting anxiously for the expected aircraft, became aware, to his dismay, that the airfield's landing-light system had packed up. By a stroke of luck, one of the few airport employees who had not already gone home was an electrician. The fuse was rectified, the plane whirled to a stop on the sandy apron and its occupants were ushered by Bolin past deserted customs barriers to a nondescript hotel for the night.

At five next morning, they found the airport as devoid of police and customs men as they had upon landing, and were able to proceed without scrutiny. As the arid Moroccan landscape passed beneath them, the general's companions followed his example, hunching in the flimsy and vibrant fuselage in silence. After about an hour, Franco stretched, stripped off his jacket and trousers, and donned the uniform from his case. They were now over the Spanish Protectorate. Ahead lay the dusty walls of Tetuán, and the Mediterranean.

Almost on the stroke of seven, Bebb throttled back over Tetuán airport, obeying Franco's instructions to circle low to examine the reception committee. Among the upturned faces below were those of Colonels Sáenz de Buruaga and Yagüe, both African Army veterans and unquestionably enemies of the government.

"All is well," said Franco. "They are friends."

The news on landing was that virtually the whole of Spanish Morocco was in rebel hands, the Moorish leaders themselves having promised support for the uprising. The one proven force in all Spain's unpredictable armies, the Foreign Legion, with its brothers-in-arms, the Moorish *Regulares,* was pledged to oppose the Republic. Within minutes of exchanging salutes, General Franco was signing orders. The designation he used was *Commander-in-Chief.*

In the government buildings off Tetuán's Plaza Mayor, a crowd of officers pressed forward for a closer view as the small general in a somewhat crumpled uniform and red sash entered to address them. His tone. was inflexible and monotonous. He leaned heavily on words such as "honor," "pride" and "spiritual patrimony"—his message: the re-establishment by conquest of Spain's "soul and glory."

Hovering beside him as he moved on to the stately office of the overthrown High Commissioner, Bolin noted Franco's manner as impassive. Engineer Captain Marín, an officer who entered shortly with the news that Spanish warships had been sighted off Ceuta, was left in no doubt that the general meant business. "Have our batteries fire a warning shot," Franco said crisply. "If any vessel acts suspiciously, sink her."

2.   Ordeal in the Desert

According to a navy witness, there was a muffled roar, the ship lurched "and men were scrambling for safety on all sides." The year was 1898. Cuba, the last outpost of Spanish empire in the Americas, was struggling for independence against the forces of Valeriano Weyler, the "strong man" sent from Spain to crush the insurrection where General Martínez Campos had already failed. On the night of February 15, the United States battleship *Maine*, in Havana harbor to protect American citizens, was rocked by a violent explosion. She sank with a loss of 262 lives.

Though the cause was never agreed, public opinion in the U.S., outraged by Weyler's regime of terror and concentration camps, was not slow to suspect treachery on the part of the Spaniards. To make matters worse, the New York *Journal* produced evidence at about the same time that the Spanish Minister to the United States, Enrique Dupuy de Lôme, had advised his government that President William McKinley was a weakling. Backed by a wave of popular sentiment, the U. S. Congress declared Cuba independent, demanding Spain's withdrawal from the island. By the end of April, the two nations were at war.

The outcome was predictable. America was rich, overwhelmingly strong at sea and fighting on her own doorstep. Spain was poor, militarily inadequate and thousands of miles from the scene of the engagement. Nevertheless, dynastic pride demanded a heroic gesture, and the Spanish navy gave it.

Though lacking the most elementary conditions for success, Admiral Pascual Cervera, commander of the Atlantic fleet sailed for Cuba where, within five hours of offering battle, every one of his vessels was lost. In the Pacific, another Spanish fleet had already been destroyed in an American attack on the Philippines. With Santiago surrendered and Puerto Rico overrun, Spain sued for peace.

The shock to the nation was deep. For more than half a century, those colonial remnants in the Caribbean and Pacific had propped up long-outdated delusions of grandeur. As the troop ships disgorged their streams of broken, fever-ridden repatriates into a near-bankrupt motherland, Spain faced the bitter reality of her impotence.

Nowhere was the trauma felt more severely than in the windy environs of El Ferrol, the main port of the Spanish navy in the extreme northwest of the Peninsula. Once among the busiest shipbuilding and naval bases in the world, El Ferrol already knew what loss of empire, coupled with treasury deficiencies, meant to her economy. In the first half of the century, the liberation of Spanish America had brought stagnation to her boatyards, starvation to her populace. Now, after a hard-won improvement of conditions, memories of the bad days returned.

At 136, in the old Calle del Sol, a street of austere terraced houses off the main plaza, Pilar Franco, nee Bahamonde y Pardo, saw the disaster as yet one more trial to overcome. Small, with an oval face and brown eyes that reflected the ancestral melancholy of so many Spanish families, Pilar possessed in full the stoicism of her conservative, middle-class background. Her father, Ladislao Bahamonde y Ortega, a naval commandant, came of a landed family in the El Ferrol vicinity. Though not himself rich, his "superior" origins were a matter of pride to his daughter, a staunch believer in traditional concepts of duty.

In 1890, Pilar Bahamonde had married a maturely handsome, but otherwise undistinguished, naval officer of thirty-six named Nicolás Franco y Salgado Araujo. Nicolás hailed from a long line of professional mariners. His father, Franco Vietti, was a sailor of puritanical habits whose spare time was divided between religious devotions and the writing of naval textbooks. Nicolás himself had other priorities. Frustrated by his father's austerity, he had shown little inclination to dedicate his life to temperance, and, even in maturity, was loath to restrict his pleasures for the sake of marital propriety.

In nature, as in name, he took after his paternal grandfather, Nicolás Franco y Sánchez, a lusty official of the navy's administrative section who had kept three wives busy with fifteen children and still found energy to spare for frequent "reviewing" trips.

Life was not easy for Pilar. From what Nicolás allowed out of his scarcely munificent income, she had not only to rear the children who came quickly in the first years of marriage, and run the gaunt stone house in its bourgeois setting of identical neighbors, but to maintain appearances befitting the standards of an officer's wife.

The debacle of Cuba brought additional problems. For her self-indulgent husband, the eclipse of the navy meant even slighter chances of promotion. For their young sons, Nicolás, Francisco, and Ramón, the prospect of naval careers in the family custom now seemed a bleak one.

Five years after the birth of Pilar's second daughter, and fifth child, Pazita (the first daughter was named Pilar after her mother), the little girl died. Through grief, as through anxiety, the wife of Nicolás Franco struggled on, loyal to husband, children, and her stubborn code of private conduct.

That she inspired the devotion of all her sons was made clear in their tributes of later times, but none was influenced more thoroughly than the quiet and sensitive Francisco, the boy most akin to his mother in manner and appearance. Francisco Paulino Hermenegildo Teódulo Franco y Bahamonde was born thirty minutes after midnight on December 4, 1892, and christened in the military quarter of San Francisco, El Ferrol, where the parish registrar noted him as the son of a "naval paymaster."

Small and slender, with his mother's diminutive hands and feet and a striking, almost effeminate combination of soft hazel eyes and a generously curved mouth, Francisco grew up amidst the so-called "Generation of 1898": a convenient historical tag for the reaction which affected Spain as a result of the catastrophic war with America.

Starting with the rejection of imperial notions, and the banishment of that cloying nostalgia which had for so long held the Spaniard a victim of his own past, the "Generation" expressed itself in a widespread climate of reappraisal in which people of many walks of life and social levels took a new look at their attitudes in the light of modern world developments.

Joaquín Costa, the Aragonese scholar, summed it up in two simple slogans: "Let us lock the Cid's sepulcher under treble keys," and "Let us look to the school and the larder." Only when educational and economic standards were raised, ran the message, would Spain find true political virtue.

Suddenly, radical ideas became fashionable. In education, the Andalusian philosopher and jurist Francisco Giner, twice outcast by reactionary university authorities as a reformist, was hailed for his liberal contributions to Spanish schooling.

As cultural horizons broadened, the intellectual stimulus, combined with the inevitable post-Cuba conclusion that Spain's future lay in peaceful endeavor at home, brought a spasm of new economic vitality. To the boy Franco, the "Generation" meant little at first, save a vague awareness that the standards of naval society in El Ferrol were not the standards of everyone.

While "progressive" education claimed the children of the smart and the well-to-do, Francisco Franco attended a local primary school, the School of the Sacred Heart, founded by a priest on conservative principles, graduating to secondary education at a nearby establishment catering for boys of a naval background and run by a former war-sloop captain.

Far from locking the sepulcher of the Cid Campeador, the pupils of Saturnino Suances, the tutorial captain, were nourished on a militaristic sense of history. In Spain's past lay achievements of arms to inflame the chauvinism and romance of any schoolboy, and Franco duly learned how Spanish warriors from the Cid to Cortés, from Cordoba to Espoz, had saved Europe from Islam—and later from Napoleon—had Christianized and opened up the Americas, and at one time made Spain so formidable a power that her rulers were held in awe by the world.

He learned, too, that while Spain, a composite of intensely individualistic regions, had advanced again and again under strong, autocratic leaders, she repeatedly had floundered under liberal, consultative government. The First Republic, he was taught, had been a bloody and ruinous fiasco. The country had been saved, he marked, by a small force of disciplined soldiers, and order restored under a young king trained at Sandhurst, one of Europe's best military colleges.

To young Franco and the aspiring heroes of his class, it was the "resolute" rulers of the nineteenth century—men such as General Ramón Narváez, with his self-expressed credo "the stick, applied heavily"—who had stood for the honor of their nation; the Liberals and assorted radicals ranged against them who had finally sacrificed the colonies and the navy to the United States.

In the last stages of Franco's preparation for naval cadetship, youthful prejudice was embellished by bitter experience. Though his older and more personable brother, Nicolás, already boasted the coveted white cap and double-breasted uniform of the Naval Academy, Francisco was appalled to learn that due to the economic straits of the country, coupled with the decimated state of the navy, further entry to the college was suspended. Not only had the "Generation" locked the Cid's sepulcher, it seemed that its lackeys had slammed the door on his fondest hopes.

Bitterly, Franquito said goodbye to the navy and, on August 29, 1907, a ludicrously frail figure with close-cropped hair, clothes neatly pressed by his mother and an umbrella almost as tall as himself, set out instead for Toledo to make the most of an alternative career in the army. His entire worldly possessions were packed in a single case.

At fourteen, Cadet Franco was, on his own assessment, "no longer a boy but a man." Certainly those who knew him during his three years at Toledo's Alcázar, the infantry college overlooking the Tagus, remembered his undisguised earnestness and the somewhat unfashionable intensity of his efforts.

The bullying he experienced at Toledo stuck in his memory. Much later, when he commanded the General Military Academy at Zaragoza, Franco took strong measures to stamp out the traditional practice of hazing. But his size was a spur to assertiveness, as was the urge to live up to a suave and gifted older brother, and on July 13, 1910, he graduated with honors.

The year was significant. In Morocco, the last theater of Spanish colonial operations, Spain's oldest enemies were honing their daggers and charging their long guns. In the vicious and protracted fighting that followed, a horde of Moorish tribesmen was to deal an already smarting Spanish army a blow of dramatic and far-reaching consequence.

Propelled from the cloistered optimism of cadetship in Toledo, with its monumental atmosphere of epic endeavor, to the less glorious reality of life at a regimental depot, the youthful Franco quickly encountered disillusion. Drawing-room officers, he discovered, were more than a fiction invented by radical journalists. In an army top-heavy with commissioned ranks (one officer to every ten men), killing time was a more important science than that of killing enemies. Administrative and technical incompetence flourished. Beyond an elaborate charade of military ettiquette, professionalism was too often a matter for well-bred indifference. Not even the convenience of a posting to the 8th Zamora Regiment at El Ferrol, on his own doorstep, reconciled his discontent.

While fellow graduates responded with distinction to the social challenge of commissioned life, Franco's preoccupation with "shop" simply marked him as jejune in smart society, and among his colleagues as something of a pedant. He was not equipped to succeed on the drawing-room circuit. What Franco needed was a market for practical merit—and, to the south, events were conspiring to produce one with promising openings.

On January 5, 1911, Alfonso XIII of Spain, accompanied by his Prime Minister, José Canalejas, paid a ceremonial visit to Melilla, in the east of the North African protectorate. Here, received with the trimmings of an oriental potentate, the King inspected troops and spoke emotionally of a new dawn for Spanish achievement. Deserts would be cultivated, mines induced to yield riches, roads and bridges built in the wilderness. Like it or not, the tribes would be made to submit to progress.

Even the radical Canalejas, forgetting for the moment that Spain could not cope with her own neglected lands and communications, was swept by nostalgic sentiments. "Today," declared the Prime Minister, "begins a new age in Spanish aggrandizement; a fresh chapter in our national history." To set the seal on the occasion, someone suggested that Alfonso be given the appellation "Africanus."

Hopefully, Second Lieutenant Franco applied for a posting to the southern continent. He arrived in Morocco in February 1912 to find a situation very different from the picture engendered by the King's visit. Beset by fever, tribal fury, and staff inefficiency, the army in Africa had suffered heavily during the interim period. In the Talusits campaign of August, sixty-five percent of all men had gone down with malaria. Though losses in combat were lighter, the tribesmen from the Rif had a special flair for picking-off officers.

Franco found Melilla a confusion of alarm, restrictions and overcrowding. Refugees jammed the native areas. Forty-four thousand troops had swamped the normal military accommodation and were sleeping in shops and even in a hospital. Terrorist attacks were so frequent that strict prohibitions were placed on movement during the hours of darkness. His attachment to the so-called *Regulares*, or Regulars, of Melilla, a force newly raised from native recruits by a resourceful colonel named Damaso Berenguer, aroused no envy among his colleagues. When the "chips" were down, said the skeptics, the Moorish *Regulares* would cheerfully side with their dissident blood brothers.

Franco took no chances. Away from barracks, he spent more than one sleepless night on guard rather than chance having his throat cut by his own troops. But, if the *Regulares* were as rough and callous as the unruly Riffs, they proved for the most part loyal to their paymasters.

By nature remote, Franco was not distressed by the racial barrier which set him apart from them. It encouraged reliance on his own judgment and gave him confidence. The piddling mustache of his graduate days now spread manfully over his upper lip, his face and chest filled out and his high, lisping voice no longer made him self-conscious.

The early Moroccan campaigns savored little of Beau Geste. Soldiering was a dull and desultory struggle, sporadically enlivened with skirmishes, but with dysentery, heat exhaustion, and boredom as the most persistent enemies. To pass the time, Franco read and reread military literature, made a close study of maps and topography and ruminated privately on the effects of stress on his subordinates and superiors.

Haddu-Allal-u-Kadir, in the eastern zone of operations, provided his first experience of fire. Here, a force of mounted tribesmen was put to flight when a fortuitous bullet killed its overexposed leader, a Moor named El Mizzian. The incident taught Franco a memorable lesson in the strategic value of self-preservation, an art many Spanish officers in the field regarded as beneath them. By the end of 1915, only seven out of forty-two officers who had joined the *Regulares* remained unwounded. Franco was among them. Survival had assured him, at little more than twenty, the rank of captain.

In June 1916, however, his colonial career was interrupted in full spate by a wound in the stomach, an enforced convalescence in the Peninsula following. For a man of Franco's imperative ambition, it was a hard test. Determined to gain some consolation in adversity, he mustered the records of his African service, capped them with a deserving notice of his war injury, and boldly applied for further promotion.

"Ever since my youth," Franco later told the American journalist Constantine Brown, "I have had to fulfill posts of command much beyond the capacity of my years and experience." Now, apparently, the obligation was so powerful that, when his superiors turned him down, he appealed over their heads to the King himself, a constitutional but distinctly exceptional procedure. Precocity was rewarded. At twenty-four Francisco Franco became the youngest major in the Spanish army.

The achievement did not increase his popularity. Separated from officers of his own rank by youth, from those of his own age by rank, and from both by his singular earnestness, the "little major," as he was now dubbed, left no one in doubt that his intention was to reach the upper limits of the military hierarchy.

In Oviedo, where he was attached on regaining his health to the Prince's Regiment, he was noted for his dapper turn-out and the habit (acquired in Africa) of frequently dabbing his forehead with a handkerchief. Each afternoon, he left his hotel in Uria Street, mounted a horse prepared by his groom, and jogged off for an elevated view of Asturias. Among his colleagues, he had neither firm friends nor firm enemies. Though experience had taught him to exploit the charm of a shy smile, and a disconcerting sensitivity when it suited, his austere rejection of such traditional soldiers' comforts as wine, tobacco, and women did nothing to humanize his reputation. Few were tempted to explore more than a formal relationship.

Not that Franco is likely to have wished it otherwise. Oviedo did not feature in his immediate advancement which, he felt certain, demanded a return to North Africa—"the best, if not the only, practical school for the army," he wrote some months afterward. "It is the testing ground of true merit, and those who succeed there will one day be the body and soul of the Peninsula Army." Meanwhile, his application for posting was on permanent file in Madrid.

In spring 1920, opportunity dropped on Franco's desk in the form of a telegraph from Lieutenant Colonel José Millán Astray. The colonel, a handsome and much-decorated officer whose swashbuckling exploits had already cost him multiple injuries (he was popularly known as *El Gran Mutilado*), had been picked to form a Foreign Legion in Spanish Morocco. He invited Franco to join him. In the moon-faced major, diligent and astute yet lacking his own masterful bearing, Millán Astray visualized the perfect second-in-command.

Franco obligingly sponsored the image. In October, he met the first volunteers for the Legion in Algeciras and accom-

panied them to Ceuta. They were a disreputable crowd of
Spaniards, Germans, Italians, and others, some discharged
soldiers, some criminals, most in one way or another socially
inadequate.

Millán Astray, eyes glinting in hard, matinee-idol features,
harangued them vividly on the theme of glory in death and
conquest—his favorite motto, "Down with intelligence: long
live death" appealed to their latent bitterness—and, if the
government that paid them figured low in their sentiments,
a rugged esprit de corps was soon astir beneath the rough
cloth of their battle dress. Franco, a dispassionate figure in the
shadow of his volatile commander, worked dourly to bring
method and discipline to the new force. With famine increasing the discontent of the tribesmen, Melilla and Tetuán
needed all the men they could muster to subdue their respective zones of the Protectorate.

In the eastern zone, General Manuel Silvestre was brashly
advancing an army of 25,000 toward the Rif. In the west,
General Berenguer, now High Commissioner, supervised a
push from Tetuán with more caution. When the first of the
Legionnaries joined him, including a banner of three companies under Major Franco, he wisely held them in reserve
to gain campaign experience.

The early months of 1921 passed with relatively minor
incident. The Legionnaries of Franco's banner, given endless
marching and submitted to a grueling discipline foreign to
their nature, fretted for the fighting which so far eluded them.
Franco's refusal to relax under such conditions was irksome.
Every hillock brought forth his binoculars, every halt saw a
rigorous posting of sentinels. While others rested in the assurance that the enemy was distant, the "little major" taxed
his subordinates with inquiries, lectures, and topographical
studies.

Beside such unremitting tedium, even the fire-and-brimstone
impetuosity of Millán Astray had merciful qualities. But

Franco was adamant. "Perfect knowledge of terrain is essential," he insisted. "Never be taken by surprise."

To the east, the bold Manuel Silvestre could have used a little of Franco's circumspection. By June, the general's expedition had established itself at Anual, west of Melilla, with a covering force at nearby Igueriben. During that month and July, a series of clashes took place with Riffs led by Abd-el-Krim, a former official in the department of native affairs who had turned against the Spaniards following a personal dispute with Silvestre.

On July 19, Berenguer, with no previous intimation of crisis, received the first of a series of astonishing messages from the eastern commander. It reported Igueriben surrounded by hostile tribesmen and stated that a relief force had been beaten back. On the twentieth, the High Commissioner received a request for naval and air support, which he passed to Madrid. On the twenty-first came a demand for troops and artillery to reinforce eighteen companies already in close reserve.

On the morning of the twenty-second, Berenguer learned that the Riffs had stormed Igueriben, ambushing another relief column in the desert, and that Silvestre had decided to withdraw from Anual.

I TRUST, the Commissioner telegraphed in reply, THAT THE PRESTIGE AND HONOR OF SPAIN WILL BE FOREMOST IN ALL MINDS.

Franco, camped in the Beni-Aros region of the western zone, was among those who received marching orders at a moment's notice. It was three in the morning when Millán Astray alerted him. After a thirty-hour forced march, Franco's banner reached Tetuán and learned that its destination was Melilla. From Tetuán, an overloaded train carried the troops up the coast to Ceuta. Here, they embarked on the steamer *Ciudad de Cádiz.*

On shipboard, Franco learned from José Sanjurjo, a bull-necked colonel with curly brown hair under whom he had served in the western zone, that the unbelievable rumors now spreading were true: "The army at Anual is routed. Silvestre has committed suicide. Abd-el-Krim is at the gates of Melilla." A single imperative dominated all radio messages: "Hurry!"

As the vessel plowed slowly toward Cape Tres Forcas, Franco and other officers urged the captain to increase speed to the very maximum. The captain replied brusquely that with any more steam the ship would blow up. Already, the Moors, their enemies in headlong flight, were overrunning dozens of outposts, seizing artillery batteries intact and hounding down the fleeing Spaniards by the trail of small arms abandoned in their wake. Nearly 15,000 men of Silvestre's army were doomed.

When the *Ciudad de Cádiz* eventually reached Melilla, the city was in panic. Franco, talking with survivors of the massacre, heard the agonizing details at firsthand. He had never seen soldiers in such a sorry state—"men," he said, "whose eyes were distorted with fear, who jibbered of Moorish pursuit, of tribal women butchering the wounded, of the utter frightfulness of the disaster." Day after day, they straggled into the city, exhausted and delirious—"naked, semiconscious, like poor depraved creatures."

In some ways, Anual shook Spain more severely than had Cuba. To have succumbed to the might of the United States was one thing; for a Spanish army to be annihilated by Moroccan tribesmen was another. Franco described the experience as "the most profoundly emotional" of his career.

Among others of the "new school" of colonial officers, the ignominy which tainted the whole force in North Africa left him with a bitter distaste for a General Staff and a government whose apparent incompetence, apathy, and prevarication seemed at the core of the whole grim scene in Morocco.

It was accentuated by the condition of the reinforcements now hastily sent from the Peninsula. Incomplete units, deficient in equipment, munitions, and capable officers, were found to be pathetically wanting in quality. Berenguer's staff did what it could to reorganize these units, but, as the High Commissioner maintained with understatement, "There is no guarantee that they will be capable of fighting effectively."

It was left to a few companies of Legionnaries, and the native *Regulares,* to stop the rot in Melilla. Clinging stubbornly to the outskirts of the city, then slowly rolling back their cock-a-hoop adversaries, they fought with a panache which became legendary in the colony. Casualties were heavy —one in three of the Legion's participants was wounded— but they gained ground steadily. Spanish Melilla began to regain its old confidence.

In the expanding offensive which followed, Franco's banner fought with distinction in the column of José Sanjurjo, who, both as commander of the advance, and later C-in-C Melilla, won considerable esteem throughout the army. The road back to Anual was grisly with the rotting carrion of massacre. At the worse scenes of carnage—at Zeluan, Monte Arruit, and Dar Drius—there were sights to sicken the most callous, and if Franco required further hardening to the brutal tasks of warfare here were the kilns that produced it.

"There were no tears left," he recalled at a later date.

Officers were still falling with monotonous frequency. Two of Franco's adjutants had been killed in the advance, and his cousin Franco Salgado wounded. The loss through injury of such colorful veterans as Millán Astray, who received a bullet in the chest, and Gonzales Tablas, commander of the *Regulares,* were of more far-reaching significance, for their withdrawal brought "new school" officers increasingly to the forefront. Franco, promoted Lieutenant Colonel in June 1923, became commander of the Foreign Legion. According to his general's recommendation: "He has a cool mind, is prudent in his decisions and acts calmly under duress."

Another to gain stature was Lieutenant Colonel Emilio Mola, the Cuban-born son of a captain in the Civil Guard. Tall and scraggy, with a peering, professorial demeanor,

Mola's appearance was in bizarre contrast to that of the squat Franco. But he came from a similarly bourgeois background, shared the same studious, calculating temperament and held formidable ambitions in his own right. Both were careerists, dedicated to improved standards of soldiering, scornful of bungling superiors, military or political, and determined to assert their professionalism to the utmost. Both had learned from early opposition to proceed with much wariness.

In October, Franco went home on leave to find Spain seething with controversy over Morocco. Two governments had already fallen since Anual, and a third was heading for the same fate. On the one hand the nation called for a diminution in the cost of the war (upward of 350 million pesetas a year against 75 millions ten years earlier) and the repatriation of Peninsula troops; on the other, it deplored the unruliness of the Rif and called for a stable and prosperous colony.

Faced with a Parliamentary inquiry into Anual which threatened to expose a whole network of top-level incompetence, the generals of Spain were set on defeating the government. In Madrid and Barcelona, a group of military mandarins plotted a coup d'etat. At the center of the furore, the foreign minister, Santiago Alba, a provocative personality known to favor negotiations with the Moors, went in literal fear of his life.

Franco returned to the Legion with mixed feelings. Departure for the front meant separation from a newly married bride, Carmen Polo y Martínez Valdés, the daughter of a wealthy Oviedo merchant and a mother who hailed from Asturian nobility. In the well-connected and striking Doña Carmen, the object of Franco's patient if distant attentions for several years, his career had acquired a valuable asset. For the rest, he was not sorry to get back to his unit.

He had barely arrived in Africa when the news broke from the Peninsula. Señor Alba had resigned and fled the country. The army had rebelled in Barcelona and Zaragoza, the government had yielded and the King, ignoring his oath to the Constitution, had condoned the establishment of a military dictator.

For all his professed admiration for Mussolini and the Fascist State, General Miguel Primo de Rivera was not himself a dictator of political doctrine so much as a jumbo-sized sample of the assertive individualist in many Spaniards. Swinging his gold-topped cane, puffing his cigars, exuding bluff sincerity, he waded into the nation's problems with a touching faith in "common sense" and his own popularity.

In constitutional matters he was Conservative, in municipal affairs Liberal while his labour program pleased many Socialists. With distracting impartiality, Primo de Rivera swung from one side of the track to the other, dispensing pragmatic remedies with a zest the country found infectious.

Stimulated by government investment, Spanish industry, agriculture and public works perked up. The railways began running to time; the road builders awoke from a long spell of torpor. For many, the new signs of prosperity and civil order were enough. For the rest, there was little chance to protest. The press was censored, the Church supported the system, the Houses of Parliament were earmarked for what the general described as "some *useful* purpose."

On the far side of the Mediterranean, the Army of Africa observed the dictator's progress with uneasy interest. Among his early measures, the squashing of the inquest on Anual pleased officers of Franco's ilk a lot less than their seniors in the Peninsula army, upon whom Primo de Rivera's power ultimately rested. Nor was there too much confidence in his guarded approach to Morocco. Officers of the colonial force remembered that he had once advocated the disposal of Ceuta in exchange for Gibraltar. Was he now intending to sacrifice their efforts in Africa to pay for his ambitious projects at home?

Primo de Rivera's arrival in the Protectorate on tour of in-

spection a little more than six months after taking office occasioned a luke-warm reception. At the headquarters of the
Foreign Legion, the gates were adorned with posters declaring THE LEGION NEVER RETREATS. In an address of welcome, Franco expressed sentiments typical of those Primo de
Rivera met throughout the colony.

"The soil Your Excellency stands on," declaimed the commander of the Legion, "is Spanish; paid for in Spanish blood
. . . We reject retreat because we are convinced Spain is now
capable of dominating the territory and imposing authority
throughout Spanish Morocco."

Primo de Rivera was not, it seems, impressed. On completing the tour he announced his own convictions: "After a
careful study, I am confirmed in my opinion that Spain can no
longer afford to keep armies in remote parts of the interior."
His intention, he declared, was a withdrawal of forces to the
coastal fringe he called "useful Morocco." As for any possible
intransigence on the part of the army, his solution was characteristically simple: he appointed himself High Commissioner and, in September, moved into Tetuán with his staff.

Franco wisely bowed to the dictator's authority. From their
first meeting, he had tempered his colonial sentiments with an
anxious regard for favor, smoothing over awkward moments in
the mess and ostentatiously placing his post at the visitor's
disposal. When it became clear that Primo de Rivera intended
to supervise activities in Morocco personally, Franco dropped
his political propaganda and assumed once more the role of
tactical prodigy.

The withdrawal of 1924 proved a critical time for the Spaniards, with Abd-el-Krim and his warriors pressing hard in the
west. Mola and the *Regulares* had fought a desperate defense
at Dar Accoba earlier, and now it was the turn of Franco and
the Legion to hold the town of Xuaen while the main force
fell back on Tetuán.

Once the retreat had been suitably covered, Franco had

the delicate task of extricating his own men. It was a test demanding all the guile and purposefulness for which his native Galicia was noted. It also placed him fully in the spotlight before Primo de Rivera. The problem was to conceal the imminence of the Legion's departure from the Moors, who could be counted on to hold back only so long as the battlements remained manned.

For two days, Franco had special squads on the unusual fatigue of stuffing straw into Legion tunics. At dawn on November 18, the enemy, growing suspicious of the immobile sentinels on the parapets, entered Xuaen to find it defended by dummies. Franco had gone in the night.

For his dangerous part in the withdrawal to Tetuán, Franco won promotion to full colonel and the generous recognition of Primo de Rivera. In the final phase of the long-drawn conflict in Morocco, now nearer than anyone realized, he was to be assigned a role which climaxed his career in the field with a prominent splash of distinction.

On the afternoon of September 8, 1925, Colonel Franco, perched on the ramp of a landing craft in the bay of Alhucemas, between Tetuán and Melilla, ordered his bugler to sound the advance and plunged neck-deep into the Mediterranean. As his men waded ashore to little opposition, the end was in sight.

Earlier that summer, Abd-el-Krim had extended his exploits to French Morocco. The new venture, prompted by the unexpected retirement of the Spaniards, proved a fatal mistake for the Moorish leader. Suddenly the French, hitherto indifferent to Spain's Moroccan discomforts, had become eager to cooperate against the Riffs. Marshal Pétain had hastened to Madrid with the promise of such good support that Primo de Rivera, reversing his previous policy, had agreed to a major combined offensive.

Its masterstroke was the landing by sea at Alhucemas, in the heart of enemy territory. The landing was commanded by

Sanjurjo, now promoted to general, and the first troops ashore were led by Franco and a bright young major from Melilla, José Varela, who regarded the commander of the Legion as something of a paragon. With them went a certain Colonel Goded, an energetic "progressive" of the Melilla staff.

This time, there was no mistake about the outcome. Modern in conception, executed by officers of the new school with seasoned troops. Alhucemas was a thoroughly professional operation. Though rough seas on the days immediately following the initial landing provided a temporary supply crisis, the Moors now began to seem what they had been all along— brave opponents, but unequal to an up-to-date army.

Bombarded by the warships of two European nations, they quickly fell back before the Spanish infantry. Goded wrote approvingly of the thoroughness with which Franco and his Legionnaries led the "annihilation" of the enemy. At Axdir, Amekran, Palomar, and elsewhere, retribution for the past was exacted with brutal efficiency.

With their settlements aflame, and Abd-el-Krim preparing to capitulate, many tribesmen hurled themselves to death from the heights of their craggy homeland rather than surrender to the tender mercies of the Legion.

The last stages of the war dragged on some months longer, but, after nearly two decades of dissipating conflict, most people in Spain were pleased to forget about Africa. Spanish Morocco, with little to show for the blood and pesetas lavished on it, quickly became a back issue for all except one group of Spaniards.

Born in violence, weaned in action, the Army of Africa recalled its campaigns with fierce pride, looking forward to peace with a certain restlessness. Its leaders, unique among the Spanish armed forces for their toughness and experience, did not relish a languid decline in the overcrowded club of Peninsula officers.

Many, including Franco, had the best part of their lives

before them. Twice holder of Spain's Military Medal, Knight Commander of the French Legion of Honor and recipient of France's Badge of Military Merit, Franco emerged from Alhucemas the youngest brigadier general in Europe. He was thirty-two: "Sniffing at glory," as a fellow officer had it, "as he might have sniffed at a flower."

3. Franco and *La Niña Bonita*

Early in October 1928, General Miguel Primo de Rivera, accompanied by War Office officials from Madrid and a batch of military and civil dignitaries from Aragon, attended the inaugural parade of the General Military Academy at Zaragoza. The old "officer factory," founded in Seville more than a century earlier but recently reconstituted on modern lines, was one of the dictator's favorite projects.

At his side strutted the stumpy figure of Brigadier General Franco, fresh from his success with the Foreign Legion and one of the most ambitious young officers from the Spanish Army in Africa. Despite indignant protests from the military hierarchy at home, Primo de Rivera had approved Franco as director of the Academy.

Among many senior Spanish officers, some now present, Francisco Franco was regarded as an objectionable upstart. Watching his beaming face upturned to that of the bulky dictator, they experienced the revulsion of old-school soldiers, reared on a code of strict seniority, confronted with an unashamedly blatant careerist.

As a whole, the officer corps of Spain felt strongly about "field-promoted" men from Morocco jumping the queue for advancement. The view was widely held in military circles that the status quo should be maintained in the Peninsula by making the colonial army a force quite separate.

For Franco, the blooded professionals from Morocco were the cream and hope of the Spanish army. He had once written a long letter to a military journal to say as much. Significantly, the editor had declined to print it.

Now, to the considerable chagrin of the traditionalists, Franco had not only used his good standing with Primo de Rivera to secure an influential training appointment, but had picked much of his staff from men with a colonial background: officers, as he pointedly reminded the assembled company, who had proven their "skill and dedication" in action.

If raw cadets took no exception to his zealously intoned warning that military life was "not a road to pleasure and delight" but one of "great suffering, hardship, and sacrifice," it was not calculated to flatter the ranks of Spain's ubiquitous "drawing-room" officers for whom martial exercise too often meant the consumption of *vino* and the discussion of shady political stratagems.

What Franco later described publicly as "a profound revolution in officer selection and training," was clearly implicit in his attitude, and, while Primo de Rivera left the parade in a good mood, reactions elsewhere to the sermon were frigid. With the dictator's backing, Franco could scarcely have cared less. It would have been hard to imagine a better vehicle for his didactic and vocational inclinations than the Academy. For the first time in his career he was plainly in his element.

The reforms he instituted were timely and, though unoriginal beyond their Spanish context, practical. Entrance tests were based on merit instead of merely on family influence; outmoded textbooks were replaced by lessons formulated upon the war experiences of the teaching staff; physical fitness was made a positive aspect of the program, while such scourges of cadet life in the past as venereal disease and the exploitation of junior trainees for the amusement of seniors were strongly discouraged.

Franco's regime was austere. Cadets were enjoined "Never

to complain, or tolerate complaints," and "To be ready for any sacrifice." For the average young Spaniard it was a novel outlook, in some ways as disenchanting as the periodic homilies of the fastidious and pedantic director. Yet it quickly inculcated a professional attitude and, given time, the General Academy must have contributed powerfully toward an improved Spanish army—a force which, as Franco envisaged, "need no longer blush" at inconstant and antiquated standards.

Time, however, was not to be granted. In 1929, the world economic crisis, aggravating the already heavy burden of Primo de Rivera's material programs, revealed the fickleness of his support. As his popularity evaporated in rising prices and taxation, the bluff dictator was exposed in chill isolation. He had never formed a party to back him; had not even bothered to have his power ratified in Cortes. Abandoned by the King, no longer sure of the army, Primo de Rivera stood alone, a disillusioned and increasingly sick man. In January 1930, he resigned. Six weeks later, he died in Paris.

In June, less than two years after the opening parade at Zaragoza, King Alfonso, reasserting his own prerogative, descended upon Franco for a swearing of allegiance ceremony. The sight of the dictator's protégé playing the fulsome Monarchist, caused sardonic amusement among old-school officers.

"The cadets of the General Military Academy know how to fulfill their oaths," insisted Franco. "We have taught them. We know our flag represents the King, Constitution, and Country. Gentlemen, bear in mind . . . the gold represents the glory of Spain and the Monarchy."

Few mistook the general for an ardent royalist. Indeed, while paying lip service to the monarch, Franco showed little compulsion to champion Alfonso against the Republican wave which now swept the country, which many active officers, including Franco's younger brother, Ramón, an Air Force pilot, supported.

"The fact that Alfonso accepted the dictatorship of General Primo de Rivera, and placed trust in it, represented the most popular development of his reign," said Franco later. He judged the King's desertion of the dictator accordingly.

"Like Spanish politics," maintained one acquaintance, "Francisco Franco's views were complex. In many ways his values were traditional, yet he despised the futility and incompetence rife among traditionalists. In other ways, he was a reformer. He certainly saw no future for a country in which ninety-five percent of the peasants still lived in serfdom, yet he could not support an alternative in which, as he might have put it himself, the "other ranks" took over the nation.

"As a soldier, he believed that all things had their rightful place."

Though an inconstant churchgoer, Franco was not anticlerical. He thought, however, that the Church should keep out of politics. Similarly, he saw no hardship in paying tribute to the monarchy, so long as the King abstained from meddling in the professional matters of the army, as many claimed he had done with disastrous consequences by encouraging the ill-fated march to Anual.

Essentially calculating and lacking spontaneity, Franco hungered for the un-Spanish quality of orderliness. As a Spaniard drily expressed it: "The Germans and the British, with their punctuality, their unifying conformity and innate social disciplines, were his spiritual brothers. People found him rather a mundane chap." Apprehensively, the director of the General Academy now watched the reaction against dictatorship sweep to its emotional, entirely Spanish climax.

As 1930 advanced, Spain anticipated her first elections in nine years with mounting excitement. By November, the polls still not open, a restless section of the armed forces led the people in demonstrations of impatience. At Cuatro Vientos, the Air Force rebelled in favor of a Republic, army units at Jaca soon following suit.

To Franco's embarrassment, the leader of the Air Force uprising was his own brother. Ramón Franco, an untidy, impetuous extrovert, had made a name for himself in 1926 by
piloting the first aircraft, the *Plus Ultra,* to fly the South Atlantic. In 1929, attempting a further crossing in another machine, the *Numancia,* he had come down in the ocean,
surviving by courtesy of the British aircraft-carrier *Eagle.*

Compared with such activities, dropping Republican pam-
phlets on Madrid's royal palace was child's play (Ramón,
it was said, would rather have dropped bombs). It had, however, dangerous consequences, and when the rising at Cuatro
Vientos was put down, the flier found himself running hot-
foot for Portugal together with a fellow rebel, a Colonel Gonzalo Queipo de Llano.

Queipo de Llano would have added color to any scene.
Hawk-faced, with a bellicose manner which overflowed in
liquor, he was an authentic survival from the old Hispanic
repertory: a disgruntled adventurer who had climbed on the
Republican wagon after being struck from a Moroccan command for conduct even his none-too-squeamish superiors had
deemed indecorous. The colonel was yet to be granted his
field-day.

Meanwhile, the fugitives were lucky to reach the Portuguese border. Their counterparts of the Jaca rising, Captains
Rodriquez Galán and Angel García Hernández, were arrested
and condemned to become the first Republican "martyrs."

Amidst the ensuing political turbulence, Alfonso's interim
government hung on. By an apparent coincidence of timing,
Francisco Franco had retired from Spain in the month of his
brother's rebellion to attend an international gathering of
senior officers at Versailles. He returned for the moment of
reckoning.

In April 1931, municipal elections produced a Republican
triumph in the cities, and Franco waited, with the nation, for
Alfonso's reaction. When General José Sanjurjo, the popular

hero of the Moroccan War (since promoted director of the ubiquitous Civil Guard), declared for the Republic, the King put an end to all speculation. "I intend most resolutely," he declared, "to abstain from any course that might plunge my compatriots into fratricidal civil war."

So saying, he sailed for Marseilles and exile on the evening of April 14, leaving huge crowds of Madrileños converging on his palace. Officials, rushed to the spot for fear of rioting, found the people singing with joy and toasting *La Niña Bonita* (The Pretty Girl), the name they had coined for the new Republic.

If the suddenness of the revolution was bewildering, relief at its bloodlessness was profound. Many who had envisaged the event as unleashing a Bolshevik deluge were encouraged by the moderate and intellectual makeup of the provisional Republican government, a body deeply influenced by the liberal philosophies of Giner and "The Generation." At last, it seemed to Republican supporters, Spain was truly shedding her feudal past for those ideals of social justice and liberty long acknowledged in other lands. The mood was contagious. *La Niña Bonita* was a smash hit overnight.

Franco remained dubious. If he had advanced under dictatorship and monarchy with equal dispassion, the prospect of liberalism disturbed him. In the conservative catechism of his youth, nineteenth-century liberalism had been responsible for the disaster of Cuba. In Morocco, he had seen Spain's antiwar Liberals as allies of the Moorish enemy.

"Liberal regimes," he held, "have always failed in this country."

Moreover, the situation was far from settled. In many rural areas, Spain was as strongly Monarchist as the cities were Republican, and Alfonso had made it clear he would return if and when the people wanted him. Sixty years earlier, his grandmother, Isabella II, had fled to France while excited Spaniards proclaimed "the downfall of the spurious Bourbons."

Their excitement had been premature. Isabella had lived comfortably to see both her son and grandson on the Spanish throne.

The First Republic had lasted less than a year—a disastrous period in which the state had fragmented into a chaos of lawless cantons, and was only restored to central authority by savage use of the army, which had duly taken over.

Franco's first comment on the new regime was discreetly ambiguous. "It is the duty of us all at this moment," he instructed the General Academy the day after the inception of the Second Republic, "to cooperate with steadfast discipline so that peace may continue and the nation adjust itself through the natural legal channels." He did not explain what he meant by "adjust." A few days later he was provoked to awkward denials by a press report that he had already been granted a Republican promotion. Linked with his reputation as a careerist, and his brother Ramón's activities, the story did not strike Madrid as implausible.

In a letter dated April 18 to the editor of the Monarchist newspaper *ABC*, Franco declared that while it was his purpose "as always to respect and revere the national sovereignty" he had no intention of accepting any posting which might be interpreted as "anterior complaisance on my part with the new regime," or "lukewarmness in the fulfillment of my obligations and loyalty in the past to those who represented the nation in the monarchical regime."

For the first time in his precocious quest for advancement, Franco was patently on the defensive. The imminent prospect of the Academy's annual summer maneuvers in the Pyrenées must have struck him as a welcome escape from the pitfalls of politics. If so, the relief he experienced was short-lived. Maneuvers were still in progress when the Republican Minister of War, Manuel Azaña, determined to prune Spain's officer-sated army, ordered the closure of the General Academy. The stroke was abrupt. Franco, learning the news from a

paper, could hardly believe it. He had not felt so heavy a blow
to his hopes since a similar suspension of training facilities
had denied him his youthful dream of joining the Spanish
navy.

In Manuel Azaña, the "new broom" at the War Office,
Franco was confronted with the ablest and most uncompromising member of the Republican cabinet. Outwardly, Azaña
was not prepossessing. Short and portly with a huge, doleful
face, and eyes that peered remotely through small, round-
rimmed spectacles, he bore a lumpish resemblance to the
wistful, middle-aged bourgeois of a Thurber cartoon.

His public manner was withdrawn and insipid. He seemed
made, as one critic had it, of damp clay; incapable of rising
to the passions of the ordinary Spaniard. Yet his mind was
versatile and brilliant. Lawyer, civil servant, and essayist by
turn, he held the National Prize for Literature and had been
celebrated, even as a young man, by the foremost liberal thinkers of Madrid.

As a disciple of Francisco Giner, his view of the past was
foreign to Franco. With the new breed of iconoclastic historian,
Azaña could point out that imperial ambition, far from being a
flame worth rekindling as in Morocco, had directly contributed
through inflation and overburdening of resources to the nation's economic impoverishment—that although the great
prophets of absolutism in Spanish politics, from Isabella and
Ferdinand to Charles III, might fairly be cherished in their
own right, the power they had created for unworthy successors had drastically offset their good works.

In the soldier politician of the nineteenth century, Azaña
and his colleagues saw little to applaud. True, external orderliness had often formed a feature under such leadership, and
one at a premium in a land of quick passions and violence.
But, as with the regal despots, they argued, strong generals
did not last for ever (witness Primo de Rivera) and the re-

surgence of conflict and bitterness which followed condemned their regimes as superficial.

Furthermore, the military mentality, regarding such implicit elements of social evolution as doubt, discussion, and argument as hostile, had caused many thoughtful and moderating influences to withdraw from Spanish politics at a time when above all such qualities were needed.

In a sense, the Spanish army, entrenched in positions of high prestige and influence, had become a political organization, its policy the preservation of its own power and privilege. This Azaña saw as a fault to be remedied. He had barely taken office when his scalpel, wielded with cool precision, bit deep into the tangled complex of military tradition. Concerned in particular with the high ratio of commissioned to other ranks, Azaña not only suspended admission to the academies but retired thousands of idle officers on pension.

The process, rationalizing the number of divisional commands to little more than a quarter of their original number and discarding up to ninety percent of field officers, produced a band of bitter military opponents to the government, by no means all of them anti-Republican.

On July 14, Franco read a farewell speech to the cadets at Zaragoza. After enumerating the achievements of the Academy under his directorship, he called three times upon the orderly ranks for "Discipline," a quality, he added pointedly, at its most valuable "when the spirit fights to rise in rebellion, or when the command is arbitrary or erroneous . . .

"I cannot say you leave a home behind you, for after today it will have disappeared. But I can assure you that, scattered throughout Spain, you will carry this place in your hearts, and that in your future we place our hopes and expectations . . . your memory and sound judgment will be our recompense."

The speech did not please the government. In a chilly interview, Azaña told Franco, "I must believe you did not realize what you wrote." Elsewhere Azaña spoke up for the general. "Franco is above all a soldier," he asserted, and, in summer 1932, by now Prime Minister, he backed his faith in the soldierly virtues by granting the general command of an infantry brigade in Galicia, Franco's native province.

There were greater problems than Franco's carping to exercise the Premier. To educate the people in the rights and responsibilities of Republican Democracy; to do away with oppressive privilege in its many forms; to raise the economic status of the nation and to share the land and its fruits more equitably among the populace, especially to give greater economic freedom to a starving and semifeudal peasantry—these, the broad aims of Azaña's government—demanded a superhuman effort of any man.

Azaña tackled them in the detached and uncompromising manner dictated by his intellectual attributes. Contemptuous alike of the emotionalism of the revolutionary Left, for whom all constitutional reform was inadequate, and that of the traditional Right, for whom it was too much, he calmly pressed ahead with a program that must have benefited the great majority of Spaniards, but which, in Spain of the thirties, pleased no one.

While the Prime Minister sat aloof in a wrangling Cortes, the old specter of violence stirred in the cities. In August 1932, while Franco was stationed at La Coruña, a group of retired Monarchist officers, still smarting from Azaña's army cuts, launched a short-lived *putsch* in Madrid. It was timed to take advantage of military and civil disturbances in Seville.

The Premier affected his most disdainful attitude. As the Madrid rebels attempted to seize the General Post Office, and the War Office opposite, Azaña calmly smoked a cigarette in a window overlooking the action and watched government forces overpower the insurgents. A shipload of the latter was banished to Spanish West Africa.

The rising in Seville, more ominous, was led by General Sanjurjo, ironically the very man whose declaration for the Republic in the spring of 1931 had been crucial at the time to the avoidance of bloodshed. A brave soldier, but lacking in political instinct, he had imprudently lent his name to an attack on Azaña, who had responded with wry humor by transferring "The Lion of the Rif" from the directorship of the crack Civil Guard to that of the Customs Police.

Incensed, Sanjurjo now attempted to sieze control of the old southern city, a move energetically exploited by local militants of the extreme Left. Unfortunately for the rebels, their intentions had been conveyed to the government in advance by a talkative prostitute.

Azaña, having dispatched reinforcements to pick up the pieces, dispassionately took his place in Parliament and called up an agricultural bill for amendment. Sanjurjo was caught attempting to flee to the coast, sentenced to death, but consigned instead to prison, thanks partly to the Prime Minister's refusal to be swayed by Left-wing blood cries, and partly by the general's own nostalgic appeal in the country.

Among other colleagues of Sanjurjo's Moroccan past, Franco had good reason for deploring his performance. The backlash of suspicion resulting from the risings did not spare the innocent, and several prominent Army of Africa officers of dictatorship vintage were discreetly "removed from temptation" by the government.

In 1933, Franco was put in charge of the military in the remote Balearic Islands. The lesson was obvious. So long as the existing regime controlled the army, the way to the top was denied him; his talents and ambitions were destined to stultify.

Would they, he wondered, find more scope in politics? For a moment, on his own evidence, he seriously considered resigning from the forces and returning to the Peninsula as a politician. The hint, dropped with a view to the winter elections, created interest in Madrid, and a representative of the conservative Popular Action party traveled to Majorca to offer the general a nomination in the capital, with a safe seat reserved in the provinces to insure his election one way or another.

The choice to be made was a crucial one. A fresh career would release him from the Balearics, but Franco had climbed a long way in the forces, and, given a swing to the Right in the elections, might well regret any decision to resign from the army. The answer rested on forecasting the main election prospects.

The government stood by the 1931 Constitution, a blueprint of broadly liberal reform, though in detail, often far from a vote-catching document. In some instances, notably in the granting of suffrage to women, whose inclinations on the whole were predictably conservative, it seemed designed to promote the defeat of its supporters.

In other matters, particularly those touching on the secularization of the state system, it seemed even further contrived to help its enemies. Its anticlerical clauses, including the disestablishment of the Church, its removal from the field of education, and the appropriation of property from the religious orders, had profoundly offended wide sections of the public, including large numbers of Catholic Republicans.

Nor had Azaña compromised in his dealings with the anti-Catholic Left. Attempts to disrupt the state by the powerful Anarchist and Syndicalist movements which flourished in the industrial cities, and their weaker rivals, the Spanish Communists, had been suppressed as sharply as had the military risings of the Right. In its measures against demonstrations, newspapers and other outlets of protest, the methods of the regime had differed little from those of the dictatorship.

Early in 1933, the particularly merciless extinction of a small group of Communist rebels trapped in the village of Casas Viejas, had provoked a wave of popular indignation which, if reflected in the polls, could auger heavy losses for the government. Despite official promises, the aspirations of Spain's regionalists had not been satisfied. The Catalans were upset over the dilution in Cortes of their much-coveted Statute of Autonomy, while the Basques complained that no statute of their own had been passed in any form.

If Franco had wanted a final pointer to the trend of developments, he might have noted the budding of a new brand of radicalism on the mainland. The so-called Falange, inspired by Fascist movements in Germany and Italy, had been founded by José Antonio Primo de Rivera, the handsome son of the late dictator, in association, among others, with Julio Ruiz de Alda, who had accompanied Ramón Franco on his successful Atlantic flight. In the autumn of 1933, several thousand people had attended the first Falange rally, and a number of rank-and-file adherents were being drawn from areas normally linked with the far Left. By November, with the elections pressing, a swing to the Right did not seem improbable, and Franco decided against precipitate action. Events proved him wise.

When the poll had been counted, the Left could claim only 99 seats in Cortes, the Rightists had 207, while a moderate group, largely Radicals under their pragmatic leader Alejandro Lerroux, held the balance. It was less a swing than a lurch, and the reformists were badly shaken.

Ardent Leftists were furious. For those who had deemed Azaña's Center-to-Left alignment inadequate, the Center-to-Right position of the Lerroux cabinet was intolerable—especially since the dominating force in Cortes, though he lacked portfolio, was the young Catholic Party Leader, Gil Robles.

In the face of conservative pressure to undo much for which the previous government had worked—a quick start was made by easing restrictions on the Church—Spain's Socialists no longer contented themselves with parliamentary opposition but veered toward open revolt. In a state of high excitement,

the balding Socialist leader Francisco Largo Caballero told an
American reporter, Mallory Browne of the *Christian Science
Monitor,* that evolutionary progress had been made impossible
by the policies of Gil Robles and CEDA (the Catholic
Party), and that Socialist leaders were almost unanimous in
favoring a rebellion.

Azaña deplored the trend, but could not stop it. When he
tried to remonstrate with Largo Caballero, his former cabinet
colleague, the Socialist spluttered: "Don Manuel, I am already jeopardizing my prestige by talking with you so long!"

Retorted Azaña icily: "Very well, Don Francisco, then I will
embarrass you no further. You need all the prestige you can
get!"

Throughout the summer of 1934, preparations for violence
proceeded in various quarters. The police found weapons in
Left-wing attics and Right-wing cellars; bombs and poison gas
were discovered at the scene of a Falange meeting; José
Primo de Rivera was impeached. On one occasion, a hundred
or so Monarchist youths were arrested for drilling with rifles.

While Largo Caballero toured the country prescribing the
dictatorship of the proletariat as a cure for Spain's ailments,
Socialists joined Syndicalists and others in political protests
and strikes, and amassed their own armaments, especially
among the well-organized and financed labor groups of the
north.

In October, Franco, having taken it upon himself to revise
the defense system of the Balearics, learned that Spain was in
the grip of a general strike. A cabinet reshuffle, introducing
three CEDA men to the government, had brought the nation
to the verge of yet another crisis.

In Madrid, gunmen appeared on the rooftops, and street
fighting flared in the Tetuán quarter. As terrorists of Left and
Right stepped up their activities, fantastic rumors spread in
the capital, including one that Trotsky had appeared in Barcelona. In fact, the rebellion in that city, though announced as

anti-CEDA and anti-Fascist, was proclaimed by the Catalan Nationalist leader, Luis Companys.

From the balcony of the Generalitat building, Luis Companys declared "the Catalan State" part of a "federal Spanish Republic." From the balcony of the Ministry of the Interior, Madrid, Lerroux replied by denouncing the Catalans and ordaining the whole country under martial law.

In Asturias, thousands of well-armed rebels, for the most part miners, besieged town halls, police posts, and barracks, and, in Oviedo, captured and operated two munitions factories. Degenerate elements, making the most of the confusion, looted, burned churches, butchered those who opposed them, and raped and killed a number of women of the middle-class.

The Republic was afforded its first taste of civil war.

On the evening of October 6, an uneasy guard at the Ministry of War, Madrid, challenged a small, paunchy man in civilian clothes who had stepped purposefully through the doorway. The sentinel's suspicions were not without reason. In the streets outside, nervous pedestrians scuttled for shelter, hands above heads, as gunmen on the rooftops took potshots at anything and anyone linked with authority. Patrolling guards fired back with abandon. At the Heidelberg Restaurant, off the Puerta del Sol, foreign newspaper correspondents lay flat on the floor to escape bullets, while, at the American Embassy steel shutters were closed and candles prepared for use should the power lines be cut.

Already, Ambassador Claude G. Bowers' communications officer, Captain Logan Rock, had had a narrow escape when his office was sprayed with gunfire. He had left the room minutes earlier to seek an urgent connection with Washington. Down the road, at Falange headquarters, Madrid's Fascists roared for the blood of the "Reds."

Largo Caballero, prudently removed from his own home to

the large Madrid studio of a supporter, the painter Luis Quintanilla, hunched anxiously beside a radio with members of his
revolutionary "cabinet." Prominent among them was Indalecio
Prieto, the man who had organized arms for Asturias. Close-
cropped, double-chinned, he had the look of a seedy all-in
wrestler. He was possessed, however, of a good, lively humor
which helped to elevate the spirits of the company. The news
Quintanilla's guests prayed to hear was that sections of the
army had joined the rebellion. It was thought they had sympathizers in the War Office.

The sentinel at the Ministry, confronted by the bustling
stranger, correctly consulted the officer of the guard, who identifying Franco, conveyed him to the office of the Minister,
Diego Hidalgo. Hidalgo, a Radical, had first met Franco in the
Balearics, where much had been made of proficiency and discipline. The Minister hoped the general's reputation was justified, for in calling Franco and his fellow "Riff-tamer,"
Manuel Goded, to organize the suppression of the rebellion,
the government had taken a drastic step.

Neither of the generals had been high on the military regis-
ter, nor were they popular, either with the traditionalists of
pre-Azaña vintage or with the staff which had evolved with
the Republic. The time had passed, however, for consider-
ing niceties. On Hidalgo's desk lay a pile of messages from the
revolutionary areas which amounted, in his own estimation, to
an emergency "the limits of which were beyond calculation."
Impatiently, he thrust them at Franco.

"I've been waiting," he snapped. "I've had people looking
for you . . ."

Franco ignored Hidalgo's agitation. Events were proving the
general's view of history. Liberalism had circumscribed the
army. Now, faced with disaster, the government cried for a
soldier. If there was little cause for complacency, at least the
element of vindication was not displeasing.

Madrid he had seen for himself. Groups of jittery young

conscripts were getting nowhere against a largely unseen enemy. The plan adopted by Franco was simple and salutary. While an infantry regiment was ordered to show its strength in the streets, hand-picked marksmen of the Civil Guard, equipped with rifles with telescopic sights, were placed on commanding rooftops where they quickly proceeded to out-snipe the rebels.

In Barcelona, the situation turned on the loyalties of the military commander, sixty-two-year-old General Domingo Batet, who, though a Catalan, decided after some vacillation not to oppose the formidable new men at the Ministry.

When Companys sent for him and demanded a pledge of allegiance, Batet blustered, "I am for Spain," then, less ambiguously, arrested the Catalan president and his government. I TAKE PLEASURE, he wired the War Office pretentiously, IN CALLING ATTENTION TO THE BRILLIANT BEHAVIOR OF THE FORCES UNDER MY COMMAND. There had been a skirmish with the rebels, before Companys surrendered, in which some twenty people, including bystanders, had been killed.

Certainly, the army in Asturias was not acting brilliantly. At Oviedo, one unit, almost a thousand strong, including four colonels and nine majors, shut itself in barracks when it heard the miners were approaching the city. There it was soon joined by a colonel of the Civil Guard and a military detachment 120 strong from a small-arms factory only a few hundred yards distant, which was abandoned to the rebels with thousands of rifles. According to evidence heard at a court-martial later, each of the colonels seems to have spent his time trying to pass the command to another.

It was left to General Lopez Ochoa, an officer of long-standing Republican opinions, to organize a rescue column less than half as numerous as the interred garrison and march to the rescue from Galicia. When he finally reached the barracks, the inmates broke ranks and rushed forward, officers and men jostling each other, to embrace their deliverers.

Franco was loath to depend upon such men. He had served
in Oviedo as a major, and he knew the Asturian miners.
Rugged, politically conscious highlanders, now well-provided
with guns and their lethal stock-in-trade, dynamite, they
would not easily be intimidated. It was not even certain to
what extent the rank and file of the Peninsula army, mostly inexperienced conscripts, was prepared to take issue against its
fellow Spaniards. According to one estimate, every fourth
Spanish soldier was a Socialist or a supporter of some other
party of the Left.

The answer, as Franco saw it, was to act unequivocably and
without sentiment. He would need, he told Hidalgo, seasoned
shock troops from North Africa, men who had learned the
grim task of suppressing armed rebellion in the Rif. General
Goded concurred. Within a few hours of Franco's arrival at
the Ministry, a reluctant government sanctioned the dispatch
of the Foreign Legion, and the first units from Africa were
under orders for Asturias.

Proclaimed Lerroux dramatically: "Spaniards, the revolution
is reaching its apogee."

Locked in the telegraph office with his aides, Franco directed the operations in Asturias by remote control. When his
long-distance calls failed to produce the required cooperation,
as in the case of the air base at León, which ignored him, he
clinically proposed the dismissal of the appropriate commander. He not only ordered naval guns to bombard the rebels, but, on October 8, personally directed the shellfire by
means of a double link with shore observers and officers of
the cruiser *Libertad.*

On October 12, the advance banners of the Foreign Legion,
together with a number of Moorish *Regulares,* were landed at
the Asturian port of Gijón, providing the directors of the suppression with guaranteed tools for success. Swiftly and without
quarter, the colonial forces established their supremacy in
Gijón, moving next to Oviedo. Against the zest and proficiency

of the Army of Africa, the miners were lost. In a last futile gesture, as callous as their treatment of many innocent and moderate citizens, the rebels blew the University of Oviedo to the
ground with dynamite, later surrendering to General Ochoa
on condition that the Legionnaries and *Regulares* were withdrawn from Asturias.

Speaking of the "melancholy plight into which our glorious
movement has fallen," the rebel Belarmino Tomás, a Socialist,
told his followers that the blame lay with the workers of
other provinces, who "did not do their duty and support us.
. . . But this does not mean that we abandon the class struggle.
Our surrender today is merely a halt on the route . . . which
must end in the ultimate victory of the exploited."

Such sentiments, together with the large quantities of arms
known to be held in the province (90,000 rifles alone were
eventually recovered), did little to reassure Franco. He had
learned in Morocco how rapidly an incompletely vanquished
foe could recuperate. Now he refused to authorize Ochoa's
personal agreement to the withdrawal of the Army of Africa.

Instead, the conquerors, reinforced, were deployed through
the region in a systematic campaign of repression until every
vestige of opposition was stamped out. "He is one of the few
men I know who never digresses," exclaimed Hidalgo of
Franco, praising what he called the general's "cold analysis of
the military requirements."

At an estimate based on government figures, and clearly
conservative, at least a thousand rebels were killed in Asturias, or about twenty for every soldier lost. The miners
claimed five thousand of their colleagues killed. Of thirty
thousand arrests made in Spain as a result of the revolution,
the majority occurred in Asturias, where prisoners were held
in deplorable conditions.

One journalist, complaining of the abuses practiced by military jailers, was himself arrested and murdered in prison by
three Foreign Legion officers. Other reporters, following the

path of the colonial troops in the province, alleged instances of robbery, rape, and murder depressingly similar to those already charged against the rebels.

In any case, government censorship kept a tight clamp on the Spanish news media. While General Ochoa's march to Oviedo was widely projected in print and on motion picture screens as an epic, mention of the Legionnaries and Moors was suppressed as long as possible, after which it was officially played down.

Among ordinary, law-abiding Spaniards, the end of the crisis came as a blessing for which Franco and Goded were held largely responsible. To such people, the attempt to overthrow the Republic by force had been inexcusable. Neither the power of Gil Robles, nor the so-called "Fascist Menace," impressed thinking people as overbearing provocation. Gil Robles, the "bogey man" of the Left, had never proved himself less than a Parliamentarian, while the Falangists—though admittedly vociferous—were no more numerous, nor representative of national feeling than the few thousand members of the Spanish Communist Party.

Moreover, compared with the social deprivations of millions of Spaniards, especially the peasants, the Asturian miners had enjoyed relatively enviable terms of employment. They had not been well placed to evoke great compassion. The truth, it seemed, was that the Left supported democracy only so long as the Left was in government. Now most of its principle leaders were in prison. A disconsolate Largo Caballero had abandoned caution and returned home to the arms of a waiting military detachment. With the exception of Prieto, who, despite his considerable substance, had vanished like a wraith, the rest of the revolutionary "government" was locked up.

Azana, treated as a conspirator despite his opposition to the uprising, had been arrested on the balcony of a friend's apartment in Barcelona, betrayed to the troops who called by a cup

of coffee on a table. With a crudity characteristic of the prevailing mood in Spanish politics, one newspaper of the Right
chided his captors for not shooting him on the spot. Ironically,
Franco could thank the Left for a good turn. Already,
Hidalgo had raised him to the rank of divisional general. On
the strength of the October uprising, he was to become Chief
of Staff at the War Office, second to the Minister alone on the
Supreme War Council of the Republic. Still in his early forties,
Franco could scarcely have hoped for such dramatic promotion had the dictatorship, and with it the monarchy, not fallen.

4. Elections and Conspiracy

In 1935, the year of such Hollywood classics as *Mutiny on the Bounty, David Copperfield,* and *The Lives of a Bengal Lancer,* Paramount Pictures produced an undistinguished movie entitled *The Devil Is a Woman.* Despite direction by Josef von Sternberg, and some diverting play by Marlene Dietrich as a beguiling harlot making an ass of a pompous Spanish general, the film caused little excitement outside the Spanish War Office.

Here, officials affected the height of indignation. If the picture were not withdrawn from all countries, threatened Gil Robles, Spain's outstanding Conservative Parliamentarian and the War Minister of the latest coalition government, the company's future in Spain would be a bleak one.

Paramount was not greatly impressed. The protest did, however, score a point for the Minister with his Chief of Staff, General Franco, who, apart from taking a puritanic view of the subject, was acutely sensitive to the comic concept held by foreigners of the Spanish army. As director of the General Military Academy in the days of the dictatorship, Franco had liked to remind his students that from Gonzalo de Córdoba, the "Great Captain" of the sixteenth century, to the Battle of Rocroi, Spanish infantry had been feared and respected throughout Europe.

With faith and application, he maintained, the army could

revive its old glory. In 1925, the forces in North Africa had pointed the way against the Riffs at Alhucemas, a minor operation in the aftermath of a world war, but one which had attracted interest in the then peace-bound officers' messes of Britain, France, and Germany, had been applauded in the *Illustrated London News* and elsewhere, and had won a modicum of international notice for Franco as commander of the Spanish Foreign Legion.

Later, in visits to military tutorials at Dresden, Berlin, and Versailles, the attention accorded him by senior European officers had encouraged his professional pretensions. Franco had yearned to promote a new and model Spanish army. Opinions varied on the role he envisaged for the forces. To Niceto Alcalá Zamora, Spain's worldly and caustic President, Franco, together with such openly anti-Republican generals as Goded and Mola, and all the rest of the "controversial" officers promoted by Gil Robles to replace Azana's trusties, was an "enemy" of the constitution.

Brandishing the list of promotions, the slightly built President, his swarthy, Andalusian features sharply offset by silvery hair and mustache, complained that only twenty out of eighty of those mentioned had paid him the respects customarily due on their appointment.

Gil Robles waved aside the protest. At thirty-seven, already successful as barrister, journalist, and politician, the well-groomed Catholic Party leader was bursting with confidence. The officers, he said, were "unfamiliar with the protocol." They might be poor diplomats, but they were "excellent soldiers."

The War Minister was not impressed by abusive opinions of his Chief of Staff. Among the defeated Leftists, Franco was reviled as a running dog of the Fascists. To a leading Fascist, José Antonio Primo de Rivera, son of the late dictator and founder of the Falange, Franco's equivocation marked him as a "chicken-hearted" coward.

"Spain," purred Gil Robles, "is a land of emotional reactions . . Franco is prudent. . . Franco is professional. . ."

To the Monarchists, Franco was frankly a puzzle. Since the Monarchist General Luis Orgaz had developed the clandestine *Unión Militar Española* (UME) in the early days of the Republic, to organize "the ambience of revolution" among army officers, Franco had consistently declined to commit himself. His rare utterances were reserved and, for a man so deliberate, perversely ambiguous. When the military conspirators were asked, "Is Franco with you?" they had to admit their uncertainty.

In an army passionately devoted to maintaining its prestige and presumptions by direct interference in politics—there had been more than forty *pronunciamientos* or army rebellions between 1914 and the military dictatorship of the twenties, not to mention a string of military Premiers and coups in the nineteenth century—Francisco Franco was regarded as exceptional.

From his earliest days as a cadet, his earnest and pedantic approach to soldiering had tended to cut him out of the extracurricular activities of less singleminded associates. Unlike the prominently "political" generals, he had no personal *cuadrilla* and gave little encouragement to sycophants. Whether harassing the stringy rabbits of Castile with buckshot, browsing among secondhand furniture for bargains to take home and do-up, or indulging his single frivolity, a taste for Walt Disney cartoons, the calculating Chief of Staff kept demurely to himself, and his family, outside official hours. To the few who observed him in off-duty moments, this somewhat prim, unprepossessing fellow seemed altogether too singular to belong comfortably to any conspiracy.

Even many of the liberal thinkers Franco deprecated—not excepting those patriots whose sensibilities had been offended profoundly by the use of colonial troops in Asturias—refused to link the taciturn general with the notion of illegal behavior, especially at the moment of realizing a career's ambition in terms of his professional status.

For all the divergence of their respective convictions, Azaña had spoken of Franco's "professional integrity"; such eminent intellectuals and democrats as Dr. Gregorio Marañón and Salvador de Madariaga believed him dependable. Gil Robles, above all, sought to harness his talent.

With the Socialists and Catalans subdued, the young leader of the Catholic Party looked to his Chief of Staff to help steady the army behind constitutional Conservative policies. "He believed," declared a Spaniard then attached to the Ministry, "that General Franco, together with the majority of hitherto frustrated officers newly promoted, would find it in their interests to work with a lawful regime which supported the reconstruction and modernization of the forces."

In a sense, it was the old army stratagem of promoting potential trouble-makers. For one short summer it seemed almost as though it might come off.

The spring following the October Revolution of 1934 had found Madrid her seasonably enchanting self. By day, the Castellana and the scented paths of the Retiro were crowded with languid promenaders. On the Gran Via, the lights of hotels, movie theaters, and cafes advertised leisurely evenings. To the relief of countless Madrileños, something very near to peace had replaced the violence of autumn.

In Cortes, an abusive attack on democratic Republicanism, launched by the former dictatorship administrator José Calvo Sotelo in an attempt to turn the discomfort of the Left into a landslide for the extreme Right, had been challenged firmly by Gil Robles in the name of Parliamentary Conservatism.

"Spain," said Gil Robles emphatically, "has no desire to bow to the superstate . . . We shall not allow any tampering with the Parliamentary system."

A further stroke of moderation had come from the government, strongly backed by the President, in its decision against death sentences for leaders of the revolution. True, thousands of October's rebels—including most of the Socialist leadership and almost the entire Catalan Nationalist government—were serving nominally lengthy prison sentences, but in a nation of frequent amnesties for political prisoners the punishment did not seem, to the majority, excessive.

At last, too, the coalition of the Right had decided to look seriously at the financial affairs of the Republic. During the dictatorship, the nation had drifted deeply into a situation of debt which had not been helped by international reaction to the subsequent upheaval in Spanish politics. The withdrawal of capital on the advent of the Republic had reduced the value of the peseta substantially at a time when export prices were still down as a result of world economic crisis.

In 1933, the budget deficit had been estimated at 783 million pesetas, since when no further figures had been studied, and now Joaquin Chapaprieta, the financial expert, was called in to restore order to a wayward economy. Great savings were expected of the brusque, hardheaded financier.

It was against this background that Francisco Franco settled to take stock of the army the Conservative Ministry had inherited. It was not a task which made him any the more complacent of foreign jocularity. Of a total establishment of some 130,000 officers and men, less than 35,000—the regular soldiers of the Army of Africa—looked anything like a modern fighting force. Even the Legionnaries and *Regulares* of the Army of Africa, though boastful of a fearsome reputation, lacked much in the way of support and mechanization.

For the rest, the failings of Spain's armed forces were flagrant. The Peninsula army, composed at ordinary level entirely of short-term conscripts, was short of everything save officers. These, proliferating excessively despite the drastic cuts of Azaña's time, were so poorly paid that a large number did at least one other job to earn a living, a situation making neither for skill nor contentment.

Dissatisfaction was not restricted to the officers. Many conscripts resented the twelve to eighteen months most of them spent in the army, and those from strong political backgrounds formed Leftist groups in their barracks. While the commissioned conspirators hatched their own plots, an estimated twenty-five percent of the other ranks in some camps was active on behalf of the "people's" revolution.

In terms of equipment, the picture was pathetic. During the October Revolution, the miners had had more rifles to spare than the army, and certainly a greater willingness to spend money on weapons than had the Spanish government.

As a result of a searching five-hour meeting of divisional generals shortly after Gil Robles took office, Franco learned that a single day of total warfare would leave the forces entirely bereft of ammunition. Many units lacked helmets and gas masks, and troops sent to Asturias had not carried first-aid kits.

Such support weapons as existed were largely obsolete. The artillery was antiquated; the few warplanes in service were of First World War vintage; the heaviest bombs available weighed no more than twelve pounds. Even for a force regarded more as a tool of power within its own country than as a guarantee against outside enemies, the Peninsula army was far from impressive. Many militant Rightists displayed their outright contempt for it. The Fascists, though numerically and financially weak, could now parade without fear of opposition from their suppressed counterparts of the Left. With their blue shirts and ominously regimented ardor, they struck a note of immediacy and glamour that made the local soldiery seem spiritless.

Among reactionaries, the Carlists, or self-styled "Pure Royalists," were training their own army. Born of the contentious succession to Ferdinand VI, and supported by doughty regressionists of both the Church and the traditionally independent Northeast, Carlism had already provoked two ferocious civil wars in a century and was not inclined to be caught unprepared by a third.

At Pamplona, in the heart of Carlist Navarre, its adherents had set up a military college to train their officers. Four hundred young members were selected, with Mussolini's approval, to learn modern warfare methods in Italy, where Carlism had many sympathizers. In fields and other open spaces outside Navarrese villages, the Carlist militia held drill sessions at weekends. Its independence contributed, in the eyes of many officers, to the case for overhauling the army-proper.

Among the most urgent needs, as Franco saw it, were a crash program for the manufacture of munitions, the reopening of the General Academy, and a plan to cope with any recurrence of armed rebellion in the uneasy province of Asturias. In July, Franco, Goded, and another member of the War Office staff, General Joaquín Fanjul, attended field maneuvers intended to rehearse the securing of Oviedo in the event of further trouble in that area.

At the same time, steps were taken to bring armaments production onto a reliable military basis, with provisions against union interference in the factories. Franco also organized a personal spy network to report on Leftist activities in the regiments. In the long term, designs were invited for pursuit and bomber aircraft, modern artillery and other ordnance, while a study of poison-gas production was ordered.

This was an ambitious and costly project, but with Franco's enthusiasm and the influence of Gil Robles to back it, a new optimism grew among the army staff. For the time being, the plots of the military conspirators were pushed to the background. In three years, Franco estimated, and within an allocated one billion one hundred million pesetas, Spain's army could be overhauled and rearmed: the Western World would no longer laugh at Spanish generals.

Like so many Spanish projects of the century, however, the scheme posed fewer problems on paper than in practice. One obvious requirement—that its government sponsors should retain their influence until the job was at least under way—could not be regarded with certainty in a Republic that had seen more than twenty governmental crises, and sixty-odd Ministers, in a little over four years.

With the field to itself, the Right was increasingly split over policies. Gil Robles, proposing the revision of a few clauses of the Constitution within its own provisions—including the modification of regional autonomy and the establishment of a senate—appeared far too moderate for those who wished the whole system abolished and a full-blooded regime of reaction established.

When the CEDA leader supported his colleague, Manuel Jimenez Fernándes, the Minister of Agriculture, in rebuking "absentee landlords living in Paris and Madrid, and interested only in profits," he surprised and disgruntled many wealthy Rightists. When he reproved the youth of the party for its outspoken, Fascist-style opinions, hotheads demanded more fire in the leadership. Amidst the dissension, the hot gospels of Calvo Sotelo won a mounting number of converts.

Another obstacle to Franco and the rearmers was the inertia and corruption which pervaded the Ministries. Chapaprieta had not increased the cooperation of Civil Servants by paring their already meager salaries, and in autumn the first of two scandals involving prominent government officials set the worst of possible examples.

This concerned a Dutch gambling operator named Daniel Strauss who, emboldened by the reputation of Spain's public servants, had offered a number of them a stake in the profits of a new-style roulette wheel, the *Straperlo*, in return for a gambling concession. Public gambling was forbidden in Spain, but the officials had not seemed pessimistic, and Strauss had been tempted into paying an advance for their "influence!"

It was the first and only gamble in Spain on *Straperlo*. Fondly believing he had cornered the market, Strauss announced the opening of a casino in San Sebastián, whereupon to his speedy distress, he had been denounced in the press and advised by his contacts to leave the country to avoid further trouble. Their concern did not run to returning his payments.

At this relatively anonymous stage of proceedings, the story might have passed harmlessly into the realms of coffeehouse humor had it not been taken up by the plump and puckish Indalecio Prieto, an outlaw of the October Revolution who, like Strauss, had taken refuge in France. Urged by Prieto, the gambler now wrote imploringly to the holders of his money, requesting its return on the grounds of dire poverty.

To the delight of the exiled Socialist, the ploy elicited a return of correspondence, photostats of which he sent promptly to the Spanish President. Among those compromised were the Mayor of Madrid and the Governor of Catalonia, both Radicals; Aurelio Lerroux, the nephew and adoptive son of the Radical leader; and, by implication, Lerroux himself.

Franco had followed the scandal cagily, aware that Gil Robles was awkwardly placed by the developments. The picture now presented in Cortes of trusted representatives of the nation fumbling to defend themselves with feeble excuses, evasions, and distortions, did not increase the general's faith in democratic institutions.

At the Minister's office in the historic palace of Buena Vista, once home of the much-maligned Godoy, the Chief of Staff found Gil Robles in an unusually distraught mood. With the whole structure of the coalition endangered, he had felt

obliged to swallow his pride and uphold the offenders. Worse
was to come. On November 29, a month after the climax of
the *Straperlo* affair, another scandal made newspaper headlines.

Once more, the Radicals were implicated, this time with a
fraudulent claim against the government for several million
pesetas. The money related to á contract for two ships ordered
by the government, but found so rotten on delivery that one
had sunk in the harbor. At first, the officials concerned had
canceled the contract. Later, however, Lerroux approved payment. The shipowner, it transpired, was influential in Radical
circles.

Again, Gil Robles bore the stench to keep the coalition together. Flushed and silent, he took his seat in Cortes to hear
José Primo de Rivera flay him as the defender of grafters. His
stock, and with it Franco's hopes of a refurbished army, fell
rapidly.

In December, with the Radicals shattered and Chapaprieta
daring to propose a tax increase affecting well-to-do Conservatives, the supporters of the Right finally turned on the government they had created and smashed it. Summer seemed
far off. The flirtation of the Militarists and the Republic was
over.

During his last hours at the War Office, the departing Minister summoned Franco and his staff to an emotional farewell
gathering. "I shall return," insisted Gil Robles fervently, "after
the elections. Our work is not finished." Franco embraced
him. The general made a short speech. Never, he declared in
an artless manner, had the army felt itself in better hands
than those of the past months. Honor and discipline had been
upheld. "Honesty has been the rule at the War Office . . ."

He did not add that "honor" and "honesty" could not kill
the army's enemies. He refrained from saying what he thought
of elections. He did not dwell on the yearned-for planes and

artillery. As far as Franco was concerned, the work was not
simply "unfinished"—it had yet to begin.

Shortly before three o'clock on the morning of Monday,
February 17, 1936, General Molero, War Minister in the caretaker cabinet steering Spain through the general elections,
was roused from his sleep by a caller. The night was fresh from
the rain which had lashed down on Sunday, the day of the
polling, but Molero was not in a mind to admire it. At sixty-six,
a man of moderate political leanings, he had not responded to
the excitement of the hustings with the passion of many other
officers.

While hardened conspirators toasted the prospects of an
army coup, and their younger colleagues danced the pre-
election nights away to Jimmy Campbell's piano at Mayer's
Club, the smokily fashionable haunt of Madrid's antidemocrats,
Molero preferred his home comforts. So, indeed, did General
Franco, his caller, for whom the hope of a Right-wing victory
shared no place with whisky bottles and scented harlots.

Franco, however, had not seen his bed that Sunday night.
As the limousines of the prosperous, specially insured against
damage by Leftist agitators, had swished last-minute Conservative voters to the polls through wet streets, he had settled by
the telephone to await results from his contacts.

Early reports had favored the Right (the National Front),
and at eight there had been celebrating at CEDA headquarters. But as the evening lengthened, the Left (the Popular
Front) had picked up victories. In particular, Azana, much-
supported since his release from imprisonment, had begun to
pile up the figures. Before midnight, the outcome was clear
enough to urge Franco to action.

Two facts were significant. In the first place, though the
electorate was fairly evenly divided in broad terms of Left and
Right, the electoral system promised the former a majority in
Parliament. As its outstanding politician, Azaña was destined

once more to head the nation. In the second place, the country had shown itself overwhelmingly in favor of the moderate or constitutional parties on either side. Not only the Marxist Left, but the Totalitarian Right had been rejected by the bulk of the electorate.

In short, the militarists were in trouble. The elements most akin to their ideals had been defeated, and a Liberal, the one man they feared more than any Marxist, was about to take charge of the government.

When Francisco Franco roused Molero at three in the morning, he knew that unless the election results could be neutralized, both his career and his plans for the forces would be shattered. Molero, reaching drowsily for garments to cover his nightclothes, was shocked into wakefulness by the urgency in the man's voice. According to Franco, revolutionary mobs were threatening the peace of the nation, their leaders declaring triumphs entirely beyond the scope of the elections. Provincial cities were exposed to disorder. Madrid was on the verge of violent demonstrations. Steps had to be taken to avert greater dangers.

"What do you advise?" asked Molero anxiously.

Franco replied that the cabinet must be induced to proclaim a State of War under the Law of Public Order of the Constitution, a measure that would effectively stop the Left taking office. When Molero asked if the Prime Minister of the caretaker government, Manuel Portela, knew of these developments, Franco volunteered to inform him.

Earlier in the evening, he had tried to persuade the chief of the Civil Guard, General Sebastián Pozas, to back his endeavors. Pozas, a Republican, had observed unhelpfully that Franco's view of events owed something to imagination. He, too, had his sources of information. According to Pozas's reports, there had been noisy celebrating in many places, and some demands that the promised release of political prisoners should take place immediately. In his view, however, the only "revolutionary mobs" in sight were Republican electors expressing their natural joy. The Prime Minister alone could force him to cooperate with Franco.

Molero did not oppose the idea of approaching the Premier, and on Monday evening Franco gained an audience with Portela at which the general pressed his case for declaring a State of War. He had already drafted the necessary orders. Portela, elderly, indecisive and lacking influence with the electorate, suggested that such a course might provoke rather than prevent a revolution.

Maybe, retorted Franco, but if the Prime Minister was firm they could crush it. "You have authority over Pozas and still control the resources of the State," said the general. "You can count definitely on the aid I promise you."

Portela said he would think about it. He was still thinking when Calvo Sotelo, elegantly tailored, black hair smarmed back, called on him with a similar argument. Harassed on one side by those who would deny the results by martial force, and on the other by those who clamored for the swift implementation of the Left's election promises, Portela dithered.

Spain held its breath. In union offices throughout the country, officials waited to call their members on strike at the first sign of a concession to the Right. Communist leaders, a mere fifteen seats salvaged from the election among more than four hundred and fifty, gazed enviously at the eighty-five won by the Socialists and prepared to make the most of confusion.

Hours passed, and rumor had it that Gil Robles was backing an army coup. In a ground-floor room at Falange headquarters, Madrid, José Antonio Primo de Rivera, long-faced and dark-suited, reflected on his rejection by the electorate. Explosive feuds between his gunmen and extremists of the Left were forcing him to make frequent changes of residence. On his desk lay a loaded service revolver.

Everywhere, wealthy Spaniards scurried for shelter. Through lands dotted with long-suffering, impoverished peasants, railway engines hauled carriages packed with rich families heading for the border. At Gibraltar, the comfortable Rock Hotel buzzed with the chatter of Spanish aristocrats.

And then the truth about Gil Robles emerged. Far from joining the antidemocrats, the CEDA leader, whose party had gained twice as many seats as the rest of the Right put together, had declared his respect for the will of the nation, resolved to press his opposition through correct Parliamentary procedures. The chance that the Right might cling to office by armed force was gone.

Two days after Franco had seen him, Portela invoked his privilege to hand over to Azaña immediately, rather than wait several weeks for the reopening of Cortes, and passed with a sigh of relief to the background. Gil Robles offered the new government his party's cooperation in maintaining public order.

But the forces the Catholic Party's leader had commanded in office were gone. Within a week, Generals Goded, Mola, Orgaz, and others, were holding meetings not with a view to cooperation but to ending it once and for all. Among them, watching, listening, agreeing, was Franco.

Conspirators who knew him of old were wary of his new warmth. In fashionable Estoril, Portugal, General José Sanjurjo, released from prison since his frustrated Seville rebellion of 1932, and now planning to return to Spain to complete the job, held reservations about his former subordinate. If necessary, he declared, confidence swelling with a mounting court of rich fellow exiles, he could do without "Franquito" ("Little Franco").

The sentiment was mutual. Sanjurjo's seniority, his nostalgic hold on many who recalled him as the "Lion of the Rif," and his Carlist connections, all contributed to his usefulness as the figurehead of a projected rebellion. But Franco knew from past experience that Sanjurjo lacked the ambition and astuteness to seize power in his own right. The "Lion's" roar was more impressive than his bite.

The main targets for Franco's attention at the February revolutionary meetings were Goded and Mola. As their junior during the Moroccan campaigning, he had followed their forceful careers with admiration. Now he studied them in a new light.

Goded, direct, ruthless, unequivocally hostile to the Republic from its inception, had been tipped by many as a future dictator. His sharp, authoritative demeanor and undoubted courage, marked him for a dominant role in any military coup. With his fiery temperament went administrative talent.

Mola was in many ways more akin to Franco, a calculating and wily officer whose early struggles against a bourgeois background had taught him caution and inclined him to Fascism of the Nazi type. The thin build, large ears and peering eyes that gave him something of the appearance of the March Hare in *Alice,* belied an ambitious and resourceful character.

Unlike Sanjurjo, neither Goded nor Mola was deluded by romantic concepts. Their minds were not tuned to royal anthems and aristocratic notions of honor. As realists they saw the future in terms of naked power. For some time, the personal ambitions of such formidable colleagues had done little to increase Franco's appetite for revolutionary investment. Now, at last, he joined the "Movement" on terms he found favorable—not his terms, or their terms, but the terms of Azana.

Predictably, Azaña had lost no time purging the army command of Rightist officers. Less predictable had been some of the details of their banishment. These, announced almost before Portela's chair of office had cooled off, consigned Mola to a provincial post at Pamplona, Goded to the Balearics and Franco to the even more remote Canary Islands.

The appointments—a reversal for Goded and Franco of their

"exile" stations under the previous Azaña government—affected the logic of the rebel leadership in several ways. As one consequence, Mola, less isolated than his rivals, was to become "Director of Organization" for the rising within the Peninsula, thus establishing his authority in the early stages.

On the other hand, Goded, geographically destined to assume responsibility on the east coast, could console himself that it was from Catalonia that Spain's last dictator, General Primo de Rivera, had swept to triumph in Madrid.

On the face of it, Franco came off third-best. The most isolated of the generals under the decree of Azaña, he was not only handicapped by the longest haul to the capital, but would be obliged by developments to retard his arrival even further by accepting charge of the rebellion in North Africa, a task for which he was outstandingly qualified. The prospect did not daunt him.

The strength of his position on deeper analysis—and it opened vistas Franco had scarcely dared ponder—lay precisely in its apparent disadvantage. Undoubtedly, Goded and Mola would unfurl their banners in Spain before he landed. But Franco did not envisage a coup as bloodless as Primo de Rivera's. In the big cities, and probably Asturias, he expected violent Leftist reactions.

Madrid and Barcelona, he told friends later, would almost certainly be the scenes of "mob" resistance. With the generals on the spot preoccupied deploying their half-hearted and unreliable conscripts, it did not seem unlikely that the honors would fall to the late arrival—especially if he brought the Army of Africa with him. Accordingly, Franco now agreed, with Goded, Mola and others, to support a military uprising if the political climate became sufficiently confused in the coming months.

It was still February. In the last days before sailing for the Canaries, the calculating general made private contact with a number of influential civilians of the Right to sound their attitudes to the situation. Among them was José Antonio Primo de Rivera, whom he met at the house of Ramón Serrano Suñer, the CEDA Youth leader and husband of Franco's wife's sister.

Circumstances had mellowed José Antonio's opinion of the general. At all events, such differences as obtained between the young leader of the Right's aggressive radical minority and Franco, the fundamentally traditional authoritarian, did not prevent the astute soldier gaining information of Fascist strengths and resources in Spain. Earnestly, Franco entreated José Antonio to keep in touch with the military movement through Colonel Yagüe, who had led the Foreign Legion in Asturias. Yagüe, it happened, was a personal trusty of Franco's.

Finally, with a nice regard for protocol, Franco called on the President and Azaña to pay his departing respects to the Republic and the government. Gravely he beseeched Alcalá Zamora, who gave him a generous interview, to beware of rebellion—from the Left. "Remember," said Franco, "the cost of suppression in Asturias . . . the army does not have the proper equipment. . . ." Nor, he hinted thickly, did the new Staff.

The interview with Azaña was brisk. "You are making a mistake in sending me to the Canaries," the general said ruefully. The Prime Minister gave him a sardonic smile. Azaña was not anticipating candor.

For the next three months, the main problems of conspiracy largely bypassed Francisco Franco, who, golfing, fishing, or simply strolling with his wife and small daughter among the banana groves of Tenerife, was content to fade into so balmy a background.

By contrast, Mola paid dearly in stress for the privilege of directing preparations. The Carlists, the best armed and drilled of the army's prospective allies, were aloof and distrustful of the scheming officer, while Sanjurjo, who managed them

better, was far from handy in Lisbon, and, worse, spent some
time in Germany where he was right out of contact. When
the Carlist representative, Manuel Fal Conde, did agree to
talk terms, his price for cooperation included recognition of
the Monarchist flag as the emblem of revolution and the dissolution of all political parties.

This hardly helped Mola in approaching the Falange, whose
purists were already hostile to any suggestion that they should
become the "ally of a confused reactionary movement." It was
one thing to issue sanguine plans for a rising, as Mola did at
the beginning of April; another to persuade people that such
plans would work.

When the first attempt to launch the coup failed at the end
of the same month because a key figure in the scheme, Rod-
riguez del Barrio, Inspector General of the Army, went sick
with what was diagnosed by many as cold feet, Franco must
have thanked God (and Azaña) that he was a thousand miles
away from it.

Meanwhile, albeit unwittingly, the Left was at least helping
its military enemies. From the first, Azaña's government, so
moderate it did not include even a Socialist of the milder
type, let alone a Communist, was in trouble with the more
extreme of its electoral allies.

For half a century, Anarchism and Syndicalism, concepts
close to the Spanish spirit and now incorporated in the powerful National Confederation of Labor (CNT), had opposed the
constituted authority of the state, whether Monarchist or Republican, conducting at the same time a running fight with
the Socialists, whose General Union of Workers (UGT) was
the great rival of CNT.

With the Right defeated, the army plotting treachery and
the Socialists torn between constitutional and rebellious action, the Anarcho-Syndicalists, especially the Anarchist secret
society, FAI, stepped up their militant activities. Armed attacks by the FAI on Socialists and Communists were as violent

as those of the Falange. Some identified the two groups for a time as the FAI-lange.

In March, Azaña arrested José Antonio, ostensibly for his own protection, but the Falange leader continued to issue directions from his not-too-restrictive prison. Oliver Baldwin, son of British Prime Minister Stanley Baldwin, who visited José Antonio in jail, found the prison yard a parking lot for the expensive vehicles of well-to-do women "bearing him flowers."

To add to the problems of the government, the thousands of political prisoners set free included many whose resentment took small heed of Azaña's declared policy of "no reprisals, no persecution."

Churches and newspaper offices were burned as acts of vengeance, employers were forced to re-employ men they had long-since replaced, gangs of malcontents swarmed onto the land to incite the peasants and terrorize not only the beneficiaries of large estates but small proprietors whose struggle to survive was already a hard one.

Among the consequences, money, and the men who managed it, abandoned the country, while Spanish financiers identified themselves increasingly with the army conspirators. "Never," moaned Indalecio Prieto on May 1, Labor Day, "have Spaniards witnessed so tragic a spectacle as that now offered to the world by their country. Spain is totally discredited abroad. Its lifeblood is being drained by strife and disorder devoid of any perceptible revolutionary purpose . . . the resources of government and national energy are being dissipated by a chronic unrest which is proving too much for the people."

Events were proceeding exactly as those rejected at the elections might have hoped. Among them, the Spanish Communists, astutely directed by Comintern agents, were working hard to gain a hold on the Left wing of the Socialist party by supporting its leader Largo Cabellero, more than ever revolutionary since his sojourn in prison.

By May, the split in the one party that could sustain Azaña's government was so bitter that Prieto and his followers were driven from a Socialist meeting in Andalusia by Largo Cabellero's gunmen—"hounded out," in Prieto's own words, "at pistol-point by our own co-religionists, who were shooting hard . . . lads of my guard, their backs to the wall of the bull-ring, protected my retreat with fire from their automatics."

Prieto responded by instigating the deposition of Alcalá Zamora, now little trusted by Left *or* Right, and the elevation to President of Azaña. His plan was to pour some of his abounding and earthy energy into the vacuum left by the somewhat remote ex-Premier, establish a Popular Front cabinet and thus frustrate his Socialist rival. Largo Caballero thundered defiance.

"When the Popular Front breaks up," he stormed on May 24, "as break up it will, the triumph of the proletariat will be certain. We shall implant the dictatorship of the proletariat. That does not mean the repression of the workers, but of the capitalist and bourgeois classes!"

A fortnight later, Mola published an undercover document outlining the shape of the dictatorship proposed by the army, promising immediate promotion for all junior officers who helped the rising. Though some concessions had been offered to the Falange and the Carlists, these were not incorporated in the written declarations.

As anticipated, Goded was allotted immediate responsibility on the east coast, Mola himself for Pamplona and Burgos, and Franco for the forces in the Moroccan Protectorate. Among others, Queipo de Llano, the army adventurer who had taken part in the early Republican risings, was enlisted to take charge in Seville. He had found the rewards for Republican service less than expected.

But the Carlists were still reluctant to agree to the program.

In some heated correspondence following a futile six-hour meeting in the Monastery of Irache, Navarre, Mola informed Fal Conde: "Everything is paralyzed by your attitude . . . The traditionalist movement is ruining Spain by its intransigence."

By the time Sanjurjo had smoothed over the problem, the political fires of the land were at white heat. The Socialist Youth had joined the Communist Youth; the CEDA Youth had joined the Falange; Calvo Sotelo had eclipsed Gil Robles as the spokesman of the apprehensive middle-classes. His speeches, veering from violent attacks on Spanish democracy to open incitements to military action, incurred the unavailing reproaches of the Speaker in Cortes. "Against this sterile State," cried Calvo Sotelo, "I am proposing the integrated State . . . an end to anarchic liberty and criminal plots against production."

Accusations of Fascism did not perturb him. "If this is Fascism," he observed of his program, "then I, who believe in it, am proud to call myself a Fascist!"

In the early hours of July 13, a police truck bearing the number 17 stopped outside 89 Velásquez Street, in the capital. The day before, an Assault Guard lieutenant had been murdered by three Fascist gunmen. Now, a number of police officers who shared his Left-wing opinions disembarked from the vehicle.

"Which is the apartment of Señor Calvo Sotelo?" Captains Condes and del Rey asked the concierge.

Having awakened the opposition leader, they asked him to dress and accompany them to headquarters. Apprehensively —his phone had been cut and he was prevented from alerting neighbors—Calvo Sotelo took leave of his wife and young children and entered the police truck. In the seat behind him sat a man named Cuenca, a professional gunman once in the pay of General Gerardo Machado of Cuba. As the accelerating vehicle reached the intersection of Ayala and Velásquez streets, Cuenca drew a pistol and fired two shots at the back of the politician's neck. The victim slipped to the floor between the seats and was shortly dumped at the mortuary of Madrid's East Cemetery.

The indignation aroused by the murder gave a final boost to the army rebellion. Mola had fixed the hour for 5 P.M., July 17. Shortly after lunch on the seventeenth, General Romerales, the Republican commander in Melilla, North Africa, and one of the fattest officers in the Spanish forces, looked up from his desk to find a revolver pointed at his nose. Having been forced to resign by his colonels, he was led away to await execution together with many others in Morocco whose opinions were inconvenient to the rebels.

The Army in Africa had launched its rebellion to a flying start. The same afternoon, the High Commissioner for Morocco, Alvarez Buylla, phoned Madrid from Tetuán to announce that he was besieged in his residence. The fleet, he was told, would be sent to his rescue. Meanwhile, he must hold out at all costs.

Speculation swept the Spanish government. If this was part of the much-rumored *pronunciamiento,* why had the Peninsula army not moved? Could it be a strictly Moroccan phenomenon? The current Prime Minister, Azaña's friend and fellow-Republican Casares Quiroga, appeared to act on that assumption, restricting his countermeasures to the colonial crisis during the afternoon.

Belatedly, Azaña recalled the man most of Spain had forgotten. "What is Franco doing?" the President asked the Prime Minister.

"Franco? He is safely confined to the Canaries."

5. The Outbreak of Civil War

Dawn on the morning of July 19, 1936, found a strange race in progress to Spanish Morocco, first scene of the army *pronunciamiento,* or rising, which Madrid radio had already dismissed as an absurd plot. Steaming south with orders to crush the rebellion was a pride of heavy warships out of the Spanish naval bases of El Ferrol and Vigo.

Flying north across African sands from Casablanca was a flimsy biplane, chartered in England, bearing General Franco, late of the Canary Islands garrison, to a prearranged post at the head of the rebel colonials.

On the cruisers *Miguel de Cervantes* and *Libertad,* and on Spain's single seaworthy battleship, *Jaime I,* the atmosphere, unlike the smooth sea, was foreboding. For the most part, the ships' officers sympathized with the rebellion; for the most part, the ships' crews did not. To aggravate the rift, a number of naval officers, following the example of their conspiratorial admiral, Javier Salas, had already pledged aid for the rebels, while a section of the seamen, bonded by political views of the extreme Left, was resolved to thwart any breach of law by their superiors. As the vessels ran south, the tension aboard had risen to breaking point.

Nor was the airborne Franco without taut nerves. After months of hedging and vacillation, the forty-two-year-old general had decided to stake everything for which he had worked on a coup d'etat. It was perhaps the first time in a masterful, but fastidiously cautious career, that he had taken a truly irrevocable step, and it can scarcely have settled easily upon a belt-and-braces temperament.

As late as June 23 he had sent a characteristically ambivalent letter to the War Office, both denying and justifying an officers' conspiracy.

Those officers who, like himself, had been removed from important commands for anti-government sentiments, were, he had pointed out, "for the most part generals of brilliant record, highly respected in the army." They had been replaced by "men who are considered by ninety percent of their fellow soldiers to be of inferior qualification."

Nonetheless, Franco had lied quite brazenly: "Those who accuse the army of conspiracies . . . are deceiving you." Now there was no turning back. Into the final deed of rebellion, Francisco Franco had poured all the resentment of Liberalism and democratic values born of his family background, and all the frustration occasioned by such values in conflict with his professional life. Above all, he was determined to see his plans for an elite, efficient and well-provided army carried at last beyond the stage of blueprint.

From "the blindness of the masses" and the "negligence of the authorities," as he now put it, the generals would "know how to save that which is compatible with internal peace and Spain's desired grandeur." The army would once more "feel proud of being Spanish." By 7 A.M., the heavy ships of the fleet were within two hours cruising-time of Ceuta.

Almost on the stroke of that hour, the twin-engined charter plane G-ACYR dropped out of a brilliant sky over Tetuán and the small general scrambled down into the dust of San Ramiel airfield. Only a few hours earlier, the last serious resistance to the Moroccan rebels had been crushed at that very station. As usual, Franco's timing was consummate.

He was met by Colonel Eduardo Sáenz de Buruaga, the

officer who had organized the coup in Tetuán itself. "All's well in Morocco, *mí General*," reported Buruaga. More than thirty thousand of the toughest troops employed by Spain, the Moors and Legionnaries of the Army of Africa, stood openly against the national government.

Franco issued some preliminary orders, then gestured to the waiting transport. "*Vamos a ver!*" he said briskly. ("Let's go!")

The journey from the airfield to Tetuán's Plaza Mayor was a swift one. At short intervals along the road, Moorish soldiers presented arms as the general's convoy swept by, while, at the gates of the *Alta Comisaría*, a motley crowd of civilians, drawn by the military presence, waited in anticipation of an important arrival.

The day before, an ancient Fokker plane in the service of the government had ill-advisedly dropped a cargo of high-explosive on the native quarters of the city. A prudent Grand Vizier, Sidi Ahmed el Ganmia, had urged his angry fellow Moroccans to side with the rebels.

Now, as the chubby, blue-jowled figure of Franco appeared, paused briefly at the gates, then disappeared inside, the curious spectators raised a cheer of support. By 8:45 A.M., Franco was comfortably installed behind the splendid desk of the deposed High Commissioner of Morocco, Alvara Buyulla, busily studying the scant news then available of the rising in Spain itself. Of prime concern was his naval intelligence, for it was on the south-steaming fleet, by secret arrangement with Admiral Salas, that Franco depended for the prompt transportation of the rebel Army of Africa to the Peninsula.

Time and again, speed had proved the essence of the successful Spanish *pronunciamiento*. Few Rightists doubted that the generals would outsmart the government. "Everything has been perfectly arranged and will quickly be over," declared one, the wealthy Count de Romanones. "Four days—five at the most."

That morning, General Sanjurjo, nominal head of the military movement, was preparing to meet the widow of the murdered Calvo Sotelo in Lisbon. Here, assured of a climate of hostility to the Spanish government, he would escort her from the station to a suitable hotel in the city. Then he planned to fly to Spain for a triumphal reception.

But though Sanjurjo, the aging "Lion of the Rif," was popular on a wide Conservative front in his country, informed observers increasingly doubted his capacity or design to rule Spain in his own right. More credible were the claims made for Generals Goded and Mola, both reputable soldiers and men with a sharper taste for real power.

As Franco took his bearings in Tetuán early on the nineteenth, Goded, a formidable anti-Republican, departed his base in the Balearics for the key eastern conurbation of Barcelona, from which city, significantly, Spain's last dictator, Primo de Rivera, had set out. At the same time, Mola, "director" of the plot and leading conspirator in Spain itself, was consolidating his support in Navarre where traditional Carlist sentiments worked against the government.

For Franco, everything depended on crossing the Straits. Once in Spain, it could scarcely be doubted on prior form that the Army of Africa would demonstrate its efficiency. The miners' revolt of Asturias had already proved the daunting superiority of the colonial regulars not only over armed civilians but over the conscripts upon whom Goded and Mola depended.

The ensuing hours, however, brought a sequence of sensational messages, three cables in particular heightening the crisis in Franco's life.

Cable 1: Counterrebellion in the Spanish fleet. At nine o'clock, two hours after the general's arrival in Morocco, Captain Marin of the Tetuán staff entered his office with news that the big warships were off Ceuta and behaving suspiciously. They had sent no messages and stubbornly refused to answer signals. In fact, the naval officers' plot had misfired. The first signs that it was likely to do so had occurred on the lighter and faster ships of the fleet.

When the captain of the destroyer *Sanchez Barcáiztegui* had called upon his men to rebel against the government, they had at first listened in awkward silence, then, acting on a single shout of "To Cartagena" (the naval base on Spain's south coast), had overpowered the officers and appointed their own committee to command the vessel. On the heavy ships, the confrontation had reached violent proportions. The *Jaime I* had become a floating battlefield, her thwarted officers resisting the crew to the last man. When the big vessels arrived off Africa, they were commanded by their senior artificers under authority derived by radio from the Navy Minister.

Cable 2: General Sanjurjo killed in air crash. On the clear afternoon of July 20, a perspiring Sanjurjo climbed aboard a small plane at La Marinha, near Lisbon, and settled to fly to Burgos in northern Spain. The pilot was disturbed by the weight of his baggage.

"I suggested discreetly that it might be better to travel light," the pilot said later. "I was told: 'They are the general's uniforms. He cannot arrive in Burgos without his uniforms, and on the eve of his triumphal entry into Madrid.'" Minutes later, the laboring aircraft crashed on the outskirts of the take-off ground and Sanjurjo was incinerated in the burning wreckage.

Cable 3: General Goded captured. Mid-morning the same day, Goded had arrived at Barcelona from Majorca and set up headquarters in the old Captaincy General overlooking the harbor. He discovered that the coup had misfired in the city. The troops, despite liberal rations of brandy, were half-hearted; the workers up in arms, and the Civil Guard remained loyal to the government. In the late afternoon, the

rebel headquarters was stormed by the Loyalists and Goded
was captured.

By the evening of July 20, only Mola survived of Franco's
serious rivals among the rebel warlords. But Mola commanded the action. Franco was isolated by the government
fleet off North Africa. Buyulla's grand desk stretched impres-
sively yet unconsolingly before him. Somehow—almost any-
how—he had to beat the blockading warships.

As critical days passed in frustrating inaction, the rebel
officers of Tetuán noticed that their commander's customarily
reserved manner had assumed disturbing proportions. Increasingly aloof from question and discussion, Franco dismissed the
concern of others with mounting evasiveness.

According to his former chief, the battle-scarred Millán
Astray of the Foreign Legion, Franco perused each unfavora-
ble cable with a studiously set smile, screwed up the paper
and thrust it immediately into his trouser pocket.

With everything to gain in Spain, but no means of getting
there, the general cast desperately about him for transport.
Already, he had dispatched a plea to Rome, the most likely
of sources, stating (according to Count Ciano, the Italian
Foreign Minister, who received it) that "twelve transport
aircraft would enable him to achieve victory in a few days."

Unfortunately for Franco, Mussolini, who had for some
time lent his sympathies to the Carlists, was not immediately
convinced that the Moroccan rising had any link with the
one he supported to the north.

Nor was Franco luckier in Germany. A mission from Morocco led by a Captain Francisco Arranz and entrusted by
Franco with a personal plea to Hitler for transport aircraft,
threw Berlin officials into a quandary. Unknown to the Moroccan party, an envoy from Mola was seeking aid from the
Germans at the same time. At one stage, noted German Foreign Office agents, Arranz and Mola's envoy actually sat in

the same Berlin cafe, manifestly ignorant of each other's presence.

That the so-called National Movement of Spain, with its claim to be replacing the Spanish government, should be thus uncoordinated and divided in leadership perplexed the systematic Berliners. By the time Franco's letter was forwarded to Adolf Hitler, the Foreign Minister, Constantin von Neurath, had decided with officials of his own department that support for Franco would not be politic.

What little fresh news reached Morocco from Spain was depressing. The government held all the major cities and made much on the radio of its command of the fleet. "They are mad," observed the Socialist leader Indalecio Prieto of the insurgents in one broadcast. "Who do they think is going to save them?"

On his own wavelengths, Franco called for "blind faith in victory." From one inveterately calculating and open-eyed, the phrase had a desperate ring to it. Asked how things were going, Franco was cryptic.

"I win or die," he snapped at the questioner.

In Spain, the announcement of the military rebellion and the government's prompt dismissal of the offending generals, brought confusion to what had started, for most Spaniards, as an uneventful weekend.

At extremes of the political spectrum, the activists were busy. But for the bulk of the people, the masses who had voted overwhelmingly in February for a constitutional government of one complexion or another, the quest was for peace and a restful break from their daily chores.

Among the higher echelons of the Diplomatic Corps, and many wealthy Spaniards, who were summering in the breezes of fashionable San Sebastian and elsewhere on the north coast, all was set for a languid Saturday at the seaside. "There was not a ripple of excitement at San Sebastian," wrote U. S.

Ambassador Claude G. Bowers, who drove east in the heat of the afternoon to Irún where, in the small local movie house, he watched a newsreel of the recent Schmeling-Louis fight.

In Madrid, men in shirtsleeves and women in cotton frocks sipped cool drinks or ate ices at the many painted tables on the pavements while loudspeakers relayed the latest song hit of the season:

"The music goes round and round, oo-oo, oo-oo, oo-oo, and it comes out here . . ."

The music stopped and a government announcer interrupted. "People of Spain! Keep tuned in . . . don't turn your radios off. Rumors are being circulated by traitors. Wild stories cause panic and fear. The government will broadcast day and night . . . Learn the truth from this station. Keep tuned in! Keep tuned in!"

At 7:20 on that evening of Saturday the eighteenth, after several assurances that the Republic had the situation well in hand, a bulletin declared that the rising had been crushed. Crushed or not, it seemed that the rebels were still dangerous, for at 10:30 P.M. Dolores Ibarruri, one of the few Communist deputies in the Spanish Parliament, broadcast an emotional appeal to the people to resist the insurgents. "It is better to die on your feet than to live on your knees! *No pasaran!* They shall not pass!" cried Ibarruri (dubbed *La Pasionaria*, the Passion Flower, by her audience).

In the early hours of Sunday morning, a high officer in the Air Force, Ignacio Hidalgo de Cisneros, shouldered his way home through packed streets from the War Office to tell his anxious wife: "You should see the crowds outside the War Ministry! Thousands of them . . . holding their trade union cards in their hands. Waiting for arms—just waiting for arms."

Thousands more had made for the Puerta del Sol chanting "Sol! Sol! Sol!" and "Arms! Arms! Arms!"

For Prime Minister Casares Quiroga, pacing his freshly gilded office in the Paseo de la Castellana, the situation was proving unnerving. Eight days earlier, he had ridiculed the idea of a military coup d'etat. Now, urgent calls to check the allegiance of garrisons undermined his failing confidence.

In some cases, inquiries went unanswered; in others, there were insults. Cables rang with exclamations of *"¡Arriba España!"* From the streets outside, the chanting of the workers reminded the Premier that the only organizations in Spain with a chance of opposing an armed rebellion of the army were the militant trades unions. The moderate and middle-class Casares Quiroga must have shuddered. To arm the workers would be tantamount to unleashing revolution on top of insurrection.

That evening, eschewing such unconstitutional action, the Prime Minister resigned. The dilemma passed squarely to the President, Manuel Azaña. Seldom can the idealism and debating skills of the intellectual and liberal Azaña have seemed quite so useless. Between the devil and the deep, his only possible path from disaster was the compromise his very nature found odious. Accordingly, through the medium of Martínez Barrio, lately Speaker in Cortes, an attempt was now made to recruit General Mola, the archconspirator whom Azaña had personally expelled from the War Office, to the cabinet of a new government.

Loftily, Mola declined the inducement. When further efforts to make a deal with the Peninsula generals proved negative, Azaña consulted the Socialists. Reluctant as were the Socialist leaders to see weapons distributed to their Anarchist rivals, their advice was that the arming of the trades unions was the remaining hope for the Republic.

The night passed in urgent and tense consultation. By morning, a formal alliance had been agreed between the divided ranks of the Left, and a scratch government formed under a friend of Azaña's, José Giral, by profession a chemist. Like its predecessor, Giral's cabinet was entirely one of moderates. Its composition, however, was irrelevant. The Left demanded only one thing of José Giral: an order for weapons. When he signed it, the effectiveness of his government was finished.

The arrival of rifles at the trade union offices was greeted by members everywhere with an excitement verging on delirium. Chanting "Death to Fascism!" and "Long live the Republic!" the crowds moved off to vent their exuberance.

Thousands made for the Montaña barracks, a forbidding edifice on the crest of a hill in the northwestern quarter of Madrid, where, on the afternoon of the nineteenth, the rebel officers were preparing to lead their men into the streets. They never left the gates, for the building was ringed by an overwhelming mob of citizens against whose fury a sally must have been suicidal.

The garrison held out until Monday with machine guns and mortars, but many of the troops were opposed to their officers, and the white flags they waved encouraged the crowd to surge forward. When it was over, the officers' mess was a shambles. "Dead officers were lying there in wild disorder," wrote an eyewitness, "some with their arms flung across the table, some on the ground, some over the window sills. And a few of them were young boys." Outside, in the glare of the sun, lay the bodies of hundreds of soldiers and civilians.

In Barcelona, the army was being defeated at the same time. Among the first refugees from the city was Joseph Friedman, a motion picture operator from the United States. "Everyone seemed to be firing at everyone else," averred Friedman. "The authorities have distributed rifles to thousands of workers with orders to shoot anyone who looks like a rebel. Anyone who has a hat looks like a rebel . . ."

Among those killed in the suppression of the rising in Catalonia were General Mola's brother, Captain Ramón Mola, and the Anarchist leader Francisco Ascaso. From Ascaso's lieutenant Garcia Oliver, a sturdy man in his early thirties wearing a Sam Browne belt and a pistol at his hip, U.S. reporter Walter Duranty gained the following viewpoint:

"The Anarchist position is exactly opposite to that of the Bolsheviks in November 1917. They seized power with a program of social revolution which knew no limits. Power was thrust upon us, but we have no such program. Our only struggle is against excessive action by the ultraprivileged classes, the great landlords, the capitalists and the clergy, which finds armed expression in Fascism . . .

"Our future political form is undecided, but Spaniards, especially Catalans, are intensely individualistic and will never accept the bureaucratic control of the masses the Bolsheviks have developed."

Many Spaniards, indeed, were now quite uncontrollable. The arming of the people, precipitated by the treason of the military conspirators, had put weapons into the hands not only of patriots but of fanatics and unrestrained vengeance-seekers. Their response was as appalling as it was predictable. As in 1934, gangs of revolutionaries roamed the country burning churches, torturing and murdering clerics, wantonly terrorizing the bourgeoisie and the upper classes. In a little over a month, an estimated 75,000 people would have met a senseless death at the hands of promiscuous and ignorant killers, the vast majority of the victims shot in cold blood with no greater provocation than belonging, or seeming to belong, to the wrong political category or social class.

Mola's instructions to the rebels to "be very violent" had rebounded with interest. Central government had become a mere token. Everywhere other than in Nationalist-held areas, the real power was in the hands of the working-class parties whose local Committees of Control were a law unto themselves.

In Madrid, Giral and his cabinet were overshadowed by the Socialists, astutely exploited by a minority of Communists, while, in Barcelona, the Catalan Nationalist government of Luis Companys survived by the grace of the Anarchists.

Vengeance was only part of the picture. While the hot-bloods had lusted to get on the rampage, thousands of sober, respectable citizens wished no more than to save Spain from military dictatorship. Old men and boys alike showed an almost pathetic eagerness to join a militia which lacked the most rudimentary training facilities. Experienced officers were largely on the side of the enemy; weapons were insufficient in numbers and quality.

"We are sending a thousand militiamen a day to the fronts," one government officer, Commandant Carlos Gomez, told observers in Madrid.

"How long do you train them?"

"Three days."

"How much of that in shooting practice?"

"What!" exclaimed Gomez. "You don't think we waste ammunition on practice. The militia will get all the practice it needs at the front."

Having wrought the utmost confusion, the military coup in the Peninsula had gone off at half-cock. Two thirds of Spain remained in Republican hands, including Madrid and the major industrial cities. "The treason of the military chiefs," wrote a *Times* of London correspondent, "was not only odious but stupid, for they must have known their men were not with them, and should have been able to discern that the era of the *pronunciamiento* is past."

Only in the north had the rebels achieved any real cohesion, and here Mola worked hard to establish a platform for his further ambitions. At Burgos, on July 24, the proclamation of a provisional rebel government was accompanied by the parading of a new figurehead, a white-bearded general of patriarchal image named Miguel Cabanellas, hastily chosen to replace the late-lamented Sanjurjo.

Cabanellas, a reluctant rebel who held no argument with the Republic as such, was calculated to appeal to the hesitant and to impress moderate opinion abroad. At a press conference in the shadow of the great Gothic Cathedral of Burgos,

Cabanellas waved a bony finger at the assembled reporters and declared in a firm voice: "There is only one thing I would like to clear up. Our National Movement is not a Monarchist movement, nor Fascist. All my life I have been a Republican, and I intend to remain one."

"Why is General Franco not named in your cabinet?" asked a correspondent.

"We have been unable to communicate with Franco," replied Cabanellas frigidly.

While Cabanellas chatted, Franco fretted. Inaction was a poor sequel to his call for "blind faith in victory," and his officers, for the most part removed from his confidences, were not above mooting the general's fallibility. The night of July 21 increased their uneasiness. That evening, the throb of engines had been heard off Ceuta and the dark shapes of two vessels were spotted heading inshore. With a crash of gunfire, the coastguards went into action; frenzied shouting ensued from the shadows on the water. Franco was quickly informed of the incident.

Sleepy and unshaven, he listened to the tales of a number of apprehended seamen. It transpired that a rebel naval officer from Cádiz, one Arsenio Martínez Campos, anxious to join the forces in Africa, had raised a party of volunteers in his home province and seized a couple of trawlers at pistol point. Luck, having steered the fugitives safely through the Republican blockade, had departed them in Moroccan waters, where they had been caught squarely in the coastal fusillade. Several had been killed, and their leader gravely wounded.

One man, a staunch Falangist named Manuel Mora, urged that the two vessels should be used to smuggle troops into Spain, and Franco heard him attentively. Indeed, he took up the advice. To the surprise and displeasure of more than one officer, the general not only insisted on loading the bullet-splintered smacks with every last man they would carry

(about two hundred, jam-packed), but ordered their departure for the Peninsula the same night.

Prior to Franco's arrival from the Canaries, the Moroccan
colonels had themselves dispatched some two hundred
soldiers to establish contact with the Nationalists in Andalusia,
but then the crossing had not been threatened by warships.
Now, the blockading vessels made the risk seem a reckless
one.

As it happened, the trawlers were lucky. Halfway across
the Strait, the battleship *Jaime I* hove in sight and, in desperation, the troops on the pitching decks of the little vessels actually fixed bayonets. To their relief, a swirling mist engulfed
them at that moment and they went on to complete the
journey in safety.

The episode, revealing Franco in a mood of unaccustomed
impulsiveness, underlined his mounting impatience. Every
day wasted in Morocco gave the other side vital hours in which
to organize its huge reserve of manpower. All the time, Mola
gained influence in the north.

That week, in the same emboldening fit of frustration, the
small general rounded pugnaciously on Tangier, an international control zone administered by Britain, France, Italy, and
Portugal, in whose harbor Republican warships were anchor-
ing. In a fighting telegram to the International Control
Committee, Franco declared that a continuation of the practice WOULD AMOUNT TO ADMITTING THE PRINCIPLE THAT PIRATE
SHIPS CAN TAKE REFUGE IN TANGIER AND USE ITS PORT AS A BASE
FOR PROVISIONING AND OPERATION . . .

If the rebel leader were oddly placed to be raising legalities,
at least he had little to lose by the impudence. Lack of a re-
buff increased his bravura. Ostentatiously moving troops to the
border, Franco proceeded to issue blunt notice to the Commission "that if within a period of forty-eight hours they have
not taken effective measures for the definitive withdrawal of

. . . all pirate warships . . . I shall consider myself at liberty to take my own measures . . ."

Suddenly, the storm had spilt out of the teacup. The rude posture of an unheard-of Spanish insurgent threw the authorities of powerful nations in a tizzy. While marine contingents were rushed to Tangier by the powers of the Commission, Giral was put under pressure to withdraw the disputed ships. He gave way before Franco did and, though the obedience of the alleged "pirates" to the orders of the Spanish government cast a telling light on the general's case, the propaganda value to Franco was considerable.

Few could remember when a Spaniard had last issued an ultimatum to a foreign power, let alone got away with it, and the effect on Nationalist morale was a profound one. To the world at large, Franco, rather than the preoccupied Mola, or the puppet Cabanellas, became the news focus of the Spanish rebellion.

Militarily the Tangier affair had not solved Franco's crisis. With the government able to maintain its blockade from ports on Spain's south coast, the Army of Africa was still contained in isolation.

The first hope of a strategic break came from Italy. On July 25, finally convinced that Franco was at one with the Peninsula insurgents, Mussolini had agreed to make ready the twelve planes requested for Morocco, with a promise of more help to follow.

Five days after *Il Duce* reached his decision, a squadron of three-engined Savoia-81s took off from Cagliari air base, Sardinia, and set course for Nador, near Melilla, in the eastern zone of the Spanish Protectorate. Excited by the prospect of adventure, the Italian pilots waggled the wings of their cumbersome aircraft, exchanging lighthearted banter with their crews as they gained height. The fliers wore noncommittal civilian clothes, the national markings on the planes had been painted out and each craft had been equipped with bombs and machine guns.

Everything had been remembered save for one detail: an adequate supply of fuel for the journey. The result was a near-fiasco. Three of the planes were forced down with empty tanks before reaching Spanish Morocco. Some of the airmen were killed, others injured. Worse, from a Nationalist viewpoint, one survivor, landing in French territory, was shaken into revealing the purpose of the mission.

Proof of Italian assistance to the rebels persuaded the French government, hitherto bent on assisting Giral, to make an urgent appeal to other interested nations for a pact of non-intervention before Spain became a source of international contention. The decision was too late.

On the evening of July 26, following a stirring performance of Wagner's *Die Valküre* in Berlin, Hitler had received the envoys from Franco and had agreed to support the Spanish Nationalists. Like Mussolini, he saw the creation of a Fascist-influenced government of the Right in Spain as a boost to his Mediterranean aspirations and a useful antidote to British and French power on the sea lanes.

He also reasoned that concern for events in Spain would distract the democratic powers of the West from the facts of German rearmament, while a Nationalist victory would ensure valuable Spanish iron ore for his munitions factories.

Hermann Goering, chief of the Luftwaffe, revealed other factors. "The Fuehrer thought the matter over," said the Reichsmarschall later. "I urged him to give support under all circumstances: firstly, to prevent the further spread of Communism; secondly, to test my young Luftwaffe in this or that technical respect."

On the evening of July 30, the nine remaining Savoias reached Melilla with so little petrol that it was necessary to siphon the residue from eight aircraft to provide the ninth with the wherewithal to fly on to Franco at Tetuán. The excitement was not over. This machine, flown by the leader of the squadron, missed its course and was soon found to be much nearer Republican Malaga than was good for its safety. Veering west, the captain engaged in voluble argument with his crew about whether the hills in the distance marked Ceuta or Gibraltar. Eventually, with daylight and fuel again running out, the Italians touched down at San Ramiel.

Franco was not amused by the Italian performance.

On August 3, when the German battleship *Deutschland* paid Ceuta a goodwill visit, he entertained her commander with a good deal more cordiality than he had shown the squadron leader of the Savoias. Nevertheless, the supplies promised by Hitler had yet to arrive, and the general could no longer restrain his impatience. After a fortnight on tenterhooks, Franco decided to ferry the Strait by the steam of his own meager shipping, using the surviving Savoias as air cover.

The nearest thing to a warship Franco possessed was a decrepit gunboat, the *Dato*. The Republican blockade comprised a battleship, two cruisers, a flotilla of destroyers and an unknown but forbidding number of submarines. Even allowing for some air support, claimed the general's advisers, the idea of sending a near-defenseless convoy against such an array was not thinkable.

For the second time in two weeks, Franco defied the consensus of opinion and his own innate caution. "I haven't called you here to listen to such things," he told naval men who advised against the mission, "but to tell you that a convoy of troops and material *must* get across . . ."

On the afternoon of August 5, Franco watched his armada sail from a vantage point on a height near Ceuta, Monte Hacho, to which he had repaired with General Orgaz, late of Grand Canary, and others. Beneath them, some three thousand troops were bound for Nationalist-held Algeciras in two mail steamers, a coastal tramper, and a tug. By way of escort, they had the *Dato*, a converted trawler and an ancient torpedo boat. Ahead, the Savoias and a miscellany of light and antiquated Nationalist aircraft scoured the sea for the enemy. Thanks largely to the undue alacrity with which the Republican warships fled before these airplanes, only two incidents of any gravity ruffled the convoy's passage.

One was a brief exchange of shells between the *Dato* and a government destroyer, the *Alcalá Galiano,* which made off for Malaga when Nationalist planes appeared above her—"a triumph for faith and discipline," as Franco aptly pointed out.

The other involved the destroyer *Lepanto* which, bombed by one of the Savoias, put into Gibraltar to land casualties. Here, her anchorage, just across the bay from Algeciras, constituted a threat to the projected Nationalist landing. Franco promptly dispatched a cable to the Governor of Gibraltar.

If the Governor allowed the *Lepanto* to stay in her neutral haven longer than strictly necessary to disembark dead and wounded, warned the general, he intended to bomb her at her moorings. It was no time for mincing words with the British.

Shortly afterward, the destroyer departed, steaming swiftly west, and that evening the Algeciras landing was completed. Not a single soldier had been lost on the crossing.

Twelve centuries earlier, in the summer of 711, the Moorish leader Tarik ibn Ziyad had led the first Muslim invaders of Spain across the Strait of Gibraltar to swarm through the hamlets and towns of Andalusia. Now, on August 6, 1936, as Franco flew from Tetuán to a new headquarters at Seville, he could see Moorish soldiers once again sprawling and brewing drinks in the gardens and plazas of Spain.

The impasse was broken. Soon Franco, like Tarik before him, would be driving his men north. Soon German transport planes would be shuttling reinforcements from Morocco while burly fellows from Berlin and Hamburg, heavily disguised in cloth hats and plus-fours, would land at Cádiz with the latest Luftwaffe fighters.

If Franco were jubilant, he expressed it clinically.

"The Spanish army," proclaimed the general with something approaching expansiveness, "may be compared at this moment with a surgeon who is operating to save Spain . . ." All the patient had to do was obey army orders. "Civilians who are now armed will be requested to hand over their weapons to the authorities and return to their schools, their offices and their factories, and thenceforth to give up taking part in politics."

6. Monarchists, Falangists, and Militarists

On August 15, 1936, just under a month from the day of the military uprising in Spain, General Francisco Franco stepped onto the central balcony of the town hall at Seville, and into as piquant a charade as was ever devised by Lope de Vega.

His fellow actors would have delighted the Prince of *Comedias*. Generals Queipo de Llano and Millán Astray, among others present to observe the ceremonial substitution of the pre-Republican standard for that of the flag of the Republic, were characters straight from the old Hispanic repertory. Each was determined to upstage the other. "The situation was very strained," wrote a witness.

Queipo de Llano, self-styled overlord of Seville, stiff-backed and mustachioed, had brought with him a prepared speech from which, according to the same source, "he gave the history of the colors of the flag and of the different standards we Spaniards have had, losing himself completely in these disquisitions . . .

"It was thoroughly ridiculous. He went so far as to talk of the Egyptians."

Millán Astray, barely having managed to restrain himself during this discourse, stepped forward to "*Vivas*" from his fans in the watching crowd. A bizarrely arresting man—the swash-buckling founder of the Foreign Legion had lost an eye, arm and leg in his early campaigning days, but still clung to the motto "Death to the intelligence"—"*El Gran Mutilado*" plunged into an emotional tirade.

"Gesticulating like a man possessed," he invited the absent enemy to "come and see what we are capable of under the shadow of this flag . . . let everyone shout with me, with all the force he is capable of: Hail death! Hail death! Hail death!"

He ended by hurling his hat high over the crowd, a gesture Queipo de Llano eyed wistfully.

Franco, by contrast, had to be urged to make a short speech. "This is our flag, the authentic one," the small general told the crowd brusquely, then, having groped for a few extra phrases, he retired to the reception room for a rare but needed cocktail before returning irrately to work.

For the dour *gallego,* never an exhibitionist and scarcely a humorist, Seville that August was a city of embarrassments.

Not the least was Queipo de Llano's insistence on dominating affairs in his own fief. Liaison between the two staffs was helped neither by the arrogance of the local commander, nor by his striking personality, which tended to obscure Franco's public image in Andalusia.

For every poster issued by Franco's office, there were a score in the streets of Queipo de Llano. The man's picture was everywhere, on ashtrays, vases, and other shop merchandise.

When, in an attempt to improve their relationship, Franco named Colonel Luis Villaneuva of his staff as liaison officer to the Seville command, Queipo de Llano dismissed him as the concierge of the city, remarking that he spent his time retailing gossip to his employer.

Not only did Queipo refuse to supply Villaneuva with a car, when even the most junior officer of the division sported one, he also instructed his propaganda office to ignore all material issued by Franco.

"I don't know why these gentlemen don't get out of here," he declared once of Franco's officers, "their skins are very thick. However, it's all the same so far as anything they do matters."

One day, promised Franco, Queipo would be put in his place. Meanwhile, he suffered his foibles with tolerance. At that stage, as Franco's own PRO pointed out, a conflict of authority would have been disastrous.

Blustering, passionate, not infrequently indiscreet, Queipo de Llano remained a law unto himself in the city. His hawklike features stared from hundreds of posters, his pronouncements blared from amplifiers in the streets, his voice was heard regularly on the radio.

It was a fruity voice—a voice, as one student of the war put it, "seasoned by many years consumption of sherry and valdepenas."

"The Movement has triumphed in all Spain," cried Queipo with more gusto than truthfulness. "Madrid will be ours in a few days . . . villages which do not lay down their arms will be leveled . . . the rabble must surrender or be shot like dogs."

Regarded variously as a joke for his often funny broadcasts (Republican listeners responded to his verbal excesses with gleeful cries of *"Viva Vinos"*), as a monster for the sanguinary image in which he reveled, and as a herald of hope by many threatened by Leftist terrorists, the "radio general" was by any standards an outstanding character among Nationalists.

A born rebel, Gonzalo Queipo de Llano y Serra had thrown over a training for the priesthood to join the army as a gunner, rising through the ranks to his commission. His tendentious escapades under the dictatorship of Primo de Rivera and the Monarchy were notorious. After conspiring to overthrow the latter, he had been forced to flee the country to Portugal, returning after the fall of Alfonso to be rewarded with the post of Chief of the Military Corps of the President of the Republic.

Foreseeably, the Republic had failed to match Queipo's estimation of his talent, and, somewhat against the better judgment of Mola, who considered him untrustworthy, he had been admitted to the generals' conspiracy. The task assigned to him was the stiff one of taking Seville.

The story of how, practically singlehanded, he succeeded, became a Nationalist legend. On July 17, the day of the rising, Queipo de Llano had roared into Seville in a Hispano-Suiza tourer accompanied by his aide-de-camp and three officers, and had set about making himself felt in the city.

At the garrison headquarters, he had bumped into General Villa-Abraille, the commander.

"I have come to tell you the time has arrived to make a decision," snapped Queipo.

"I shall always remain faithful to the government."

"Very well! I have orders to blow out your brains, but since I am your friend and hope to avoid violence, let us hope you will see the error of your ways."

Having arrested the other staff officers one by one, Queipo de Llano had pushed them into Villa-Abraille's office, torn out the telephone wires and instructed a corporal to shoot anyone who tried to escape. He then moved to the infantry barracks where he repeated the procedure.

When General Allangui, the commander of the barracks, tried to break away to address his troops, Queipo de Llano had grabbed him shouting, "Don't make me use violence!"

"I was holding him firmly by the wrist," the rebel general recalled afterward, "and all the time my other hand was in my pocket and my finger round the trigger of my revolver. In a voice which must have sounded like thunder, I shouted: 'Please understand, we shall stop at nothing!'"

Then, taking the revolver from his pocket and gesticulating at a nearby group of officers: "You are my prisoners! Follow me!" roared Queipo.

It was not until he had locked up these oddly sheepish fellows, and placed a friendly captain in charge of the regiment, that he had realized there were only 130 men in the whole barracks. Outside, the city population numbered a quarter of a million.

Undaunted, Queipo de Llano had ordered artillery to be leveled at the municipal buildings, offering the civil government the choice of surrender or destruction. By nightfall, a substantial portion of the city had fallen into rebel hands though, in some parts, workers retaliated savagely.

"Union officials," warned Queipo in his radio debut, "will be shot if they do not give the orders to resume work."

Scores of union and party officials of the Popular Front, among others, were to be slaughtered in the grim days which followed. A correspondent of the *Times* of London reported "a great many ugly stories of shootings without even the barest form of trial and at least one case of a 'shooting party' in Seville which members of the public were invited to attend . . . The hand of military dictatorship in Andalusia is anything but gloved."

Franco himself, according to a U.S. interviewer who found the general "personally a kindly man," saw "no inconsistency in killing peasants for their own good, or in eliminating opposition through murders masked as military executions."

Firing parties were to rid the military leaders of many of their most active political opponents. Though the number of Nationalist executions in the war—estimated at around 40,000 —remained substantially lower than the number of slayings on the other side, the process was more discriminating, more "efficient," in its choice of victims.

Franco had much to gain by the process. Two years earlier, during the miners' rising in Asturias, he had recognized the long-term value of repression to his own concept of political stability and had overruled a pledge of no reprisals to the rebels. Then, however, democracy had proved inhibiting. Now, the generals had carte blanche.

While the promiscuous terror of the people's revolution worked against its leaders by strengthening the opposition, the more selective slayings of the self-styled "forces of law and order" effectively contributed to the dictatorial aims of General Franco.

Meanwhile, the remarkable Queipo de Llano, mustache bristling, threats and promises crackling on Seville's radio, continued to dominate his own fief.

Franco's early problems with his allies were not confined to military rivalries. In the deeper hostility of Seville's Monarchists and Fascists, as potent a combination as the odor of oranges and dried fish in the back streets, he saw revealed starkly a major dilemma of the Right.

Next to the ubiquitous posters of the Militarists, the banners of the Spanish Fascist party, the Falange, proliferated in the city. *WITH US OR AGAINST?* demanded Falange streamers spanning the entire façade of buildings. *THERE IS NO MIDDLE COURSE.*

Patrols of Falangists, bristling with guns and wearing their familiar blue shirts and the medieval yoke and arrow insignia of Castile and Aragon, roamed the streets with contempt for other authorities, especially for their "decadent" rivals, the Monarchists. These, represented at their most formidable by the *Requeté* militia, replete with red berets, prominent crucifixes and royal banners, looked with equal distaste upon the break with crown and tradition represented by Fascism.

Alongside Fascist hoardings, the *Requeté* had raised huge posters emblazoned with the crown and such slogans as *OUR FLAG IS THE ONLY FLAG; THE FLAG OF SPAIN. OUR COLORS ARE ALWAYS THE SAME.*

On some public occasions, the feud became ludicrous. At Nationalist concerts, and other patriotic gatherings, both the Falange and the *Requeté* were adamant that their respective hymns should conclude the performance. Bands were often obliged to play one tune after the other until none but a small group of fanatics from each side remained to hear them. Eventually, exhaustion would resolve the conflict until next time.

Franco bestowed his favors with discreet impartiality. For the Monarchists, he held out "Spain's great imperial tradition," carefully vague on the point of restoration. For the Fascists, he talked of class reform and restriction of capitalism. For the third force, the army, he promised a new deal, with a strongly "authoritarian" government. Like Primo de Rivera before him, he seemed far from dogmatic in the party sense.

To democrats, Franco posed as a man of the people. "I want to keep Spain from falling into the hands of one class," he told an American correspondent. "I want to erase the abuses of centuries by giving all classes an equal opportunity . . . We are going to divide the landed estates . . . establish more schools and keep the Church out of politics."

For his foreign supporters, there were other tidings of comfort. "The reorganization of the State," declared Franco in Seville, "will be based on a corporate system resembling that of Italy and Germany—with traditional Spanish characteristics."

In short, as *New York Times* man F. L. Kluckhohn reported succinctly, the general demonstrated "a willingness to use any tools, foreign or domestic, and make any pledges the needs of the moment dictate. The end justifies the means: he has declared himself a liberal, a Fascist and an advocate of strict military dictatorship as expediency has demanded . . ."

With increasing fascination, Spain's Nationalists studied his postures. Where, when and how would Franco strike his true colors?

In the first week of August, reinforcements now arriving in regular batches from Morocco, Franco pushed the Army of Africa north toward Cáceres, whence it would be able to wheel up the Tagus Valley on Madrid. Though his strike column was only a few thousand men strong, the general reckoned on Republican unpreparedness to help him.

The advance, led by Colonel Blanco Yagüe, a burly, bespectacled Falangist who currently commanded the Foreign Legion, was accomplished in dusty, fast-traveling trucks, and, for some way, met little opposition. Here and there, groups of trade unionists and loyal government supporters made a spontaneous stand, but the bulk of the militia was still "training" for want of a better word.

Franco had been correct in his surmise.

"The so-called instruction," wrote George Orwell, who personally endured the experience, "was simply parade-ground drill of the most antiquated, stupid kind. It was an extraordinary form for the training of a guerrilla army to take . . . this mob of eager children, who were going to be thrown into the front line in a few days' time, were not even taught how to fire a rifle or pull the pin out of a bomb."

The Spanish writer Ramón Sender, who held an infantry command with the Republicans, wrote with resignation of the usefulness of his pistol in impressing decisions upon subordinates, remarking of the welcome services of a veteran artillery lieutenant: "When a professional soldier had his heart on our side, his efficiency was instantly noticed."

Not until it reached Badajoz, the old walled town near the Portuguese border, did the Army of Africa encounter appreciable resistance. Here, Franco learned, an assault force of the Foreign Legion, singing its regimental hymn as it advanced, had been decimated by machine-gun fire. Fresh attacks had carried the fighting to the streets where the Legionnaires and Moors killed everyone bearing arms. Others were shot in the bullring later.

"We drove out along the walls to the ring in question," wrote Chicago *Tribune* reporter Jay Allen on August 23. Files of men, their arms in the air, were being brought in. "They were young, mostly peasants in blue blouses, mechanics in jumpers. 'The Reds.' They are still being rounded up."

As elsewhere, the conquerors reopened churches closed by the Leftists, held services for victory and generally contrived to promote their cause with stern and moral conviction.

"The main objects of the revolution," Franco informed the people of the army-dominated areas, "consist in the establishment of a military dictatorship to last as long as necessary to restore order and the national economy . . ." Strikes would be outlawed, "the idea of license of thought" restricted, the press "trained to serve the cause of truth in Spain," the Church respected in a movement likened itself to a crusade against "intellectuals, Marxists, and atheists."

On the afternoon of August 26, the general happily left Seville by plane for Cáceres, where his new headquarters was established in the Palace of the Golfines de Arriba, a solidly fortressed edifice in the San Mateo district of the township. It was a well-chosen setting. South, across the Sierra Morena, the highway led to the disembarkation points for Moroccan reinforcements and Axis supplies. To the west, the road was open to Lisbon, a vital post for foreign aid and intelligence.

North, through the twisting valley of the Tormes, the route led through Salamanca to Burgos, a now unimpeded connection with the military junta, while, to the east, the flat bed of the Tagus beckoned to the ultimate prize of Madrid. Along this last path, the Army of Africa now rolled the ill-prepared militia of Estramadura through Trujillo and on towards the capital. When the government commander in the west, General Riquelme, tried to stand before the oncoming regulars, his inexperienced units repeatedly were outflanked.

With characteristic Spanish independence, his militiamen disdained to engage in an activity so unheroic as the digging of trenches, while a substantial number of Anarchist combatants ignored orders altogether in favor of futile counterattacks on their own.

By the beginning of September, Talavera de la Reina was the only town of importance between Franco and the capital, and ten thousand Republicans prepared to defend it. Madrid, loath to risk more of her unready army in a major engagement, waited anxiously. On the evening of September 3, an official of the War Ministry phoned Talavera for news. To his dismay, he was answered by a Moroccan.

With the road to the capital open, Franco's staff was jubilant. The uprising was six weeks old and for many the venture seemed practically over. In Seville, Queipo de Llano anticipated the high office he hoped to hold in a new central government.

"The day the command sees fit," Queipo boasted, "we will enter [the capital]. General Mola will address us very soon from the Puerta del Sol; I give you my word of honor. The Marxist rabble, the sons of *Pasionaria* can count their days numbered in Madrid."

He underestimated Franco.

At Cáceres, Franco, already completing his design for the coming weeks, envisaged nothing so magnanimous as halving the honors with Mola, Queipo, or anyone else. He was not, he informed his lieutenants, going straight for the capital. The news was disturbing. Alfredo Kindelán, the Nationalist air force chief and a strong Franco supporter, warned that a delay could cost them the one city they wanted above all others.

"I know," replied the general, "I have meditated long on the consequences . . ."

Franco's sanctum at Cáceres was comfortable and modestly elegant. The floor was of polished brick decorated with a motif of helmets and lions, there was a framed genealogical chart above the fireplace, a purple-shaded lamp for night work and a table bearing papers weighted with mineral samples. The window, iron-grated, was reassuringly screened by a blank wall. Outside, guards of the army and various paramilitary Nationalist forces prowled alertly in pairs.

In this room, the general planned his army and political strategy, received the homage of local Falangist chieftains and gave interviews to approved foreign journalists, who found him courteous, relaxed but seldom informative. More importantly, it was here that he conferred in September with three people intimately involved in his next step.

The first was General Kindelán. Kindelán, who had been with Franco in Morocco, was convinced that the forces were not well-served by a junta. He was a strong advocate of the appointment of a supreme military commander, and was eager to promote the candidature of Franco. His motives were twofold. On the one hand, Kindelán genuinely admired the *gallego* and looked forward to being chief of his air force. On the other, he wished to curtail the power of such generals as Mola, Queipo de Llano and Cabanellas, all of whom were by philosophy anti-Monarchists while Kindelán himself was a staunch restorationist.

It was interesting to note, at a stage when Franco's appeal among Fascists was rising, that for the second time since the rebellion he was being abetted by a Monarchist. His dash by air from the Canaries had been engineered by the proprietor of a Monarchist newspaper, *ABC*—now Kindelán clearly imagined him a king's man. Franco disillusioned nobody. Instead, responding with delicate modesty, he left Kindelán to the smooth devices of the second actor at Cáceres, his elder brother Nicolás.

Nicolás Franco had come into his own since the rebellion. A bulkier man than the general—his lugubrious manner and taste for sartorial sobriety once earned him the title of "the general's butler"—he had generally outshone his brother as a young man, gaining the naval commission the other had coveted to rise comfortably, if unspectacularly, on the administrative side of the service. Nicolás had never lacked social and organizational talents. Already, these had proved useful to the Movement in the establishment of an import agency for armaments at Lisbon. Now, he took Kindelán aside and talked earnestly.

On September 23, while Franco was in conference, the third person of importance arrived at Cáceres. Carmen Franco and her husband had been parted since the flight from Grand Canary, and the general had undoubtedly missed the one person to whom he could turn for reserves of assurance. Moreover, if Kindelán were to play the "kingmaker," a "queen" was appropriate, and it would have been hard to conceive an actress more fitting than the darkly aristocratic Carmen. The reunion marked a high note of confidence.

The same day, Franco gave orders for his army to divert to Toledo. At Toledo, lying some twenty-six miles off the Madrid road to the south, a small Nationalist garrison had been holding out against heavy odds since the earliest days of the rebellion. For its dramatic rather than its strategic implications, the siege had stirred millions of Spanish hearts.

On July 20, Colonel Ituarte Moscardo, military governor of the Toledo area, had barricaded himself in the environs of the Alcazar, a fortress-cum-palace above the Tagus, with some three hundred officers and cadets, about a thousand other Nationalist supporters, mainly Civil Guards, and several hundred women and children. There, hopelessly cut off in Republican territory, the colonel had stood to the flag of rebellion, defying all calls to surrender, even when threatened by the death of his hostage son.

As September drew on, with half the Alcazar garrison killed or wounded, the position grew critical. To eke out food rations, the horses and mules in the stables were eaten. One by one, the towers protecting the Alcazar were mined and demolished by the Republicans, forcing the defenders to live increasingly in the foundations. On the twentieth, the Social-

ist leader Largo Caballero personally visited Toledo to hasten
the fall of the citadel. Fire engines loaded with petrol were
brought forward, the buildings drenched and set on fire. The
northeast turret, one of the remaining bastions, was mined
and blown into the Tagus.

Finally, Republican reinforcements arrived from Madrid for
the overwhelming effort. It never took place. On September
27, the hapless defenders saw the spearhead of Franco's army
on the hills to the north, and the besieging forces began to
vanish. The niceness of Franco's judgment was about to be
apparent.

Kindelán had already been at work on the junta of Burgos,
where the principle opponent of a scheme to appoint an over-
all military commander was the white-bearded president, General Cabanellas. "A war," insisted the veteran Cabanellas, "can
be run equally well by a generalissimo or a directory . . ."

"Sure," replied Kindelán. "The first way you win; the second
way you lose."

At an off-the-record meeting of the generals on September
12, the matter had been put to the vote, and Cabanellas defeated; whereupon Kindelán had promptly proposed Franco
for the post of Generalissimo. Mola, mindful of his political
chances, and seemingly regarding the military command as a
full-time assignment, had actually seconded the nomination.
At all events, it was agreed to conduct the business officially
at the next meeting of the National Defense Junta, September
29, at Salamanca.

On September 28, a bleary-eyed and hollow-cheeked Moscardo paraded his band of bedraggled survivors in front of
their rescuers, saluted and gave the password that had first
signaled the military uprising. He was greeted by a barrage of
flashlights. Franco had ordered every available reporter and
photographer to the Alcazar for the occasion.

"I have never had a greater ambition," declared Franco,
"than to rescue the Alcazar."

Next morning, as he flew north to Salamanca for the generals' meeting, Nationalist Spain hailed Franco as a savior, the hero of the moment. So avidly was the news digested, so immense the mood of elation, it seemed hard to some to believe that the war was not won. As Franco landed at Salamanca airport, two hundred Falangist and Monarchist warriors, specially organized by the efficient Nicolás, greeted him with shouts of "Generalissimo!"

Tactfully, Franco declined to attend the ensuing discussion. The remaining generals, uncomfortably seated on hard wooden chairs in a building on the airport, called upon Kindelán to put his proposal. It seemed no more than a formality. It proved to be much more.

The draft Kindelán quoted had been worded by himself and Nicolás Franco shortly after the relief of Toledo. The decree comprised four brief articles, the longest a mere four or five lines, the last simply canceling contrary provisions already endorsed by the junta. Articles one and two were much as expected, the former providing for a supreme commander of land, sea and air forces in the Movement, the latter establishing his style as "Generalissimo."

Article three, however, was a bombshell.

"The post of Generalissimo," Kindelán read out, "will be combined with the office of Chief of State for the duration of the war, and in the latter capacity his authority will extend over all national activities: political, economic, social, cultural, etcetera."

The protests were loud and immediate.

Mola, a sudden vision of his fondest plans crashing, attacked the proposal bitterly. Others, including Cabanellas, joined him. Kindelán countered heatedly, claiming he already had Mola's support. The argument was not resolved when the morning session ended. Over lunch, uninhibited by committee-room procedures, Kindelán and his supporters brought their full persuasiveness to bear on the dissidents. Outside, the

whole of Nationalist Spain hailed the victor of Toledo.
More immediately, Nicolás Franco's two hundred armed men
awaited a pronouncement.

One thing was indubitable: it would be a determined man,
perhaps even a rash one, who left the meeting stigmatized as
an anti-Franco-ist. None, as it happened, was to vote himself
the label. Even Mola settled for prudence. If the meal for
some was indigestible, at least Kindelán enjoyed the flavor of
its irony. When the session resumed, "the purest gold of patriotism and disinterest shone in the eyes of those present,"
he wrote.

All the same, Kindelán did make one concession. In the
agreement duly signed by Cabanellas, Franco was appointed
"Head of the Government of the Spanish State" rather than
"Chief of State" as the draft had put it. The relegation was
fleeting, for Franco forthwith styled himself Chief of State
regardless. He also scored a bonus into the bargain. When the
final text of the decree was delivered from the printers, the
phrase limiting his office to "the duration of the war" had mysteriously been dropped. In the excitement, few noticed and
perhaps fewer cared.

The first day of October found Burgos *en fête*, the Nationalists still elated by the news from the Alcazar. In the throne
room of the sixteenth-century Captaincy General, the palatial
headquarters of the outgoing junta, a subdued Cabanellas re-
linquished his trappings as provisional president. Drawing a
sword and flourishing it over his stocky successor, he declared
in an austere voice: "General Franco, in the name of the Lord
and by the will of the Spanish people, I hand to you full power
over the Spanish State."

Franco was straight-faced. "My General and Generals," he
responded, "you may be proud of yourselves . . ."

Outside, he was unusually animated. A large and enthusiastic crowd had gathered to applaud his appearance. The insurrection, Franco told them amid repeated cheering and

clapping, had as its motive the salvation of Spain, "the land of hidalgos and nobles."

His regime would govern, he cried, for the good of all Spaniards. "Believe me, the fate of civilization is being decided in Spain. We are defending the heritage of our ancestors. You are about to revive the Spanish empire, itself a legacy of the past . . . have faith in God and the Fatherland."

Franco, it seemed, lacked no faith in Franco. He had become the second Spanish dictator of the century. It remained to reduce the whole land to obedience.

7. Franco as Supremo

On October 20, 1936, three weeks after becoming supremo, Francisco Franco issued a general order for the capture of Madrid, the project delayed by the relief of Toledo. With the exception of the routes to the east, all the city's lines of communication had been straddled by the Nationalists, whose nearest columns were within twenty miles of the capital.

Threatened on three sides, the Republican position in Madrid was precarious. In the first week of November, as the sound of battle drew closer, the government, now headed by Largo Caballero, quit the city for Valencia, on the east coast, leaving the extreme Left to dominate the beleaguered capital. At the same time, General José Miaja, a bald and aging Republican officer in retirement, was recalled to service to defend the great central conurbation against Franco.

On November 5, Franco declared that the occupation of Madrid was imminent and warned its populace to stay indoors while the Nationalist forces took over. All citizens "guilty of crimes", he declared, would be punished. Two days later, his artillery began softening the western approaches of the city, and the Generalissimo announced that he would "hear Mass" in the capital on the eighth.

Nothing, it seemed, could prevent a rebel victory. In the United States, preoccupied with presidential elections, Franklin D. Roosevelt had curbed his instinctive Republican sympathies in favor of the strict neutrality advocated, among others, by the influential Cordell Hull, Secretary of State.

In a Britain on the verge of the Abdication crisis, a Conservative government held firmly . to the policy of nonintervention to which much of Europe paid lip service.

"Ever since the outbreak of the Spanish campaign," Foreign Minister Anthony Eden would declare later, "His Majesty's Government have had two main objects before them: first, to prevent the conflict spreading beyond the frontier of Spain; second, to preserve, whatever the final outcome . . . her political independence and territorial integrity."

Even Stalin was reserved on the matter of aid for the Republicans. Russian arms were slow arriving, payment was demanded in advance and Russian technicians and other experts were ordered to stay away from the front line.

The main contribution by Russia was indirect, namely the Comintern's role in organizing the International Brigades from Republican sympathizers in many countries. These foreign volunteers, including Communists, democrats, liberals and others, went into training at Albacete, on the southeasterly Spanish plain of La Mancha. But none had reached Madrid when Franco's columns bore down on the city.

In Lisbon, the Nationalist propaganda office took Franco's promise to be in Madrid on the eighth with such certainty that it announced the capture of the capital as a fait accompli. More than one correspondent with the Nationalists prepared a communiqué to the same effect.

Nationalist anticipation was complete.

In Seville, the mayor decorated the reception rooms of the town hall with appropriate festivity and ordered a buffet to mark the occasion. "Everything was prepared," vouched one Sevillian. "Champagne, cakes, sandwiches . . ." The same witness described how the *Requeté* organized an expedition, including women, children, and old men, "to enter Madrid behind the first troops with the object of setting up an altar in

the Puerta del Sol and celebrating the sacrifice of the Mass
. . . Taking everything necessary, down to the smallest details, including nails . . ." The party, embracing two carpenters
and four priests, left Seville in high spirits by truck.

Meanwhile, in Madrid, the Leftist authorities repeatedly
urged the people to the barricades. Children helped to raise
barriers, women formed a defense battalion and La Pasionaria
broadcast fervent appeals for those at home to resist attacks
on their dwellings, if necessary by pouring boiling liquid from
the windows.

Others hastened to follow the government along the yet
open road to the east. Mothers, infants, official documents and
artistic masterpieces from the national repositories mingled
indiscriminately in the departing convoys. When journalist
Louis Dalaprée of *Paris Soir* asked two little boys in the back
of a truck what was in the case upon which they perched,
they answered with dignity: "The first edition of *Don Qui-
xote.*"

Many were destined never to get out. At Madrid's Model
Prison, the guards, contemptuous of government orders to
evacuate hundreds of detainees to Valencia, appallingly stood
them by trenches and shot them en masse.

As Franco's Moors and Legionnaries prepared to assault
through the northeasterly Casa de Campo, heading for the
university quarter of the city, an army of workers waited to
oppose them, some armed, some hoping to arm themselves
from the dead. They did not lack numbers. What they lacked,
as General Miaja knew better than most, was the training to
render their ardor effective.

Throughout November 7, the Nationalist shelling intensified
and the defenders braced themselves for the worst. Then,
through the center of the city on November 8 there proceeded
the briskly efficient sight of men marching in military order,
steel-helmeted, well-equipped and accompanied by cavalry.
To the amazement of the onlookers, they were not, as feared,

Nationalists. The first of the International Brigades had arrived. There was new hope.

The battle for Madrid raged more than a fortnight. The Army of Africa penetrated the outskirts; the International Brigade countered to close the breach; the Nationalists came on again through the university quarter. The continuing struggle, fought foot by foot, floor by floor through lecture halls and laboratories, devastating libraries and shattering scientific equipment, violently symbolized the cost in civilized progress of Spain's inveterate disunity. Franco's bombers extended the holocaust.

Not until the last week of the month did the attackers fall back and admit their exhaustion. In Seville, the mayor's victory party had been canceled, the stale food eventually distributed to soldiers. The *Requeté* expedition to the capital, having reached the front, had had its transport commandeered by the army and was compelled to struggle home the best way possible. Many of its members suffered considerably.

For the first time, Franco's professional troops had been repulsed; the tide of invincibility halted. By the month's end, he realized that a knockout blow was impossible. In September, he had chosen to seize power instead of the capital. Now it was too late. A long and debilitating war stretched ahead.

At the back end of 1936, Franco was nominated with heavy irony as "Man of the Year" in a U.S. magazine. Many observers thought he had spent his powder, and increasing doubt was cast on his capacities. Not the least of his critics was General Wilhelm von Faupel, the first German Chargé to the rebel government, who scarcely endeared himself to Franco's entourage.

Von Faupel, at sixty-three an austere and conscientious Nazi, passed summary judgment on Franco. The Generalissimo, he reported after initial discussions, was "incapable of

measuring up to the needs of the situation"; his "military training and experience do not fit him for the direction of operations on their present scale." Moreover, considered the radical
Faupel, Franco's regime, embracing many Monarchist and
Catholic enthusiasts, was downright reactionary.

In this disparaging assessment, the German was joined by
an early Italian Ambassador to Franco, the Count Guido Viola
di Campalto, who considered the Spaniard of only moderate
caliber and lacking a single officer or civilian official of notable
ability. With Franco in charge, feared Campalto, the fighting
might go on indefinitely.

The Generalissimo tolerated such men under duress. When
an overenthusiastic Nationalist sentry put a bullet through the
window of Campalto's car in the dark, narrowly missing the
Ambassador, Franco observed sardonically that the soldier
was a poor shot. Failure at Madrid, however, had increased his
dependence on foreign aid, and he had to conceal his feelings
with politeness.

One of Franco's first actions on gaining power at Burgos had
been to cable Adolf Hitler with best wishes for the Fuehrer's
"well-being as chief of the great German nation . . . with
which we are united by so many bonds of sincere friendship
and deep gratitude." He spoke of the "flag of civilization" the
Fuehrer had hoisted.

In November, the fulsome phrases were rewarded by official recognition of the Nationalist government by both the
Germans and Italians, and that month Faupel arrived at Salamanca. Significantly, he was accompanied by a propaganda
specialist, and another for the "organization" of Spanish Fascism.

At about the same time, the shooting of the captive Falangist leader José Antonio Primo de Rivera by the Republicans
left a staunchly radical Fascist, Manuel Hedilla, at the head of
the party. Hedilla, a former mechanic of working-class origin,

shared Faupel's "pure" demands of the movement (anti-religious, anticapitalist, antiupper-class), and the German set out to subject him to the best Nazi influence.

As the months passed, Salamanca seemed more and more like a Fascist citadel. The town swarmed with smart German and Italian officers, their splendid uniforms making the Spaniards look slovenly. As ever, Spanish pride was quickly offended by foreign arrogance. In particular, the traditionalist element of the Nationalist forces resented German patronization, and the fact that Hitler's men took instructions from no Spanish commander but the Caudillo himself.

In hotels and on the streets, the exchanging of Fascist salutes was incessant. Repeated broadcasts of the Nationalist anthem brought everyone to rigid attention, right arm aloft. One British diplomat later related how he contrived a schedule of lavatory visits to avoid these critical moments.

Von Faupel's gratification was Franco's embarrassment. By the end of the year, the tightrope the Generalissimo walked between Monarchist and Falangist allegiance was strained to breaking point by a partisan atmosphere which had already convinced foreign observers that he was a Fascist.

On December 8, having drawn their own conclusions, the Carlist authorities went so far as to announce the establishment of an independent "Royal Military Academy" for the training of army officers. Franco, unconsulted, was icily furious. Extravagantly accusing the traditionalist leaders of planning a coup d'etat, he ordered Fal Conde, the Carlist chief in Spain, to leave the country within forty-eight hours. Prudently, Fal Conde packed his bags and departed for Lisbon.

It was a bonus for Faupel's propagandists. While the German conspired and the Monarchists fretted, the Italians also brought pressure on Franco. Like the Germans, they had no wish to fight under Spanish generals, and, early in 1937, Franco conceded the humiliating prospect of a joint Italian-German General Staff on Spanish soil. Contemptuously, the Spaniards spoke of the "macaroni eaters"; the latter pronounced Franco's men "a crowd of scruffy Berbers."

In January, nine battalions of Italy's vaunted "Black Shirts" under General Mario Roatta, a trusted Mussolini man, prepared to capture the Republican port of Malaga in the far south. General Queipo de Llano of Seville, who also had a force employed against Malaga, was as keen as Roatta to claim the honor of seizing the city. After a punishing aerial and naval bombardment of the hapless populace, many of whom fled east along the coast, the Italians and Spanish Nationalists entered the town simultaneously on February 8. Friction was immediate.

A few hours after the entry, Queipo de Llano broadcast from Seville that all Marxists in Malaga would be "instantly executed." The wave of shootings which followed genuinely horrified Roatta's men, and the Italian Ambassador reported to Rome his fear lest the "indiscriminate *fucilazioni*" wrought by the Nationalists, which could not go unmentioned in the foreign press, "might be attributed to the Italians and prejudice their standing as a civilized nation."

His orders were to enter a strong protest with Franco. It was intolerable, the Italian informed the Generalissimo, "that barbarities of the kind should soil the fair name of the Italian troops, particularly when Roatta had treated his prisoners with unfailing generosity."

For those who had studied Spanish history, there was no surprise in the pattern of violence. The savagery unleashed by the Carlist Wars of the nineteenth century had shocked Europe. Often, fighting had taken second place to the murder and torture of prisoners, and at one stage Britain had been moved to send an emissary of mercy to appeal against the wanton murder of Spaniards by Spaniards.

There was no evidence now that Franco disapproved of such ruthless destruction of his enemies, and Italian interference was not appreciated. Nevertheless, Mussolini had to be humored. It was not always possible, Franco explained to the Ambassador, to control the men at the front. For all that, the *fucilazioni* in Malaga stopped.

As a result, the prisons became jammed with men awaiting trial and sentence by hastily improvised tribunals. Two years later, when Count Ciano visited Spain as Italian Foreign Minister, he would estimate that there were between eighty and 250 executions a day in some Spanish cities, depending on their size, and that some 10,000 condemned Republicans were awaiting death at any given moment.

Both the German and Italian authorities were concerned about the international reporting of atrocities, and their Ambassadors were at pains to disassociate their nationals from the dubious etiquette of Franco's war.

The bombing of the historic Basque market center of Guernica placed the Germans in an especially bad light. Though far from the only Spanish town to be torn by bombardment, Guernica's ordeal brought the plight of defenseless civilians vividly to the notice of millions, rousing public opinion throughout the world.

When the German Ambassador received urgent orders from Berlin to press Franco for "an immediate and energetic denial" of reports involving German airmen, the harassed Generalissimo was obliged to produce an official press release on the subject. This stated that Guernica had been "set afire and reduced to ruins by the Red hordes." Many subsequent versions were bandied, the German air ace Adolf Galland, who served in Spain in the Civil War, eventually claiming that the Germans bombed the town by mistake. By the winter's end, tension between Franco and his foreign allies was running high.

In March, Roatta's Italian troops, now more than 50,000 strong and operating to the northeast of Madrid, were ordered toward Guadalajara in an offensive that would further tighten

Franco's grip round the capital. With the easy capture of
Malaga in mind, they advanced in high spirits.

Their confidence was misplaced. For a few days all went
well, then, with bad weather suddenly denying them the benefits of Nationalist air supremacy, they found themselves faced
with a resolute Republican counterattack. Two weeks and a
day after its initiation, the Italian offensive deteriorated into a
rout.

Roatta's (and, indirectly, Mussolini's) humiliation was not
consoled by the ill-disguised glee of many Spanish Nationalists, whose officers toasted the downfall of their more glamor-
ous allies as delightedly as if it had been a victory. One
popular joke translated the initials of the Italian army—known
as the *Corpo Truppe Voluntarie*—into the Spanish query
¿Cuando te vas? (When are you going home?)

For Franco, it was a singularly tactless inquiry. The last
thing the Caudillo could afford was a withdrawal of Italian
aid, and his efforts to placate his allies plumbed new depths
of desperation. In response to Roatta's protest that the
Nationalist commanders on the western front should have advanced to relieve the pressure on the Italians, the Generalissimo promptly dismissed from their commands two of his most
loyal generals, Orgaz and Varela, despite the fact that their
troops had been fully extended.

Orgaz had been with Franco from the first Canaries rising,
and Varela was a highly popular officer among the Spaniards. The expedient sickened a large number of Nationalists.

Six months after his appointment as supremo, Franco's
stock had plummeted dramatically. Ominously, conservative
newspapers abroad reported signs from Rome that the Generalissimo was under pressure to "give up the military direction
of the war." According to London's *Daily Telegraph*, well-
informed quarters in Berlin confirmed diplomatic activity on
the same lines.

Even more ominously for the Caudillo, General Mola, the rival he had outsmarted but not discredited in his recent coup, was strongly tipped to replace him.

One warm day in what, for Franco, was the critical spring of 1937, the small Generalissimo strolled in the garden of his Salamanca headquarters, the Archi-Episcopal Palace, and took a long-term stock of his predicament. Surrounded by factional rivalries and conspiracies, his personal safety was constantly at high risk, and one visitor observed that few headquarters had been better guarded. Apart from the sentries on every corner, the entrance was protected by two city police with rifles, two Civil Guards with rifles, two white-robed Moors with rifles and an assortment of plain-clothes men with revolvers. In the bare anteroom where callers were further screened, a stark poster proclaimed arrestingly: "SILENCE! ENEMY EARS ARE LISTENING!"

In the garden, however, the general had privacy. He looked a worried forty-five. With his dark hair graying appreciably, a comfortable spread to his waistline and reflective lines around hazel eyes, he had the manner less of the gnomish pipsqueak of the democratic cartoonists than of a reflective and avuncular merchant.

While the mainstream of Western opinion increasingly regarded Franco as a monkey of the two major Fascist organ grinders, few fellow countrymen (even among enemies) saw him in quite such a feeble light. That an obscure soldier should be claiming absolute control of a broad and tradition-conscious European nation seemed considerably less absurd in Spain than it might have done elsewhere. For in the self-assertiveness of the Spanish individual rested not only much of the country's historic inclination to anarchy, but also her familiar remedy, the patriotic despot.

Every Spaniard, wrote historian Salvador de Madariaga, is a

dictator at heart. Little in Franco's background urged his exception.

Franco's view of history (and he was an avid reader of military and political studies) favored a paternalistic standpoint. Looking into the past, it seemed to the Generalissimo that the constructive peaks of Spanish history corresponded to the individual authority of her rulers, while representative government had too frequently led to destructiveness.

To this extent, he was in rapport with the companion who now joined him in his palace garden musings. Ramón Serrano Suñer formerly leader of the Right-wing CEDA Youth, had been imprisoned at the outset of the war by the Republicans, but, having eventually eluded his captors, had recently joined Franco at Salamanca. At thirty-five, slight and stylishly turned out, he possessed a sharp wit which illuminated remarkable blue eyes.

Being also ambitious, Serrano enjoyed the good fortune of having married Zita Polo y Martínez Valdés, the attractive sister of Doña Carmen, Franco's wife. He now shared the Caudillo's reflections on past and future Spanish politics.

According to Serrano Suñer, Franco saw the existing situation in Spain as comparable to that in the fourteenth century at the coming to power of the redoubtable Isabella the Catholic. Isabella had created unity from anarchy by her grace, her industry, her perception and by punctiliously executing those who defied her. That she had scarcely recognized the Cortes did not detract from her achievement in Franco's eyes.

Again, though Philip II, who had ruled "the Southern Hemisphere" from his solitary desk in the Escorial, had cast legislative crumbs to the people's representatives, he had largely bypassed their demands in his lugubrious efforts to make Spain an unchallengeable world power.

Even Charles III, perhaps the greatest of Europe's "Benevolent Despots," had persisted in reforming Spanish society in virtual opposition to his subjects. "The children," he observed, "do not like to have their faces washed."

The fact was that Spain, despite claims of an early democratic tradition, had seen little of such a tradition in practice by the time the French Revolution shook Europe. The nineteenth century, with its sudden diversification of ideology and the resulting confusion among Spaniards long accustomed to paternalistic government, had found anarchy reclaiming the country. At that stage, the generals had begun to take over.

The suppression of doubt, discussion and argument which returned with the military ethos had paved the way for a new form of autocracy: instead of the absolute monarch, the supremo. In Franco's mind, the soldier politician, exemplified by a range of forceful generals from Narváez to Primo de Rivera, had tended toward discipline and honor in government, symbolizing the nation's desire to be free of disunity, corruption, and foreign intervention.

On one point, the Caudillo and his brother-in-law were without doubt: whatever the success of democracy elsewhere, it was wrong for Spain and could exist there only, as Serrano put, "in a brute and explosive state." At the same time, they were agreed, no man, military or otherwise, could retain power for any considerable duration without an organization to back him. Indeed, General Primo de Rivera's swift downfall when his personal popularity ran out had owed much to the fact that he had failed to establish a party to shore him up.

True, Franco's authority derived from the army, but it could not overtly remain so indefinitely. In time it would be necessary to shift the emphasis from what Serrano Suñer called "pure force" to a somewhat less raw situation.

None of the component parties in the Nationalist setup, Serrano now suggested, was adequate to this need in itself, nor, it was clear, could the uneasy alliance continue much longer in its present state.

Such unity as prevailed reposed largely in a negative

quality, the common detestation of all Nationalists for what seemed to them the alien doctrines of the enemy. Through history, Spaniards had sunk their differences to fight foreigners.

"One of the advantages neighboring rulers envy you," Isabella's confidant Pulgar had once assured the queen, "is having within your frontiers people [the Moors of Granada] against whom you can wage not merely just war but holy war to occupy and exercise the chivalry of your kingdoms. Your Highness should not think it a small convenience."

The lesson had been lost neither on Franco, nor his own confidant, Serrano. Franco's constant reference to the "foreignness" of the enemy, and the "Communist menace" (Serrano Suñer spoke of the "crusade against Asiatic barbarism") reflected such an awareness, as did his increasing emphasis on piety.

Scarcely noted for his religiosity as a serving soldier, Franco had become surprisingly devout since the rebellion. His first act upon landing from Morocco had been to attend Mass in Seville Cathedral. Priests had begun to appear in his entourage. Even his nine-year-old daughter, Carmencita, whose mother had always been pious, was prevailed upon to issue a public appeal through the Nationalist press bureau for all Spanish children to pray for papa's victory.

Finally, to complete the image, the Generalissimo had acquired (through its capture from the Republicans, who in turn had stolen it from Avila) the remains of the hand of the sixteenth-century mystic and reformer St. Teresa. Franco pointedly carried the relic on all journeys and made it known that he kept it, at night, beside his bed.

But crusades, as Serrano knew, had their limits, not infrequently ending in dissidence. The time was near, it was now decided, for Franco to stamp his authority as firmly upon the politics of the rebellion as he already had done on the military structure.

So far, he had appointed his brother Nicolás as Secretary of

State and set up a "technical junta" with seven departments (finance, justice, trade and industry, agriculture, labor, education and public works) to run the domestic affairs of Nationalist Spain under the presidency of a general, Fidel Dávila.

Franco believed that, with careful handling, the more moderate among traditional and Fascist elements could be brought together to suit his purpose in a single corporate entity. The problem lay in the uncompromising cores of Carlism and the Falange, whose adherents looked beyond a mere Nationalist victory to a strictly partisan triumph.

For them, Franco's prescription was ruthlessness. In expelling the influential Fal Conde from the country, the Generalissimo had already introduced the old lion of Carlism to its tamer. Now, with the nimble Serrano beside him, he prepared to draw the claws from a growing and increasingly troublesome tiger.

For a number of reasons, among them Wilhelm von Faupel's taste for conspiracy, the posthumous worship of José Antonio and the uncompromising stand of the "old shirts," or radical Fascists, the Caudillo's brother Nicolás had never really looked like holding the Falange to the Franco line. Serrano advocated new tactics.

In mid-April, ostensibly motivated by disturbances concerning a dispute in party leadership, Franco's men swooped on lodgings in Salamanca and arrested the Secretary General of the Falange, Rafael Garcerán, and a member of the National Council named Sancho Dávila. The two were accused of plotting against the Generalissimo. The arrests, provoking an immediate meeting of party executives, left the radical Hedilla with a narrow margin of support for the leadership. That Franco was gunning for the "old shirts" was manifest, and Hedilla determined to fight it out.

When the Caudillo fired his next salvo by directing that all Falange officials should in future recognize only his own orders, Hedilla countered by proclaiming his first right to party loyalty, encouraging radicals to set up their own junta.

Encouraged by responses in his favor, the ex-mechanic from Santander metaphorically strapped on his gunbelt and took the walk at high noon to Franco's HQ, intent on a showdown. The reception took him off balance. Smoothly, the General-issimo congratulated him on his following, waved amicably to a number of Falangists gathered outside the building and sent his visitor away in an ill-advised mood of confidence.

The next day, April 19, Franco struck.

In a decree which took almost everyone by surprise, the Caudillo pronounced the subjection of all political parties to a single movement. Though its title—*Falange Española Tradi-cionalista y de las Juntas de Ofensiva Nacional-Syndicalista*—contrived to suggest something for everybody, he and none other would be the party leader.

Asserted the decree unequivocally: "We shall abolish the political party system and all that it leads to . . . As the au-thor of this momentous epoch in which Spain has realized her historic destiny, simultaneously achieving the aims of the Movement, the Caudillo exercises absolute authority to its full-est extent.

"The Chief of State is responsible before God and History."

Astutely, Franco also ruled that all commissioned and non-commissioned officers would automatically become members of the new party, a step materially reinforcing the army's in-fluence on Nationalist politics. In a broadcast shortly before publication of the decree, Franco urged his listeners not to be deceived by propaganda invoking the ideals of democracy and human brotherhood. Above all, he demanded, Nationalists of all complexions should unite in self-sacrifice for the new state, which must not be endangered by quarreling, selfishness, stub-bornness, or pride.

The rest followed quickly. Hedilla was placed under guard, charged with rebellion and sentenced to death (though, thanks partly to the intervention of Faupel, this was later commuted to imprisonment). A score of radical Falangists were rounded up. Their propaganda was halted and Carlist radio stations were closed down.

Stunned by the speed and scope of the action, Falangists, Carlists, and orthodox Monarchists alike accepted the merger with surprisingly little protest. Indeed, few had any idea what was happening until it was virtually over, when such likely dissenters as Generals Mola and Queipo de Llano were summoned to Salamanca and faced with the accomplishment. In a single stroke, the man who had belonged to no party had made himself head of them all.

Meanwhile, Franco had diverted his foreign allies with a barrage of ingratiating statements. The Italians, mollified by much soothing and flattery, quickly recovered from their humiliation. Among other promises, the Generalissimo had declared his intention of fashioning Spain "into a close approximation of the Italian Fascist Corporative State as set up and run by Il Duce." He also affirmed that his government would negotiate a concordat with the Vatican, insuring that Spain remained Catholic.

Mussolini, in turn, telegraphed his assurance that Franco could depend on his further aid.

Even the interfering Faupel had been treated to undiminished blandishments. At a public meeting in Salamanca, Franco, already planning to bring the work of Faupel's propagandists to nought, had put an arm round the German's shoulder and unblinkingly expressed his "profound gratitude" for the other's "sympathy and moral support."

"Today," declared Franco, "Spain has the honor to be the bulwark of humanity on which breaks the attack of destructive Communism. She will fulfill her mission in the gigantic work of liberation with the admirable German example to assist her and renew her strength."

The crowd roared "Viva Franco! Viva Hitler!"

Eventually, thwarted in his desire to see radical Fascism thrive among the Nationalists, Wilhelm von Faupel would turn his proclivity for minding the business of others upon the German field force in Spain, the 6000-strong Condor Legion of General Hugo Sperrle, whose subsequent complaints to Berlin resulted in the Ambassador's recall. His replacement, a genial giant named Eberhard von Stohrer, proved more to the liking of Franco and his hustling brother-in-law Serrano Suñer.

By the start of the summer, the Caudillo's "winter of crisis" was history. One event remained to complete his greater security. On June 3, General Emilio Mola, the last officer with a technically superior claim to the rebel leadership than Franco, was killed in an air crash.

Franco received the news with composure.

"His feeling is of relief," wrote one Spanish-accredited diplomat. Few pretended that the Generalissimo's formal mourning beside the red-and-yellow draped coffin of his old colleague of Moroccan days was an ordeal of any great anguish.

8. Deadly Confrontations

The storm threatening the Gredos Mountains, south of the Sierra de Guadarrama, had stacked black towers of cumulo nimbus in the sunset, presenting a sky that winter 1936–37 as lurid and as menacing as the Civil War raging beneath it. In front of the clouds, seeking a clear break to the northwest, cavorted a lone Nationalist aircraft bound for San Fernando airfield, near Salamanca.

On board, Generalissimo Francisco Franco, weary after a long tactical conference with General Varela at Escalona, Province of Toledo, was becoming increasingly dissatisfied with the pilot's progress. It was growing dark with disturbing rapidity. Neither the crew nor its equipment was geared for night flying, let alone a blind landing. At last, Franco could repress his discomfort no longer.

"We had banked and turned over the peaks for quite a while," he said later, "when I went to the cockpit and said to him [the pilot], 'Do you know the opening words of the Falange hymn?'"

"Yes sir," replied the pilot. "*Cara al sol.*" ("Face the sun.")

"Then let's face the sun and get out of here!" snapped Franco.

To the agitation of the second pilot, the Generalissimo now ordered him to give up his place and join the other passengers, who included Franco's cousin, Colonel Franco Salgado, and a subaltern named Eusebio Torres Liarte. Whereupon, Franco, taking the vacated place, began issuing directions to the harassed pilot in the manner of a fussily earnest back-seat driver.

Somehow, they found San Fernando and contrived to land safely. But not before everyone concerned was shaken. Officers waiting at the airfield had become extremely anxious. "The pilot lost his way," Franco told them shortly.

Next morning, the second pilot climbed into the same aircraft, took off from San Fernando and flew at top speed to a base of the Republican air force, in which he eagerly enlisted.

Whether, in view of this remarkable sequel, Franco had had a luckier escape from the storm, or from the disaffected flier, can never be known. One thing was certain: both misadventure and subversion posed very real threats to the small general in his new life as Caudillo.

Contrary to the image cultivated by his apologists, Franco had never despised personal safety, and now, with the heritage of Spain, as he saw it, in his keeping, he took careful precautions to remain with the living. Not long after his visit to Varela, he gave up all flying, a decision finally clinched by Mola's air crash.

He was also sensible to the dangers from Republican artillery. Once, during a later visit to Varela on the central front, the field commander advised him that the position was exposed to enemy fire and that he (Varela) did not wish to be responsible for any accident. Franco bade him farewell and left without argument.

Assassination was a constant possibility, and rumors of plots and purges abounded. According to the German Ambassador, Eberhard von Stohrer, less than half the people in Franco territory were sympathetic to its ruler. In Stohrer's opinion, the fearfulness of the executions carried out by the regime could only alienate the masses and further endanger the Caudillo.

Franco, on the other hand, placed faith in the thoroughness of his repressive measures, taking as his lesson the futility of half-hearted reprisals in the wake of earlier Spanish rebellions.

Stohrer underestimated his system and efficiency. In May 1937 Franco established a special organization, the *Delegación del Estado para Recuperación de Documentos*, whose innocuous title belied an important part of its activities, namely the compilation of a list of "Red criminals" the Nationalists were anxious to eliminate.

When Stohrer later asked if it were true that the Generalissimo had claimed to possess a list of two million "wanted" Spaniards, he was told evasively that there was a "long list."

Meanwhile, when the Generalissimo had to travel, he considered it in the best interests of security to move unostentatiously by fast car with a minimum of formal arrangements and announcements. With good reason, his advisers were happiest when Franco was safely cloistered in his well-guarded headquarters at Salamanca—not the least of them, that influential member of his entourage, Doña Carmen Polo de Franco.

Even dictators, it has been observed, defer to their wives, and while it was not true that Franco was dominated, as some have suggested, by Señora Franco, at least that lady could claim to be the only Spanish Nationalist not actually ruled by the Caudillo. Unlike her husband, whose life to date had been a quest for authority, Doña Carmen had been born to take the quality for granted. It had come, as it were, with the silver spoon in her mouth.

From childhood onward, everything about her, from the regal tilt of her dark and handsome head to the confident steps of her elegantly shod feet, was expressive of well-bred assurance. Carmen had grown up among servants and prosperity. The post-Cuban War depression which had cast its blight upon the naval background of Franco's youth, leaving his mother to scrimp and save for her children, had left the prosperous Oviedo family of Polo untouched. While papa Franco repudiated the "Generation of '98," Carmen's papa, Felipe Polo y Flórez, had adjusted to the modern outlook and flourished.

From her mother, Doña Carmen had inherited aristocratic breeding; on her father's side there was scholarship. Grandfather Claudio Polo had been a professor of literature. To these circumstances of affluence, privilege and intellectual refinement, her beauty had added the final touch. It would have been strange had Carmen not learned to accept admiration and deference as her prerogatives early in her life.

To Franco, then a gauche and impecunious subaltern in his twenties who did not smoke, did not drink and did not fraternize with "good-time" girls, her class, in the social sense, had stood out like a beacon. In this teen-aged goddess, still at school when first he met her, had reposed all he dreamed of attaining, a living symbol of his intention to escape the confines of humdrum bourgeois status.

To the object of his affection, on the other hand, the earnestness of that singularly abstemious young officer must have been touching. If he was too short in stature to make the graceful Carmen an ideal beau, too awkward and sometimes too pedantic, his unquestionable loyalty and ambition were both moving and flattering.

Predictably, the blunt opposition of her parents to the match had increased its intensity. Señor Polo's mind, it seemed, was quite clear. Young Francisco, the son of an undistinguished naval officer, with few apparent prospects and fewer social graces, was not his dream of an ideal son-in-law. Moreover, Franco's obsession with soldiering for its own sake, particularly for soldiering in Morocco, lent appreciable edge to the older man's antipathy.

"We were pacifists at the time," Señora Franco explained later of her family.

In the lengthy stalemate which had followed, Señor Polo's stubbornness had been equaled only by the persistence of his daughter's suitor. So the years passed, and each leave from his military duties Franco renewed his respects in Oviedo, now as a captain, now as a major. Señor Polo had faltered. He had even begun following the Moroccan war maps. Eventually, on October 12, 1923, after the best part of a decade of courtship, Lieutenant Colonel Francisco Franco married Doña Carmen Polo in the Church of San Juan el Real, Oviedo. The colonel was thirty. Characteristically, he had got what he wanted in the long run.

As its sole promoter and executive had known from the beginning, the fast-rising Franco enterprise could scarcely have acquired a more desirable partner. At ease among the airs and graces of the tradition-bound higher social reaches of the army, a *milieu* for which the young Franco had never been well equipped, Señora Franco added a new dimension to her husband's qualifications.

Her effect upon his morale was enduring. Not only had Franco gained an ally who fully shared his faith in himself, but in some ways her faith was more sublime than his own. It was through his wife's piety that he first came to appreciate the practicalities of identifying his mission with divine will. "Her certainty," said a friend, "was his strength in many moments of loneliness."

His wife's role, however, was not without embarrassments. Lacking a family of size to keep her occupied, Señora Franco's lively mind and self-assurance urged a participation in public affairs which, within weeks of her husband's elevation to supremo, caused him considerable mental discomfort.

The occasion was a ceremony to celebrate the festival of the Spanish Race at Salamanca University, where a variety of professors, dignitaries and Nationalist officials was gathered before a large audience under the chairmanship of the Rector, the respected author and philosopher Miguel de Unamuno.

Franco had never had time for philosophers. For years, he maintained, Spain had suffered the influence of "a horde of mistaken intellectuals, despising the true and acknowledged thinkers of our race, peering beyond their own frontiers and absorbing the exotic and destructive in other countries."

The result of this "raging rationalism," as he called it, this savoring of "decadent literature," had been the erosion of patriotism in the minds of the teaching classes. Forgetful of the past, he insisted, they had lost "the most prominent characteristics of our race" and were shameful of the present.

The Generalissimo did not attend the university ceremony, but Doña Carmen was there in his place. The scene was impressive. The walls were hung with magnificent tapestries, there was a band to play hymns; the sunlight shimmered through the old windows, glittering on military braid, ecclesiastical finery and the ubiquitous blue shirts of the Falangists.

Prominent among the public figures present were Dr. Plá y Daniel, the Bishop of Salamanca, General Millán Astray and the Civil Governor of the Province.

When the opening formalities were over, Millán Astray rose stiffly to harangue the assembly. Gaunt and scarred, one arm of his tunic pinned across a bemedaled chest, his single eye glinting fiercely, "*El Gran Mutilado,*" the founder of the Spanish Foreign Legion, was almost hypnotically impressive. He spoke stridently, as though, according to one report, "bursting from that heroic chest."

On this day of the Spanish Race, declared Millán Astray fervently, one-half of all Spaniards were criminals, guilty of revolution and high treason. He was not, of course, referring to the Nationalists.

"*¡Viva la muerte!*" ("Long live death!") shouted a Falangist, offering the general his favorite battle cry.

Millán Astray continued unperturbed. "Catalonia and the Basque country," he said, touching on two regions of stubborn anti-Nationalist sentiments, "are cancers in the body of the nation. Fascism, which is Spain's health-bringer, will know how to exterminate both, cutting into the live healthy flesh like a resolute surgeon free from false sentimentality . . ."

"Spain!" cried the Fascist cheerleader in the audience.

"One!" roared his blue-shirted friends.

"Spain!" he repeated.

"Great!" came the trained response.

"Spain!" he persisted.

"Free!" the crowd clamored.

As one, the Blue Shirts rose, right arms aloft, and saluted a portrait of Franco on the wall. "Franco!" hailed the leader, and they all chanted, "Franco! Franco! Franco!" The rest of the audience rose uncomfortably, but one man, the chairman Miguel Unamuno, remained motionless, seated. Perhaps, for the first time, Señora Franco grew uneasy.

At seventy-two, an ailing but still active academic, Unamuno had devoted thirty-five years of his life to Salamanca University. His hair and his beard were white, and he peered sharply through spectacles perched studiously on an arched nose. Arrayed nearby in black gowns, colored tassels hanging from their mortarboards, his colleagues looked apprehensive.

Miguel de Unamuno rose slowly The hall was now quiet. His speech has been recorded in essence as follows: "All of you are hanging on my words. You all know me, and are aware that I am unable to remain silent. I have not learnt to do so in seventy-three years of my life, and now I do not wish to try any more. At times, to be silent is to lie . . .

"I want to comment on the speech—to give it that name—of General Millán Astray . . .

"Let us waive the personal affront implied by the sudden outburst of vituperation against Basques and Catalans in general. I was born in Bilbao . . . The Bishop of Salamanca, whether he likes it or not, is a Catalan from Barcelona."

He paused, and Señora Franco must have willed him to stop. But he did not.

"Just now," he continued, "I heard a necrophilous and senseless cry: 'Long live death.' To me it sounds the equivalent of '*Muera la vida*' ('To death with life'). And I, who have spent my life shaping paradoxes, must tell you, as an expert, that this outlandish paradox is repellent to me.

"Since it was proclaimed in homage to the last speaker, I can only explain it to myself by supposing that it was addressed to him, though in an excessively strange and tortuous fashion, as a testimonial to his being himself a symbol of death . . .

"General Millán Astray is a cripple. Let it be said without any slighting undertone. He is a war invalid. So was Cervantes . . . Unfortunately, there are all too many cripples in Spain now, and soon there will be even more if God does not come to our aid.

"It pains me to think that General Millán Astray should dictate the pattern of mass psychology. That would be appalling. A cripple who lacks the spiritual greatness of Cervantes . . . is wont to seek ominous relief in seeing mutilation around him . . .

"General Millán Astray would like to create Spain anew, a negative creation, in his own image and likeness. For that reason he wishes to see Spain crippled, as he unwittingly made clear."

Here, Millán Astray, who had restrained himself with difficulty, shouted wildly: "*Muera la inteligencia!*" ("Death to intelligence!")

Señora Franco was ashen-faced. On all sides, the audience broke into a hubbub. At last, voices shh-d and called for silence.

Unamuno, having waited for the disturbance to subside, arms folded, spoke again, coolly.

"This," he said, addressing Millán Astray personally, "is a temple of the intellect, and I am its high priest. You are profaning its sacred precincts. I have always, whatever the proverb says, been a prophet in my own land. You will win, but you will not convince. You will win because you possess more than enough brute force, but you will not convince because to convince means to persuade. And in order to persuade you would need what you lack—reason and right in the struggle. I consider it futile to exhort you to think of Spain."

He paused, then added quietly: "I have finished."

In the moments of astonished silence which followed, one of the professors at Salamanca, Esteban Madruga, diplomatically seized Unamuno with one arm and Señora Franco with the other and ushered them out of the assembly hall.

Franco's wife, it seems, "was so stunned she walked like an automaton."

This explosive clash between humanitarian and nihilist has been seen as "one of the great confrontations of history." At all events, it was the last time Unamuno made, or Señora Franco witnessed, a liberal oration. Franco, supplied with a report of the incident, determined that nothing like it should happen again.

Unamuno, perhaps spared a worse fate by Nationalist fears of a universal outcry, was placed under house arrest, only to die a few weeks later of a brain stroke. Among the last of his utterances was a condemnation of Republican atrocities.

Henceforward, Doña Carmen Polo de Franco tended to concentrate her energies on good works. She organized charity bull fights, patronized the Nationalist Red Cross and applied herself earnestly to the dispensing of food to the famished in newly won areas. She did not return to the halls of controversy.

Franco followed the University of Salamanca episode with a firm choke on liberal studies. A month later, he decreed that all books of Leftist tendencies should "be destroyed as a matter of public health."

Even Hollywood, it seemed, could affect the national hygiene. Turning a censorial eye on the movies, he banned from his territories all films to which the following "radicals" had contributed: writers Upton Sinclair, Clifford Odets, Liam O'Flaherty, Dudley Nichols, and Humphrey Cobb; film stars Paul Muni and Luise Rainer; directors Lewis Milestone and Frank Tuttle, and producer Kenneth MacGowan.

"Having posed as a crusader," observed one Spaniard, "logic prevented Franco from admitting that he could be wrong, the foe ever right. That is why objective voices, such as Unamuno's, annoyed him so excessively. By suggesting that there could be wrong on both sides, they damaged his cause more fundamentally than did the enemy."

It was also why Catalonia and the Basque lands, Millán Astray's "cancers in the body of the nation," provoked so much virulence.

Neither Basque nor Catalan regionalists who opposed General Franco could be dismissed as "Reds" or accused of foreign motivations. Nor could they be reviled as anti-Christ. The Basques in particular were among the most ardent of Catholic peoples. Indeed, the historical paradox which had brought them into the war as allies of the Popular Front government became an increasing embarrassment to Franco as the year 1937 progressed.

"Basque and Catalan separatisms are artificial movements with which the public is not in sympathy," Franco explained to a puzzled world. "Catalonia is as much part of Spain as Lancashire is part of England or Pennsylvania a state in the Union."

It depended, however, upon which public he meant. To many, "artificial" seemed a far-fetched description of phenomena rooted in five centuries of Spanish history. To others, the killing of co-religionists and fellow conservatives, albeit separatists, seemed a good deal less acceptable than the killing of revolutionaries of the Left.

In France, many prominent Catholics were already expressing strong doubts about the ethics of Franco's war. Elsewhere, the counterclaims of Spanish ecclesiastics filled members of the same faith with confusion.

While Cardinal Goma, the Nationalist Archbishop of Toledo, issued a letter to the "Bishops of the whole world" in which he admonished the Basque priests for ignoring "the voice of the Church," the Basque clergy projected the situation in its own terms. Neither the Bishop of Tarragona nor the Bishop of Vitoria subscribed to the Archbishop's attitude, the latter complaining sharply of a denial of religious freedom under Franco and protesting against executions without trial.

To many non-Spanish Catholics, the Nationalist assault on the pious peasants and fisherfolk of the Basque lands meant a reappraisal of original sympathies. In the United States, polls suggested that Catholics were divided six to four against the Archbishop.

Mounting religious feeling against Franco in Britain prompted the Generalissimo to draft a letter to *The Times* of London to the effect that there would be freedom of worship in Spain when he won the war. Meanwhile, he pressed urgently for Papal recognition, profering as inducement the opposite assumption, that is his power to enforce an exclusive official religion on the country. To Franco's delight, the Vatican, perhaps less impressed by the Caudillo than by the atrocities committed against the Church by the Spanish Left, formally recognized his regime on August 28.

A few days later, in a ten-thousand word letter to all Catholic bishops, Pope Pius XI and his co-signatories ruled the election of the Popular Front government void "because of the arbitrary annulment of votes." While "Marxist-held Spain is living without God," declared the Vatican, the Nationalist territories enjoyed "the tranquillity of internal order under real authority . . . Divine Worship is celebrated profusely . . . Christian life abounds and flourishes . . .

"We affirm that the war has not been undertaken to build up an autocratic state over a humiliated nation, but simply that the national spirit should arise with strength and the Christian liberty of older times."

It was a telling stroke for Franco, whose concessions to Catholicism that year included the banning of secular marriage and divorce and whose interpretation of "Christian liberty" would later include the abrogation of the Republic's Law of Religious Confessions and Congregations, the closing of Protestant schools and the outlawing of all public manifestations of worship which was not Roman Catholic.

By the autumn of 1937, Basque opposition had crumbled. Allowing for the improvised nature of its resistance and the substantial advantage in matériel available to the attackers, the Nationalist victory could hardly be attributed to military genius. The Germans complained particularly of the length of time Franco had taken in capturing Bilbao, which fell on June 19.

But the job did bear the mark of thoroughness and foresight. It was necessary, Franco pointed out, not only to reduce the number of enemies in front, but to ensure there were "fewer behind, too."

By any standards, the repression of Basque independence was savage. Early in the fighting, Franco had refused offers of a separate peace based on a limited measure of provincial autonomy, and he went on to destroy the least signs of the separatist spirit.

According to José Antonio Aguirre, President of the Basque Republic, more than a thousand Basques had been executed by November, and a further eleven thousand were under sentence of death. His people, he said, had done their duty, "I only wish I could say that Britain and the western democracies had done theirs."

Spain's "health-bringer," as Millán Astray had put it, was indeed uninhibited by "false sentimentality . . ." The Basque clergy was subjected to fierce persecution. More than four hundred clerics were deprived of their posts or imprisoned, and at least sixteen were shot with extraordinary callousness a few minutes after first learning of their impending death. Among them were the sexagenarian Joaquin Arin, Archpriest of Mondragón, and an authority on Basque culture named Father Aristimuño.

Remarked the Bishop of Vitoria of their execution: "Everyone in Franco's army, from the Generalissimo downward, would have done better to kiss their feet."

On the morning of May 3, 1937, two cars, Klaxons blaring, filled with Anarchist gunmen, turned into the Via Layetana, Barcelona. Since the military coup had failed in the city, the Catalan capital had become a powder keg of conflicting revolutionary ardor.

In their respective lairs in Parliament House and the Palace of the Generalitat, Manuel Azaña, President of Republican Spain, and Luis Companys, President of Catalonia, fumed at the arrogance of the Left-wing extremists whose internecine battles had bedeviled all proper law and order in the city.

The men in the cars scrutinized the streets carefully. Barcelona had the air of a camp under siege. "Practically every building of any size had been seized by the workers and was draped with red flags or with the red and black flag of the Anarchists," wrote George Orwell who was there at the time.

"Every wall was scrawled with the hammer and sickle and with the initials of the revolutionary parties; almost every church had been gutted and its images burnt . . .

"No one who was in Barcelona then, or for months later, will forget the horrible atmosphere produced by fear, suspicion, hatred . . ."

The cars reached the intersection of the Via Layetana and the Calle de la Princesa. Suddenly, a Communist machine-gunner opened fire from the rooftops. The cars swerved wildly, their doors flew open and the occupants jumped out.

"They did not jump out in any recognizable way," recalled an eyewitness. "It was as though, in each car, an enormous compressed spring had suddenly been released. They hurtled out, they seemed to fly in the air while assuming fantastic attitudes and gestures, waving their arms and feet like dancers. It was incredible to see them spinning in the air, and then falling slowly on the road . . ." The machine guns did not stop. "They continued firing until all the men were shot to pieces."

Rain was falling, and slowly a stream of red stain spread away from each body until the whole square was tinted with blood. The Klaxons on the cars were still screaming, leading the inevitable call for revenge. Few vehicles ventured through the streets of Barcelona in the days that followed. For the best part of a week, peaceful citizens stayed indoors while a secondary civil war flared among the hard-pressed Republicans.

Twenty-four hours before the shooting-up of the two cars, Azaña and Companys had been discussing affairs on the telephone when the exchange, which was Anarchist-controlled, had interrupted. "This conversation will have to stop," a voice had announced. "We have more interesting things to do than listen to your stupid conversations."

When government officials saw him soon afterward, Azaña was quivering with fury and frustration. "The situation is intolerable," the fat President spluttered.

Together, Azaña and Companys now decided on a showdown with the Anarchists. Assault Guards were sent to strategic positions and reinforcements requested from Valencia. The telephone building was rushed and secured by the police. The Anarchists responded with barricades and the full mobilization of their members.

For three days, Barcelona was torn by bitter street fighting in which Communist elements, with little love either for the

Anarchists or Companys, interposed on both sides. In the resulting confusion, many adopted the safest policy and shot at anyone sufficiently close to be dangerous.

Among other foreigners who had become involved with the Anarchists, Orwell tried hard to obtain a weapon for his defense, but was regarded suspiciously by the Spaniards. At last, in desperation, he broke into their make-shift armory. Every rifle had been distributed. Climbing to the roof of the Trotsky-ist headquarters, he looked down on the terrorized city and marveled at "the folly" of what was taking place.

"The whole huge town of a million people was locked in a sort of violent inertia, a nightmare of noise without movement. The sunlit streets were empty. Nothing was happening except the streaming of bullets from barricades and sandbagged windows. Not a vehicle was stirring in the streets; here and there along the Ramblas the streetcars stood motionless where their drivers had jumped out of them when the fighting started.

"And the whole while the devilish noise, echoing from thousands of stone buildings, went on and on like a tropical rain-storm."

It was a storm that killed five hundred men, injured a thousand and revealed the numerically imposing Anarchist movement as a force essentially lacking cohesion. By May 6, Garcia Oliver and its other leaders were anxious for a cease fire. When, at 8:20 next morning, a convoy of trucks bearing police reinforcements from Valencia rumbled down the Via Durruti to the *prefecture*, Luis Companys could feel that his government had reasserted its authority.

The true beneficiaries, however, were the Communists. Not only had they seen their revolutionary rivals dealt a sharp blow, they had gained from the manifest disunity among Left-ists a welcome excuse to oust Largo Caballero, the Socialist Prime Minister of the Popular Front government, from office.

Francisco Largo Caballero, prophet of the dictatorship of

the proletariat, the "Spanish Lenin" as he was inaptly dubbed, enjoyed a reputation among many Spaniards for having done as much as any man, perhaps barring Franco, to strike a death blow at Spanish democracy.

For a while, the Communists, bidding hard to usurp the revolutionary lead of the Anarchists, had been glad to cultivate the bald and fiery Socialist, and he to accept their support for his own ends. But, like Franco, he had nursed a typically Spanish independence.

Both Franciscos, in their assault upon the Republic, had of necessity resorted to dangerous allies; each had determined nonetheless to preserve his autonomy. The difference, as it turned out, was that while Francisco of the Right held his own against the Fascists, Francisco of the Left was now losing ground at speed to the Communists.

From his chambers in Valencia, the sixty-five-year-old life-long trades unionist had followed the "Battle of Barcelona" with a sinking heart. Colleagues, noting his increasing gloominess, had put it down to his high blood pressure and its attendant headaches, exacerbated by the execution of his son by the Nationalists in retaliation for the shooting of José Antonio Primo de Rivera.

But Largo Caballero already sensed that the Stalinist minority in his government held the upper hand. Not only in Barcelona was there anarchy. Persecution of technicians and other skilled men of the middle class, coupled with incessant ideological strife among the workers themselves, had left Republican Spain in economic and administrative chaos.

With food to spare in the country, people went hungry for want of efficient distribution. With munitions factories geared for production, assembly stagnated while unions endlessly argued political precedence. While the value of Republican currency plummeted, Leftist organizations elsewhere in Europe exploited the supply needs of the Spaniards, careless of providing good measure for money.

By spring 1937, a government which had entered the Civil

War with gold reserves worth £90,000,000 had already been reduced to cutting open private safes and transporting the loot to its own cellars, often in conditions of the sketchiest security. More than two thirds of the gold had actually been dispatched to Moscow as a basis for Russian aid and was later exported by that country in such quantities that talk of new Soviet gold mines in the Urals became a familiar joke in world banking circles.

As a result of this outstandingly inept expedient, amidst a climate of general mismanagement, the Republican government had become critically dependent on Russia for its ability to maintain resistance to Franco. Still, Largo Caballero defied the Stalinists. In April, he had taken steps to undermine the Communist grip of Madrid's defenses and to bring such political commissars as had established themselves in the army under his direct control. He had even engineered the recall to Moscow of the Soviet Ambassador, Marcel Rosenberg. Largo Caballero, the Russians decided, would have to go.

Accordingly, on May 13, the Communist minority in the government forced a cabinet crisis by demanding the dissolution of the anti-Stalinist Marxist party, POUM (*Partido Obrero de Unificíon Marxista*), which had sided with the Anarchists in Barcelona. Largo Caballero refused, and the Communists walked out.

When Moscow simultaneously intimated her refusal to provide urgently needed aircraft to the Republican Premier, his fate was thrown into the hands of the moderate Socialists—never his best friends—who alone could now save him from Communist pressure. Instead, they looked for an alternative leader among their own ranks.

On May 17, the aging firebrand was ousted and the mauled body of the Spanish Republic placed in the hands of one Dr. Juan Negrín, a politician of sufficiently limited resources to satisfy the string-pullers of Moscow.

The tussle of the Franciscos was over. It remained for Franco to complete the demise of their victim.

9. Nationalist Victory

For many months after the start of the Civil War, the western world—especially Washington, which had known him well as the Spanish Air Attaché—puzzled over the whereabouts of General Franco's younger brother, Ramón. Shockheaded, extrovert, and impulsive, Ramón had been the first member of the family to make headlines, storming the news in 1926 with a nonstop flight from Cádiz to Buenos Aires. A decade later, he had just as abruptly disappeared.

When reporters failed to unearth him, the news media was tempted to speculate. According to some stories, based on his early and militant activities in support of the formation of the Republic, Ramón Franco was on the opposite side to his brother.

"Somewhere in Rightist Spain today," declared one American journal mysteriously, "brother Ramón is sitting in jail, for his Leftist sympathies."

In fact, Ramón Franco was not in Spain, but Majorca. Having returned from America at the outbreak of hostilities, he had received the rank of lieutenant colonel from his brother and been appointed commander of the Nationalist air base on that island.

Thus discreetly removed from the spotlight by the cautious Caudillo, impetuous Ramón awaited a cue, as it were from the wings, while Francisco struggled for control of the stage itself.

Perhaps "ring" provides a better analogy, for in the second half of 1937, and through the coming winter, the Spanish contest hardened from what Georges Kopp, the Trotskyist leader, called "a comic opera with death" to a dour and bloody slogging match.

Militarily, each side had put on weight, the fight becoming both numerically and qualitatively more even. By intensive recruiting and the rapid training of new officers, the Nationalists had made good their deficiency in manpower until, in November, Franco could boast 600,000 (640 battalions), 290 artillery batteries and 400 aircraft. The Republicans, though deprived of numbers by defeat in the north, had raised the efficiency of their arms dramatically, especially where supported by the International Brigades, and could claim almost as many trained battalions as the Nationalists. Toe to toe, the rival armies traded punch and counterpunch.

In July, the Republicans had answered the Nationalist capture of Bilbao with a punishing offensive in the Brunete area of the central front. The same month, Franco struck at Santander on the north coast, entering the port on July 26. His opponents hit back in December at Teruel.

Here, in the eastern hills of the Peninsula, men who had sweated in the sun of the central plains now froze in a temperature forty below zero. Vehicles slid off icy roads, hands stuck to the guns they strove to haul manually and everywhere the limbs and heads of dead soldiers rose from the drifted snow.

The Republicans took Teruel; the Nationalists seized it back. To and fro the fight swayed, but the only real winner was the elements. Neither side was equipped to endure such conditions.

"Of all my memories of the Spanish Civil War," wrote one witness, "the most vivid and pathetic is the vision of Franco's

soldiers around Teruel, thinly clad, wearing shoes made of
canvas and esparto grass . . ." Of one Franco battalion more
than seven hundred strong, less than two hundred survived
the winter.

In March, the Republicans scored a telling blow at sea, sinking the Nationalist cruiser *Baleares* by torpedo. Though many
of the crew were picked up by British vessels, 761 officers and
men, including the admiral in charge, went down with the
ship.

Republican jubilation, however, was short-lived. Since November, Franco had been massing forces and supplies for a
hefty assault on Catalonia, aiming to knock-out the eastern
Republic as surely as he had dealt with the equally independent Basques. While his men had fought for their lives at
Teruel, German and Italian matériel had poured into the Nationalist ports. Franco planned to add Barcelona to Bilbao,
Santander, Malaga, and Cádiz.

As more and more battalions were marshaled in the northeast, the Generalissimo braced himself for the big punch. But
first, the Catalan capital, the heart of the target, needed softening. The cue had arrived for Majorca's air base to give
Franco its full worth.

On the morning of March 17, 1938, several waves of Italian
Savoie-Marchelliti bombers, flying in sixes, took off from
Palma, Majorca, climbing north, flying high for Barcelona.
They carried the latest development in Axis aerial weaponry
—bombs designed less for penetration than for their capacity
to devastate wide areas. Before long, Warsaw and London
would experience the technique, but as yet there was scope
for experimentation.

Beneath the droning warplanes, the Mediterranean
stretched brilliantly west across the Gulf of Valencia to the
distant sierras. Ahead lay the rugged peaks of the Pyrénées.

Within minutes, the busy sprawl of Catalonia's splendid capital was in sight.

At the United States Consulate in the Plaza de Cataluña, Barcelona, the Military Attaché, General Stephen Fuqua, was talking on the telephone. His attention was drawn to the window, not by the approaching planes, which were obscured from him, but by the sight of people running in the street.

Without further warning, Fuqua simultaneously heard an explosion and was flung across the office. The window was shattered. He was lying on the floor surrounded by fragmented glass. The building shuddered as more bombs fell on the city. Europe, three years hence, would view such a raid as commonplace, but now in Barcelona horror mingled with astonishment. The devastation, hurled at random at the heart of the capital, was widespread, and the people were quite unprepared for it.

As Fuqua ventured out to investigate, the bombers were already heading back for Majorca; another wave loading its cargoes. Everywhere, citizens had been caught in their daily stride—stricken on the pavements, in shops, on buses. One crowded bus had suffered a direct hit. At a sidewalk cafe, the American discovered the shocked waiters sweeping the mangled remains of customers into baskets. He found himself staring at a woman's shoe. A severed ankle protruded from it.

According to Fuqua, who made a note of each attack, the waves of aircraft struck the city at intervals of from one to several hours, dropping their bombs from a considerable height. In all, there were seventeen attacks in three days, killing hundreds of civilians and wounding some three thousand.

Even Hitler's Ambassador to Franco was horrified. The raids, protested Stohrer, were "nothing less than terrible . . . Almost all parts of the city were affected. There was no evidence of any attempt to hit military objectives . . ."

Among others, France and the Vatican protested in strong

terms. The British Foreign Office, viewing the episode "with horror," reminded Franco that "direct and deliberate attacks on civilian populations are contrary to International Law as based on the practice of civilized nations, as also to the laws of humanity and the dictates of public opinion."

Stung by the adverse publicity, Franco retorted that Barcelona was jammed with "Red" supplies and munitions, thus presenting an important military objective. He had, it was claimed, attempted to wage the war as "humanely" as possible, but, as his own Foréign Department put it, "his noble designs had been frustrated by the perfidy and bad faith of the Reds" who had contrived to install depots, offices, and training centers in areas screened by civilian populations.

"General Franco, whose noble and lofty feelings are well known, has endeavored, and will continue to endeavor, to restrict to the maximum degree the effect of aerial activity upon populous towns, limiting its use to those extreme cases when imperious military necessity makes recourse to it unavoidable."

Mussolini was less displeased with reactions than the Spaniard. On the evidence of Count Ciano, he expressed himself gratified that his warriors "should be shocking the world with their aggressiveness." It made a change, boasted the Italian dictator, from "charming it" with guitar music.

This attitude supported Franco's approach to the less delighted of his allies, whom he soothed by privately blaming the Italians for the bombing. Meanwhile, the world remained puzzled by the role of brother Ramón. Eight months later, his contribution to the cause still unsung by the Nationalists, Ramón Franco was pronounced dead, killed in a seaplane crash off Majorca. His demise, along with those of Sanjurjo and Mola before him, completed a remarkable trio of air accidents in Franco's life.

Had Francisco Franco been other than a nondrinker and a nonsmoker, he must have sat back with a cigar and a bottle

of cognac that June and toasted the Nationalist breakthrough.
The bombing of Barcelona was still under discussion when the
full import of the general's new offensive had swept the matter to the background. Strongly supported by German tanks
and Italian troops, the Nationalist forces had swept the Republicans aside and raced to establish a diagonal salient from
the western Pyrénées to the east coast in the region of the
province of Castellón. Unprepared for the onslaught, the defenders had offered only patchy resistance.

With the coming of summer, Franco commanded a front
from the Pyrenean border above Sort, through Lérida to
Amposta on the east coast. Catalonia was surrounded—completely cut off from Madrid and Valencia. Moreover, both the
foreign and domestic affairs of the Caudillo's regime were better than he might have dared to hope just a year ago. Thanks
substantially to the iron ore deposits in his territories (much
coveted by Hitler, who hoped to monopolize the industry),
Franco had maintained a fair export business.

The capture of ports on the north coast had meant outlets
for trade in ore with Britain, and Franco was no longer entirely dependent for aid upon Italy and Germany. With his
new earnings he had bought trucks and other supplies from
the western democracies, feeling strong enough the same year
to place a ceiling of twenty-five percent on foreign shares
in Spanish industry.

This serious upset to German plans infuriated the Nazis,
and Goering advocated "holding a pistol" at Franco's head.
But it meant new contacts for the Nationalists in other countries.

At the end of 1937, the British government arranged to exchange "trade agents" with the Generalissimo in the persons
of the Duke of Alba and Sir Robert Hodgson.

For Franco, the representation of a major democratic world
power at Salamanca was a valuable key to respectability. Already, Poland, Czechoslovakia, Holland, Rumania, Switzer-

land, Yugoslavia, Turkey, and Uruguay had similar agents with his regime, while Greece, Hungary, Japan, Manchukuo, and Eire were among those who had accorded him full recognition.

While the Republican peseta fell, the Nationalist peseta gained in value. While the Republican government became increasingly vulnerable to Russian whim, Franco became less dependent on his allies. He brought an aristocratic soldier with American and British affinities, General Gómez Jordana, into foreign affairs to help offset the pro-Axis bias of his brother-in-law, Serrano Suñer. And he made it clear he wished no truck with possible rivals.

Both the Alfonsoist and Carlist heirs had offered their services to the Nationalists, only to be sent packing with rebuffs, and when Franco's old political boss, Gil Robles, turned up at Salamanca from Lisbon he was given the same treatment.

Gil Robles returned to Lisbon to charge the Caudillo with insulting him. Franco's Spain was no place for a Parliamentarian, especially a Monarchist.

Meanwhile, Juan Negrín, the Communist-backed Republican Premier, was struggling to match the Generalissimo's authority. In many ways, this moderate Socialist, thickset and darkly handsome with a taste for good living, seemed an odd candidate for Communist support. It was the acceptability of his image to the democracies that appealed to Moscow. He turned out to be stronger than expected. Transferring the central government to Barcelona, Negrín had proceeded to exercise increasing control over Catalan affairs and the rival clans of the Popular Front.

At last, some sort of unity was served on the Left, and the Communists did not get it all their own way. Indeed, for a while it seemed they might even have supported the wrong man. Negrín had an experienced Socialist in Indalecio Prieto at his Defense Ministry, and Prieto was a staunch anti-Communist.

Army officers were forbidden to attend Communist Party meetings, the post of Chief Political Commissar was abolished and so were many of the commissariats, including that of one Commissar Anton, a fervent party man who had become the lover of La Pasionaria. For this, the demogogic woman deputy did not thank the strong-willed Prieto.

Communism, however, held two powerful weapons: its external control over military aid to the Republicans, and the persuasiveness of its strong-arm agents inside the Republic, notably those of the Communist dominated SIM, or *Servicio de Investigación Militar*. Ostensibly a counterespionage organization, SIM was used increasingly in Negrín's time to terrorize and eliminate Communism's rivals.

The need for foreign aid bore heavily on Negrín and, with the commencement of the Generalissimo's offensive to split the Republic, the Prime Minister flew to Paris to seek the opening of the French frontier with Catalonia for the passage of Russian and other arms to his government. The approach was timely, for the Nationalist breakthrough had coincided with Hitler's assault on Austria and the formation of Léon Blum's Popular Front government in France. The French cabinet not only agreed to Negrín's request, but contributed to the supplies which now began to flow over the border.

Franco came very near to a confrontation with the French. At one point, Blum actually proposed issuing an ultimatum to the Caudillo demanding his immediate renunciation of Axis support, but withdrew on the advice that a unified policy between Britain and his country was imperative in the face of the Fascist threat.

Negrín's satisfaction was short-lived. On returning to Spain, he found Barcelona bombed, Franco's advance continuing and Prieto slumped in a chair confiding to reporters, "We are lost . . ." The Defense Minister's long and punishing fight against enemies on both sides had not left him in a mood to mince words. Like millions of other Spaniards, he saw himself trapped between Franco and the Communists, and he wanted neither.

Negrín could not tolerate such pessimism. At the end of March, backed by popular demonstrations organized against Prieto by La Pasionaria and her fellow ideologists, the Premier deposed Prieto from his defense post and the veteran revolutionary resigned the government. Reluctant as he might be to do so, Dr. Negrín was dancing to the tune of his sponsors.

Summer, wedding pessimism to stark reality, urged Negrín to desperate action. Accordingly, on the morning of July 24, he called an extraordinary council of war in Barcelona. The plan agreed among the ministers and officers present was to launch an all-out offensive across the Ebro river from the north in the hope of restoring contact with the Republican forces to the south of Franco's salient. That it was a counsel of do-or-die there was no doubt, for the French, falling back into line with British policy, had reclosed the frontier, and Catalonia's war resources would be committed to the utmost.

The same day, an army of 100,000 men—the so-called "Army of the Ebro"—was alerted, and that night the advance units moved off to cross the river to cries of "Forward, sons of Negrín!"

Smoothly as his own cause appeared to be proceeding in the first half of 1938, Franco was conscious of being jostled by greater events. Elsewhere in Europe, the storm clouds were gathering, and though he had seldom missed an opportunity to congratulate Hitler on his postures—the Caudillo's latest message of blessing had been an enthusiastic response to the Nuremberg Rally—the small dictator lived with a mounting dread that his "big brothers" of the Axis would push their luck too far. The one thing, as Franco saw it, that could now prevent his victory was a larger war in Europe, a war that must bring either a French army over the border to restore the Republic, or an Axis occupation to end his independence.

As the year had opened, a great deal depended on London where the British Premier, Neville Chamberlain, was locked in stubborn disagreement with Foreign Minister Eden over policy toward the dictators.

Chamberlain's desire for appeasement versus Eden's espousal of a firm role had come to a head over Italy's part in the Civil War. Reviled by totalitarian apologists everywhere, the elegant Anthony Eden had held his ground, demanding the withdrawal of Italian troops from Spain before Britain could think of befriending Mussolini.

Wrote Eden's counterpart, Ciano, in his diary: "The crisis is on . . . I have authorized Grandi [Italian Ambassador in London] to take any steps which may add an arrow to Chamberlain's quiver. An Eden cabinet would have as its aim the fight against the dictatorships . . ."

On February 20, Franco's fears were dispelled, at least temporarily. That morning, Chamberlain called Eden to Downing Street and dismissed him. The British Prime Minister was set on a policy that would sacrifice one country after another to the Fascist powers, and, if it did not bring "peace in our time," certainly gave Franco time enough to complete his own war before the rest of Europe erupted. When Ciano heard of Eden's removal, he went out in festive mood to drink "several toasts" with the Prince and Princess of Piedmont. Franco was scarcely less relieved.

Through his agent in London, the Duke of Alba, he now pressed for closer links with the Chamberlain government, asserting that Republican Spain had lost the war and hinting that improved relations with the Nationalists would be in Britain's best interests if she wished to safeguard her access to the Mediterranean.

One way in which relations could be improved, the Generalissimo suggested at the end of April, would be for the British government to persuade France to reclose the French border to military supplies for the Republicans. The border was shut in a few weeks.

Later in the year, Lady Chamberlain toured Franco's Spain to the acclaim of the Nationalist press. Though her visit, like that she had paid to Mussolini, was unofficial, Franco saw to it that she received a splendid welcome at Burgos. British papers reported her progress; Falangist papers described her as "one of us." One foreign correspondent asked if she intended to seek a complete picture by visiting the Republicans.

"Why should I?" replied Lady Chamberlain.

Franco was in good form, staying at the Duke of Villahermosa's country seat north of Zaragoza, when the Ebro offensive hit the unsuspecting Nationalists. It had been a dark night, and the vanguard of the attack had crossed the river safely under the noses of the enemy, some by boat, some on pontoons, some wading and swimming in their eagerness to strike a long-awaited blow at the other side.

In the vicinity of the bridgeheads, the weight and ferocity of the offensive overwhelmed the Nationalists and, within a few hours, the "Sons of Negrín" had driven a salient thirteen miles deep into enemy territory.

Franco's immediate concern was to promote calm among the volatile Spaniards around him. To this end, his first activity the morning the news broke was to attend a lengthy church ceremony to celebrate the feast of St. James, the patron saint of Spain. Afterward, he treated his agitated staff to an impromptu dissertation on the earning capacity of operatives in the Galician fishing industry before, eventually, starting for the battle front.

The Republicans had gained important heights along the river and, ominously for the Nationalists, were fighting with a fury they had not shown for some time. The viciousness of the clash shocked participants on both sides.

In a hollow known as "The Valley of Death" a young American, Edwin Rolfe, attached to the Lincoln Battalion of the

Army of the Ebro, jotted some hasty impressions of the grim
fight.

"Place stank with dead. Enemy shells over our ridge into
valley beyond, killing evacuated wounded, men with can-
teens at waterhole . . . As dark came, enemy began to use
tracer . . . Bodies stank. Bullets popped overhead, red tracers
seemed to move slowly through air. Men screaming: '*¡Socorro,
socorro!*' ('Help, help!') or groaning '*¡Madre Mía!*' long drawn
out . . . Men dead by hundreds, mostly the enemy . . .

"Longest day I've ever spent . . ."

Franco set up his headquarters in a large truck at Alcañiz,
a town on the tributary of the Ebro not far from the fighting,
with road communications to north, south, east, and west. The
fact that this time he ignored advice about his personal danger underlined the seriousness with which he viewed the crisis.

His plan, however, was a cool one. It was to concentrate on
holding the flanks, allow the enemy advance to extend to the
front, then, at length, to pinch in the bridgeheads and cut off
the Republicans.

"In this way," he explained, "our troops would maintain a
stranglehold on the Red salient and in due course destroy
their opponents on the very ground chosen by them."

The scheme, calling for patience and the acceptance of considerable losses, did little for Nationalist morale. Though the
impetus of the Republican charge died out before the Army
of the Ebro achieved its objective of a land link with the central forces of the government, the "Sons of Negrín" held on to
their early gains and the approach of winter saw both sides
bogged down in savage trench warfare.

Franco was to lose some 41,500 men on the Ebro, and as
the figures mounted, his handling of the campaign was increasingly questioned. This time, the Caudillo could not remain
aloof from his subordinates, and violent arguments flared at
his headquarters.

Visitors found the customarily composed *gallego* in a rare

and peevish temper. "They don't understand me!" he burst out. "They don't understand me! I have the best of the Red army locked up in an area twenty-three miles long, and they don't understand me!"

It was not only his own officers who doubted his methods. The Germans, pointing out that he had learned his tactics against Moorish tribesmen in the desert, complained that he was old-fashioned, especially in the use of tanks which he was reluctant to use en masse—"in a concentrated way," as Colonel Ritter von Thoma, the Condor Division's tank commander, advocated.

Stohrer, the German Ambassador, had become sufficiently pessimistic to urge a negotiated peace between the two sides before the nation's tolerance of Franco was too far undermined by his terror tactics against Leftists in occupied territory.

Franco, he reported, bridled at the suggestion with nervous intensity.

"There will be no mediation," Franco snapped stubbornly. "Criminals and their victims cannot live together . . ."

Even Mussolini was downcast. "Put on record," he told Ciano as the Ebro stalemate continued, "that I predict the defeat of General Franco."

On top of everything, the Sudetan crisis had brought friction in Europe once more to the danger point. With conflict seemingly imminent, the French warned Franco point-blank that they would advance through the Pyrénées and Spanish Morocco if he did not make his neutrality in such a conflict explicit.

"Tell them," Franco ordered his agent, "that Spain will be neutral if they keep out of our war."

He had little option. Though Axis aid was crucial to his own victory, he could scarcely hope at that stage that Germany would be strong enough, whatever the eventual outcome of a larger conflict, to prevent the French army implementing its threat. And if it did, his regime would be finished.

"The Government of Spain," he told Britain accordingly, speaking of the Nationalists, "intends to maintain complete neutrality in the event of the outbreak of war in Central Europe on condition that no power provokes war in Nationalist territory. Their [the Nationalist] air and armed forces will in no circumstances cross the Spanish frontier so long as Spain is not attacked."

Chamberlain's Munich appeasement again eased the tension, but the Germans were not pleased with what they regarded as Franco's overenthusiastic pledge of neutrality, and his urgent need for supplies for the Ebro front was used by them to extort larger holdings in his war industries. A seventy-five percent interest was obtained in three companies.

Hitler's occupation of Czechoslovakia, coming as a further revelation of his methods and attitude to treaties, did nothing to improve Franco's peace of mind in the foreign sphere. By now, however, he had overcome the home crisis.

If Nationalist losses in the Ebro offensive had been high, the Republican cost had been higher. Too much had been spent in the initial blow to allow for an effective follow-up. Bogged down in trench warfare, the "Sons of Negrín" had lost both heart and initiative and could only wait apprehensively for Franco's counterattack.

When it came, in October, those who scrambled back across the river could count themselves lucky. Some 20,000 prisoners had been taken by the Nationalists and more than twice as many casualties suffered. Those who tried to stand on the plains north of the Ebro were swept aside. "It was a rout," declared the Republican general Vicente Rojo.

Two days before Christmas, the Generalissimo ordered six army corps to converge on Barcelona, mopping up Catalan resistance as they went. On January 26, 1939, Moroccan and Navarrese troops, cautiously probing the outskirts of the city, discovered it bereft of military opposition. The streets were bleak and dirty, torn by Franco's bombs and the bullets of feuding Leftists. Many people, hungry and sick of bombardment, were positively welcoming.

When Franco made his entry in a column of fifty thousand soldiers, including the Italian Littorio Division, the city's Conservatives could at last come into the open. There was wild applause and loud shouts of "Franco!" and "Duce!"

By February 10, the border with France was manned exclusively by Nationalists and practically all Catalonia subdued. Later that month, Britain and France recognized the regime, while Azaña, his orderly and civilized mind distracted by the chaos and brutality of events, resigned the office of President, a post which had ceased to be meaningful. In the United States, another President was coming to the conclusion that recognition of Franco was inevitable.

"But let him stew in his juice for a while," pronounced Roosevelt.

In Catalonia, the Generalissimo had seized seventy percent of the enemy's munitions output, destroyed the army on which his foes had pinned their last hopes, and severed the remnants of the Republic from its land link with the rest of Europe.

Madrid still held out. But Franco had thirty-two divisions and six hundred aircraft deployed against the capital while, within it, the populace was faced with near-starvation rations.

At the beginning of March, Colonel Segismundo Casado, commander of the Republican Central Army, outlined the hopelessness of the position to Negrín. The army commanders were almost unanimously in favor of negotiations with Franco, the air commander agreed with them and the chief of the Republican fleet intimated that his crews would rebel if steps were not quickly taken toward peace.

On March 5, the fleet at Cartagena, defying the Negrín government, put to sea and headed for the safety of Algiers. Only Dr. Negrín and the Communists were for fighting on.

On March 6, Colonel Casado acted openly against the Prime Minister, assembling a Council of Defense at his headquarters in Madrid's Calle de Alcala to discuss an end to hostilities. The most influential of its non-military members was the Socialist Julián Besteiro, whose refusal to leave the capital during the war had endeared him to many Madrileños.

There ensued a remarkable public dialogue, followed by millions of Spaniards on both sides. "The moment has come," declared Besteiro on Madrid's radio, addressing himself to the Nationalists, "when we are disposed to undertake negotiations for an honorable peace. We await your decision." From Burgos radio, next day, came the Nationalist reply.

"We can answer only that we desire victorious peace," intoned the voice of Franco's brother-in-law, Serrano Suñer, Minister of the Interior. "After victorious peace we will show our generosity."

There was an impasse, it seemed, between honorable and unconditional surrender. Meanwhile, the Council, having suppressed a Communist coup in the capital, strove privately for a compromise. In preparation for the worst, secret plans had been laid for the evacuation of Madrid when, to the surprise of Casado and Besteiro, Franco invited talks on a cease-fire.

Hopes for genuine discussions proved abortive. On March 23, the Council's envoys arrived at Burgos only to find foreign photographers posted at the airport and Franco's representatives in a frigid mood. His demands were unaltered: surrender without pact or signature.

The Caudillo was happy to play cat-and-mouse.

On March 25, Franco launched a new offensive, at the same time reiterating promises of "generosity" by radio. For the despondent Republican troops, they were enough. Acting on their own initiative, many disbanded their units and went home. Orders to return to the lines were ignored. By the evening of the twenty-seventh, the Central Army had melted away; only its General Staff remained in the contest.

According to one correspondent in Madrid, C. D. Gallagher, the first Franco troops to enter the city came by Metro, actually paying for their own tickets. Wrote American reporter Gallagher of the end of hostilities: "I knew when I had written my last word on the subject. It was when my runner came back and returned my last telegram. He said: 'Italians are in the radio station. They looked at this and said, "Take it away, we don't want it."' I packed up my typewriter and began to think of London. My job was finished."

On April 1, Franco published his final bulletin of the Civil War. "Today," it ran laconically, "the Red Army having been disarmed and captured, the National troops have reached their final military objectives. The war is over."

ᴸ Including exiles, Spain had lost a million of her population in three years and spent the equivalent of 3000 million ill-afforded pounds on her own destruction. Something like six hundred thousand people had died as a result of the Civil War, of whom perhaps a hundred thousand had been executed without proper trial, or otherwise murdered.

It was a far cry from the coup d'etat the generals had planned in 1936. Few then had foreseen a struggle of more than a few weeks; fewer that the three principal plotters would die in the contest while the devious "Franquito" emerged as Spain's Caesar.

Of the Republican principals, most escaped to exile, but the would-be peace-maker Besteiro stayed with the people. His fate belied Franco's "firm guarantee for all Spaniards who are not criminals." Placed on trial by court-martial, Besteiro was condemned to thirty years imprisonment and, in due course, died in a Nationalist jail. Luis Companys, the Catalan President, met a less protracted end. He was executed by the triumphant Caudillo. Hundreds of more humble men were shot day by day. Prisons in the newly conquered territories, like those already held by the Nationalists, were quickly filled by Leftists awaiting a like fate.

In Ciano's book, Franco was engaged in "very drastic and painstaking housecleaning. Many Italians (Leftists who had fought as volunteers with the International Brigades) also were taken prisoner . . . The Duce . . . .ordered that they all be shot, adding 'Dead men tell no tales!'"

Perhaps symbolically, the victory celebrations were marred by torrential rains. As Franco took the salute of 160,000 picked troops in Madrid, drenched members of the diplomatic corps watched ten thousand Italian and five thousand German soldiers swing past with Fascist-trained precision.

On his head, the small general sported the red beret of the Carlists, while, under his campaign jacket, he wore the blue shirt of the Falangists, an odd compromise he had already made effectively his own and was to carry forward to a new era of Spanish politics.

Next day, he strode solemnly under a white canopy held by six priests into the suburban Church of Santa Barbara for the religious ceremony. Ten thousand palms had been strewn on the steps and a choir of monks chanted antiphons from the days of the nation's imperial splendor. On the high altar stood a crucifix commemorating the sixteenth-century Christian victory of Lepanto over a Muslim fleet.

Stiffly, the Caudillo halted. Unhitching his sword from a bulging waist, he handed it to Cardinal Goma, the Primate, and, with bowed head, offered thanks for his triumph over "the enemies of truthfulness."

10. "We Three"—Franco, the Duce, and Adolf Hitler

Six months after the end of the Spanish Civil War, Hitler's Panzers detonated the second world conflict of the century, and Franco dropped out of the international headlines—though not for long from the minds of Europe's new belligerents.

On May 10, 1940, the alarming distress of the democratic Allies produced the resignation of Britain's Neville Chamberlain and a fresh government under Winston Churchill. Among the first measures of its foreign department was an urgent, if not altogether optimistic, attempt to establish some rapport with the Caudillo.

"It is essential," Britain's Deputy Chief of Naval Staff, Admiral T. S. V. Phillips, informed the chosen envoy, Sir Samuel Hoare, "that the Atlantic ports of the Peninsula should not fall into enemy hands. With the probable loss of France and the French fleet we are stretched to the utmost in our battle with the U-boats. If the Atlantic ports of the Peninsula, and with them the coast of northwest Africa, go over to the enemy, I do not know how we shall carry on.

"It is essential also that the naval base of Gibraltar should remain available to our Mediterranean and eastern communications. If you can do anything in support of these fundamental needs of the war, your mission will be of the highest importance."

Hoare, slight of build, a figure of quiet respectability in a very English tradition—he had been educated at Harrow and Oxford, spent some thirty years in the House of Commons and hailed from the oldest banking family in the City of London —had been unemployed since the collapse of Chamberlain's cabinet, of which he had been a member.

After pottering disconsolately between his home and the Carlton Club, and the Carlton Club and the Houses of Parliament for a few days, he had been taken aback by the offer of what seemed a most onerous mission. Chamberlain, told of the assignment, doubted if Hoare should accept it. "You may never get to Spain," exclaimed the ousted Premier, "and if you do, you may never get away.

"The French army is in hopeless rout, our own army is already being evacuated from France and is leaving behind most of its equipment. Go to Spain if you wish, but do not expect that in the midst of these defeats your mission can be successful."

Hoare decided to chance his luck with events and with General Franco. It was eloquent of the suspicion felt in London for Franco's Spain, however, that the conservative Sir Samuel took instruction in the use of an automatic pistol before leaving, and not only carried this during his journey, but also retained the services of an armed bodyguard from Scotland Yard for his visit. The British aircrew which flew him to Madrid was ordered to remain there in readiness for a quick return if it were needed.

The welcome of the Franco regime was not heartening. On the morning of June 1, the expected time of Hoare's arrival in the capital, noisy crowds organized by the Falange were out in the streets shouting "Gibraltar Español!" and other anti-British slogans. As it happened, the plane did not appear until the afternoon, and, well before it touched down, the demonstrators grew tired and dispersed.

Hoare's first refuge was the Ritz Hotel, Madrid, where the

ambience proved somewhat less than to his liking. "It was, for instance, filled with very aggressive Germans. Gestapo agents listened to our conversations and hung around us at every turn. Our telephone was regularly tapped." Sinister events stalked the white and gold corridors. "A Spanish ex-Minister was decoyed from the restaurant and brutally assaulted by Falange gunmen. The wife of a German diplomat threw herself from the top floor when she heard that her husband had been ordered back to Germany. A discreet management shrouded such embarrassing episodes from the visitors . . ."

But "the atmosphere of enemy espionage could not be mistaken." Hoare began looking for a house in which to set up headquarters. He found one in the Castellana, now the Avenida Generalissimo Franco. It had one drawback: it was next door to the German Embassy.

While waiting for the all-important audience with Franco, Britain's self-styled Ambassador "on special mission" consulted his American counterpart, Alexander W. Weddell. Weddell, a cultured and pleasant-mannered man who collected old books and possessed in Virginia a Tudor manor house transported from England, lived in one of the finest residences in Madrid, the Montellano Palace, surrounded by Goyas and Guardis. Amongst such splendor, Sir Samuel found him not optimistic.

The United States had eventually opened relations with Franco on April 1 of the preceding year, since when Weddell had been subjected to systematic discourtesy from the regime to which he was accredited. He warned Hoare especially of the pro-Axis sentiments of Franco's forceful relation Serrano Suñer, dubbed for his dominating posture within the hierarchy the *Cunadisimo*, or Brother-in-Law-in-Chief.

Late in 1939, Serrano Suñer had become Franco's Foreign Minister, showing a marked antipathy toward the United States and Great Britain. With prematurely white hair, blue eyes and a penchant for colorful ties and snappy attire, the *Cunadisimo* could turn on dazzling charm when it suited him, but he displayed little in his dealings with Alexander Weddell.

A particular subject of contention between the two men was that of food supplies offered by the United States for Spain's starving populace. The Civil War had left the land in dire fear of famine. "In any other nation except Spain," as Hoare observed sympathetically, "I should say the country is already very near it."

Among other preconditions, the American government sought assurances of recognition for such aid in the Spanish press and a declaration of Franco's full and continuing neutrality. Weddell also pleaded for some leniency toward the Generalissimo's ill-fated political opponents. Instead, Serrano Suñer boasted the increasing solidarity between Spain, Germany, and Italy; America was castigated in Falangist newspapers, and the execution of prisoners continued unabated.

From Weddell, Sir Samuel also learned of the difficulty of talking to Franco. While the German Ambassador had access to the Caudillo almost for the asking, the American had been kept waiting for weeks on end, to be dismissed after all with the most brusque of interviews.

Hoare contrived to arrange an audience in three weeks, each of which seemed an interminable length. In the second, resistance to Hitler ended in Norway, Mussolini made his declaration of war on the Allies and Franco altered his status of neutrality to the equivocal one of "non-belligerent."

In the third, Marshal Pétain sued for an armistice and the Germans drew ominously near the Spanish frontier. Madrid teemed with rumors. The Germans had crossed the border and were advancing through Navarre. Nazi tanks had been seen in San Sebastian.

One night, Hoare was awakened and informed that Hitler's troops would be in the capital in a few hours. Since he had reluctantly sent his plane back to London, there was nothing he could do at that moment. He turned over and completed his slumbers. Meanwhile, he had met the Generalissimo fleetingly in the formality of presenting his Letters of Credence—a stiff march up the staircase of the Madrid Palace, a short pause in the splendid suite at the top, a formal exchange of introductions in the throne room with its Tiepolo ceiling, then a few minutes of desultory conversation with the Caudillo.

Franco was correct but unbending.

"I was accorded no personal interview such as he invariably gave to the Axis Ambassadors and to several of the neutral chiefs of mission," complained Sir Samuel.

"When I afterward reflected on these experiences, the Gibraltar demonstration, the ubiquitous signs of German interference . . . and the evident disinclination on General Franco's part to enter into any serious discussion . . . I began to wonder whether Chamberlain had not been right, and my mission had not started too late."

By June 22, the day fixed for the audience, Hoare was more than impatient to find out. Franco received him in the library of the Palace of the Pardo, last occupied by Azaña, across a desk on which reposed signed photographs of Hitler and Mussolini. Hoare found the dictator "small, rather corpulent" and "bourgeois" with "the voice of a doctor with a good bedside manner."

His prescription met the worst expectations of the Englishman. "Although it was common knowledge that the country was on the verge of starvation," recalled Sir Samuel later, "he brushed aside my remarks by declaring that Spain needed nothing from the British Empire, and that any imports that were required would come from North Africa . . .

"As to the course of the war, it was clear from almost everything he said that he regarded an Allied victory as entirely impossible.

"'Why,' he asked, 'do you not end the war now? You can never win it. All that will happen if the war is allowed to continue will be the destruction of European civilization.'"

In Hoare's view "such staggering complacency made any serious discussion almost impossible." With democracy fighting for its life beyond Spain, the Generalissimo impassively advocated surrender to the assailants. The Englishman departed Franco's presence astonished at the Spaniard's apparent conviction that he had been marked out by Providence to save his country at all costs and "to take a leading part in the reconstruction of a new world."

Such a world, it seemed, would be ruled by dictators.

Franco and the Pardo Palace were well met. The secluded, modestly sized building first erected by the Emperor Charles V as a hunting lodge for the Spanish kings, appealed to the Generalissimo's insular, unostentatious nature. Palm-shaded terraces embraced the red-brick and blue-tiled château in shadows of privacy; the quiet, intimate interior was mellow with fine old carpets and tapestries.

Here was to begin a reign more remote and cloistered from the ruler's subjects than that of any Spanish autocrat since Philip II. Outside, in the remains of the ilex forests through which Charles III and Charles IV had so zealously toted their shotguns, rabbits, partridge and fallow deer still abounded. It was the setting in which Franco had always fancied himself, complete with twelve-bore, Scottish tweeds and English Spaniels—the distinguished but understated squire of *Country Life*.

The village itself was something of a let-down. From the end of the road, on a slight rise beyond, could be seen Madrid and the terracotta plain of Castile. But the Velázquez aspect was not improved by the poverty and squalor in which the people of Pardo lived, nor by the barracks at each end of the village street.

As usual where Franco went, Moorish and other armed guards were prominent. Hoare, familiar with the trappings of statesmen, found the protective measures exceptional.

"I seemed to be visiting an oriental despot in the East rather than a Spanish General in the West," he wrote. "Indeed, the impression of grim seclusion given me by the environment of this chief of a police state was far stronger than any I had felt in visiting the last Sultan of Turkey in Constantinople."

Such precautions were circumspect. With the end of the Civil War, bands of Leftist guerrillas had taken to the hills and woods to continue their resistance to military dictatorship. They had little alternative but summary trial and sentence.

"The steady toll of life taken by the tribunals set up in many of the principle towns," reported a *Times* correspondent after the war's end, "is driving to desperation the Republican militia-men who have hitherto succeeded in avoiding capture or have escaped from concentration camps."

Spain, in exhaustion, cried out for an amnesty, "a great and noble voice," as one Spaniard expressed it, "to put soul into the peace," but Franco was not the man to raise it. Too often, in the belief of the pragmatic general, peace from Spanish civil strife had been bought by equivocal armistice leading, after a breathing space, to rebirth of the conflict.

This time, there would be no rebirth if Franco could help it. The general's decree on the treatment of political offenders, announced early in 1939, covered not only his opponents of the Civil War, but reached back to the period of the October Revolution of '34. Its terms, proposing "guilty of subversive activities" all who had "opposed the National Movement in fact or by grave passivity," left little room for complacency in anyone who had not actively supported the rebellion. Informants were granted a heyday, and private grudges found a new form of settlement.

All Republican officials and servicemen were detained as a matter of course, and any soldier with rank was normally con-demned to a long prison sentence. Those pronounced guilty of killings, or of failing to have stopped them, were sentenced to death. Trials and executions took place daily, and every twenty-four hours Franco and his Assessor-General, Martínez

Fusset, discussed and approved the execution lists. A small proportion of those sentenced was reprieved by the general, whose sense of chivalry appears at times to have been touched by the pleas of mothers or wives who appealed directly to his mercy.

In four years following the Civil War, it has been estimated that an average of slightly less than a thousand executions were performed a week, the figure being higher for the first two years, when shootings were daily; lower for the next two, when the mass killings took place weekly. The International Committee of Jurists put the total figure for the period at 192,684 victims.

Lesser "criminals" were incarcerated in prison where Franco magnanimously offered them redemption through "labor and good behavior," one day of good behavior to be "equivalent to reducing the sentence by two days." Many died of disease and other factors before, as Franco put it, they had "paid for the crime."

While the Caudillo bought security at home with the firing squad, security in the foreign sphere called for more subtlety. On the eve of his victory, Franco had blustered: "After the Civil War, Spain will be organized as a nation in arms . . . she must and shall have an army equal in efficiency to those of other countries." This was a long-standing Franco dream.

Again: "It is sheer fantasy to discuss Mediterranean equilibrium without taking Spain into consideration. We have in our hands, irrevocably in our hands, the entrance to the Mediterranean, and, in view of modern armaments, this acquires an unthought-of significance.

"When other European states discuss the Mediterranean, we will not be left out of any talks on this problem. I shall consider, and Spain herself will consider, completely invalid any plan which may be formulated regarding the Mediterranean without us."

Bold words, but the boldness was not backed by substance. Franco was unquestionably master of Spain, but he had won something suspiciously like a Pyrrhic victory. Nationalist expenditure during the war had equaled 480 million gold pounds against a revenue of 148 million for the same period.

Mussolini was owed 56 million pounds for his assistance, and Hitler had yet to render his own bill. Spain's capital had been squandered on self-destruction, her gold had disappeared abroad, vast agricultural and industrial assets destroyed. Almost all her merchant fleet had gone, half her railway rolling stock, a third of her road vehicles. Worse, the skilled workers vitally needed for reconstruction were largely alienated from the regime. Many were dead; more in prison or exile. The fury triggered by the general's rebellion had brought the country to the verge of ruination.

When Franco talked of an efficient army, modern weapons and Spain's role in the Mediterranean, he was talking to a people on the brink of starvation who had seen enough fighting to last them a lifetime.

In June 1939, he came down to earth with a tacit admission that the crusading general had returned to his old role of cautious opportunism. "The chief feature of our foreign policy," Franco announced then, "is its *hábil prudencia* (adroit prudence)."

Franco had always been a prudent officer. Whatever his private reservations, he had in the past marched in step with the Monarch, the dictator Primo de Rivera and the Republic alike, so long as his professional ambitions had been well served. Only when these were rudely terminated by the advent of the Popular Front government, had Franco shown signs of rebellion, and then he had been a most cautious conspirator.

Nothing about Franco was rash or spontaneous; no route chosen without lengthy recourse to the maps. Even the one great gamble of his life, the act of rebellion, had been plotted with the odds well in favor of paying prompt dividends.

It was significant that his calculations for a swift coup had been confounded by the one factor least comprehensible to his nature—spontaneity on the part of the people. If one attribute above others had enabled him to triumph, it was his chameleon-like ability to adopt in turn the colors of the rival groups which supported him. Now he was faced with a wider test of the facility. Upon it depended the survival of Franco's Spain.

Centuries of Spanish history demonstrated the dangers to the nation of involvement in foreign wars, and whatever attention the Caudillo may or may not have paid to the short but constructive reign of Ferdinand VI, one of Spain's rare pacifist rulers, he could scarcely have failed to be impressed by the profit accruing to the nation through neutrality during the last great war of Europe.

Yet neutrality, too, posed its problems.

On the eve of the gathering conflict, Franco confided to Ciano the crux of his dilemma: a "miserable future," as he put it, for a neutral Spain if Hitler won; the end of the Nationalist regime, he avowed, if the democracies gained victory.

This bleak outlook was further aggravated by the Hitler-Stalin pact, an event which staggered Franco to an extent he had not known in many years. Not only did it make a mockery of his Civil War relations with the Germans in the defense of "the Catholic and Spanish heirloom of civilization against the Marxist heresy and the Russian plague," but it revealed starkly Hitler's appalling cynicism, a quality the earnest Franco found profoundly disturbing.

September 1939 saw the Generalissimo calling urgently for a settlement in Europe before things went too far, but his thin voice was lost in the crescendo of gunfire, and the sweeping German successes of summer 1940 swept him on a new tack before the wind of prudence.

"The broad view that I then formed and that subsequent

events did not modify," recalled Sir Samuel Hoare, "was that Franco definitely wished for an Axis victory, but not for an overwhelming victory. A peace of negotiation seemed likely to give him the chance of projecting himself into a European position of importance . . . a broker's part between the belligerents . . .

"If he was to enter the war, he must . . . be quite sure that any serious fighting was over before Spain became a belligerent."

In the seclusion of his sanctum at the Pardo, Franco strained his wits both "to have his cake and eat it." Like Philip II, he fought his case largely on paper.

On August 15, Britain now standing alone against the complete totalitarianization of Europe, Franco wrote to Mussolini expressing his "greatest admiration for the brave Italian comrades who had fought so gloriously," asserting his intention to join the war at a favorable opportunity *so far as he had means at his disposal.*

To this end, he declared, he had requested from Germany the conditions for action. These, as the German Ambassador saw it the same month, comprised territorial demands including Gibraltar and parts of North Africa (notably of French Morocco and Algeria), and military and economic aid from Hitler.

Mussolini replied that, in his opinion, Spain's participation in the war would not depress her economy, though he understood Franco's desire for a breathing space. However, he added, circumstances were against this. Soon, Britain would be defeated; indeed, her government survived solely on the element of untruth. Then Franco could depend on Fascist Italy to back his objectives.

The Duce was advising what Hitler would reiterate: that Franco should join the Axis first and bargain later.

On September 22, Franco wrote to the Fuehrer, protesting

"unchangeable and sincere adherence" both to the Nazi leader and the cause in which he was fighting. Spain's first military action, he stated, would have to be the occupation of Gibraltar, for which, he confided, he had been preparing in secret for some time. The seizure of The Rock would only take a few days. But he omitted to say when he thought of effecting it.

Meanwhile, he had sent Serrano Suñer on a goodwill mission to Germany, during which the *Cunadisimo* talked with Ribbentrop and Hitler, and quaffed champagne left over from Molotov's visit. It was his strong impression, he informed the Caudillo, that the Germans had designs for North Africa and were not enamored of Franco's ambitions there.

By autumn, the Fuehrer, tired of Franco's dallying, decided to use personal persuasion on the Spaniard. He wanted Spanish bases urgently, and that October the Great Dictator crossed occupied France to Hendaye, on the Pyrenean frontier, to settle matters with Spain's small and prevaricating despot.

Adolf Hitler had not helped Franco to power for nothing. Now the creditor was coming to collect.

The German leader told Mussolini afterward that he would rather have his teeth out than submit to another confrontation with Franco, and there is little doubt that the Fuehrer was unprepared for what took place at Hendaye.

For the last four years, the Generalissimo had missed few opportunities of conveying admiration to Hitler, who might well have assumed he was dealing with a sycophant. On his scant knowledge of the Spanish, the Fuehrer rated them emotionally susceptible, and his long and unusual journey to Hendaye smacked of a winning gift to the ego of the Spaniard.

For the rest, was he not the lord of half a continent and Franco the head of an impoverished and defenseless land? There can have been few misgivings in the Nazi's mind as he traveled south about the outcome of the meeting.

Yet, things went wrong from the start. To Hitler's annoyance, Franco arrived for the appointment an hour late. Strutting the red carpet to the conference coach which was parked at the railway station, the Caudillo gave a gratifying Fascist salute, but, once inside, perched stiffly on a seat in silence and seldom opened his mouth but to carp.

According to the Fuehrer's interpreter, Paul Schmidt, who was present, Franco did not even look like the man they had expected. Stout and swarthy, "with vivacious black eyes," the Caudillo struck Schmidt as a candidate for a burnoose: an Arab rather than a top Spanish general. His high-pitched voice was like that of "a muezzin summoning the faithful."

Hitler felt that the man was "not cut out to be a politician." For all that, Franco needed no lessons in obstructiveness. When the Fuehrer announced that the war was almost won, the Caudillo reminded him shrilly of America. When Hitler declared proudly that his troops would clear the British from Africa, Franco chimed in that Africa was a large continent. When the Nazi generously offered German troops for the storming of Gibraltar, Franco would not hear of it. National pride demanded Spaniards for the job, he protested.

January, cried Hitler, was the time for Spanish action; now, the time to seal the alliance.

But first, bemoaned Franco, he needed grain and heavy armaments. More grain and armaments, perhaps, than Hitler could afford at the moment?

And so the meeting went on. For every positive point by the Fuehrer, the small Spaniard trilled an objection. And when he could not conjure one fast enough, he claimed he could not understand the interpreter. According to Schmidt, at one point Hitler leaped to his feet with impatience, but, on second thoughts, sat down again, drumming his fingers.

As the discussions at Hendaye evolved, the main barrier to an alliance seems to have turned on Franco's stipulation of territory in North Africa. According to the Caudillo, Spanish expansion in Africa, like the recovery of Gibraltar, was "a duty and a mission." He had seized Tangier in June, while the other powers were preoccupied.

But Franco knew that Hitler cherished North Africa for his own ends, and if the shrewd *gallego* sought a further delay in developments he had picked the right subject. He had also picked the right moment, for the guns Hitler needed for an advance through Spain to Gibraltar had been diverted east by the British campaign in Greece.

When the German leader refused to discuss Spanish claims until Franco had committed his country to belligerence, the result was an impasse. Franco returned to Madrid with his hand intact; Hitler fumed over a wasted journey.

"I fear," he told Mussolini afterward, "that he [Franco] is making the greatest mistake of his life . . . it does not correspond to the help you and I, Duce, gave him when he found himself in difficulties."

But perhaps, added Hitler, there was still time. "Perhaps at the last moment he will realize the catastrophic effect of his behavior and will find, even though it be late, the path to that front whose victory will determine his own destiny."

Franco followed Hendaye with every sop to Hitler short of belligerence. German agents were allowed to swarm freely through Spain. The Spanish press beat even the Nazi press in extolling the Axis war effort.

German reports from the Peninsula told of the Caudillo's obligingness in the business of refueling U-boats in secluded Spanish bays, a facility that was to be extended to the Germans throughout the Battle of the Atlantic to the cost of many Allied lives and supplies.

Early in 1941, his anger now faded, the Fuehrer wrote Franco amicably but chidingly: "We three, the Duce, you and I, are bound to one another by the most rigorous compulsion of history that is possible. This being so, we, in this historical

analysis, should obey as a supreme commandment the realization that in such difficult times *not an apparently wise caution
but the bold heart can save nations."* (author's italics)

There was an added threat:

"The mightiest military machine in the world stands ready
for every additional task it may be put to to solve. And how
good and reliable this instrument is the future will show."

On February 26, Franco replied in obsequious terms, stress-
ing his "utmost enmity against England." He wished to dispel,
he said, the slightest doubt that he stood with the Fuehrer, at
his disposal, "united in a common historical destiny, desertion
from which would mean my suicide and the death of the cause
I have led and represent in Spain.

"I need not confirm my faith in the triumph of your cause,
and I repeat that I shall always be its loyal follower."

That summer, Hitler's invasion of Russia was warmly wel-
comed by Franco. Not only did it represent a comforting diversion of German arms from the Pyrénées, it gave the
Caudillo the added satisfaction of posturing once more in his
familiar role as the enemy of Communism and anti-Christ.
Spain sent a division of volunteers to the Russian front.

In July, in the most outspokenly antidemocratic speech he
had yet made, Franco warned the United States to keep out
of Europe, repudiated economic aid from America and Britain, denounced "outworn democracy" and categorically stated
that the Allies were beaten.

Speaking to an audience of army officers in Seville, he
averred that for twenty years Germany had been the defender
of European civilization, and that if Berlin were ever to be
threatened a million Spanish soldiers would be ready to help
the German people. Serrano Suñer made the most of the prevailing climate, insulting America, congratulating the Japanese
on Pearl Harbor and inciting a crowd of supporters to attack
the British Embassy.

Meanwhile, American and British attempts to win Spain's friendship through economic aid were rebuffed. Though many Spaniards, perhaps the majority, at heart preferred the Allied cause to that of the Axis, Franco allowed no such sentiments in public. He even preferred to reimpose bread rationing rather than accept wheat from the United States government. Unable to turn down one shipload of grain from the American Red Cross, the regime refused to acknowledge it openly, instead exploiting the gratitude of the hungry by acting as distributors.

While President Roosevelt's initiatives were snubbed, and the American people continued to be offended by the killing of Spanish Republicans, Serrano Suñer vented his personal animosity toward the United States on Ambassador Weddell.

When Weddell had cause to complain that a letter posted and delivered in Spain actually bore a German censor's mark, the Foreign Minister was furious. The stand-up row which ensued between the two men resulted in a breach for several weeks between Franco's Foreign Ministry and the American Embassy.

Britain was finding the going no easier. Having extended a generous trading loan to the Caudillo, the war-battered island was repaid by constant villification in the official Spanish press, the abuse of British diplomats and the refueling of Nazi U-boats in Spanish bays.

Not everyone was willing to suffer Franco silently. In Washington, Cordell Hull summoned the Caudillo's Attaché to his office and expressed himself bluntly. "While it is most disagreeable to recall our experiences when dealing with the Spanish government," growled the American, "I must state that in all its relations with the most backward and ignorant governments in the world, the American government has not experienced such a lack of ordinary courtesy or of the consideration prevailing between friendly nations as it has at the hands of the Spanish government."

The policy of the regime, he pointed out, had been "one of aggravating discourtesy in the very face of our offers of aid . . . bearing in mind the coarse and extremely offensive methods and conduct of Serrano Suñer in particular and, in some instances, of General Franco."

Winston Churchill would be equally succinct in his war memoirs. The British leader called Franco a "narrow-minded tyrant" whose "policy throughout the war was entirely selfish and cold-blooded."

11. "The Hour for Changing the Guard Approaches"

As 1941 drew to a close, the promised Axis victory did not seem to Franco any closer. Watching the German army grind to an icy halt in the Russian snows, the Japanese demolish the monuments of *Hispanidad* in Manila and the United States rise in arms against the Fascists and their allies, the cautious Caudillo dropped a hint of appeasement here and there to the democracies.

One result of this modified attitude was a more critical appraisal of his brother-in-law Serrano Suñer, whose dislike of the western powers was proverbial.

Sir Samuel Hoare, the British Ambassador, placed the Spanish Foreign Minister with Ribbentrop and Ciano as "the three musketeers of totalitarian intrigue." Little love was lost between the Briton and the Spaniard.

"If I wrote a psychological study of his personal character," Hoare informed London, "I should find my model in the novels of Stendhal . . . The love of power, the struggle to achieve it, the determination to maintain it and the delight in displaying it, he describes in particular with a penetrating cynicism that almost always ignores the higher motives of the human mind and heart.

"In Serrano Suñer, Stendhal would have found a personality that fully conformed with his conception of the ambitious ca-

reerist whom he so often made the central figure of his novels
. . . Count Mosca in the *Chartreuse de Parme* was Serrano
Suñer's prototype . . .

"Looking myself at this strange man, nervous, sensitive, with
the sensibility of a jealous woman, prematurely gray, metic-
ulously careful in his personal appearance, I once thought he
was something of a pinchbeck Robespierre.

"For behind his pleasant family life and his obvious delight
in smart society, he had a ruthless nature. More than once he
spoke to me of shooting men and women as if it were a matter
of no account, and never did he display the least symptom of
human kindness toward the protestations that I constantly
made to him about the iniquitous treatment of innocent
people."

Serrano, who reputedly blamed the United States and Britain for not intervening to save the lives of two brothers shot
during the Civil War by the Republicans, made a scarcely
better impression on the new American Ambassador, Carlton
J. H. Hayes, who had replaced Weddell that summer. Of the
redoubtable brothers-in-law, it was Franco rather than his
Falangist Foreign Minister who first deigned to put a serious
case to the American.

The Caudillo began by lecturing Hayes, himself a distinguished historian and former professor of Columbia University, on Spanish achievements in America across the centuries,
in which he indicated the selflessness of Spain's missionary
efforts in the New World.

Hitler, insisted the Caudillo, was "an honorable gentleman
who had no quarrel with Great Britain and no thought of im-
pairing its independence." The real enemy of the United States
and Great Britain was not Nazi Germany but "barbarous and
oriental Communistic Russia."

"He insisted upon the 'impregnability' of the 'fortress of
Europe' which German arms had constructed and against

which all efforts of the British and the Russians and 'even the French' had proved vain. France was utterly defeated. Russia was being conquered. The British Empire was spent.

"Even if we could now train and equip large armies, we couldn't repeat our feat of 1917–18 and get them across the Atlantic by reason of the vastly increased effectiveness of German submarines, and in any event there would now be no such possible landing place for us as France had provided in the First World War.

"The moral [Franco asserted] was that we should concentrate our strength against Japan in the Pacific and come to terms with the Axis in Europe."

When Hayes stressed in reply the futility of treating with the Nazis, pointing out the succession of broken pledges and treacherous aggressions in their wake, Franco listened impassively. He had said his piece and did not elaborate.

Serrano Suñer slouched in his chair, his eyes on the ceiling. He kept, it seems, a "cynical" countenance. "On the few occasions on which I saw him in the spring and summer of 1942," wrote Carlton Hayes of the Foreign Minister, "he impressed me as having something inscrutable about him. He seemed mysterious and never frank. We knew of his intimate associations with the German Ambassador . . . and we had plenty of evidence of his fostering of Falangist activities against the United States in Latin America."

But where did he stand in relation to his leader? Was the Falange's most conspicuous chieftain aiming to usurp the powers of his less flamboyant relative and raise the party to omnipotence in the regime? Certainly the conservative wing of the Nationalist system distrusted him, and rumors of unrest in the army, ever jealous of its own power, abounded. Its fears were not unfounded.

Apart from being the only legally recognized party in the country, the Falange was militantly organized and well established in government, where its members held three vital Ministries embracing press control, the syndical unions and the police. The Civil Governor of every Spanish province was a member of the party, and Serrano Suñer spent much of his time on visits to the branches where he took the Fascist salutes of its blue-shirted minions. His photograph overwhelmed all others in the pages of Spanish newspapers.

By the summer of 1942, the man Spain dubbed the *Cunadisimo,* the Brother-in-Law-in-Chief, had undoubtedly overstepped his usefulness to Franco, so dominating the political stage that many Spaniards wondered if the influential Foreign Minister were not in fact already the master of his remoter relative.

This view was not diminished by the small dictator's disinclination to parade in public, nor by the secluded method of personal rule from El Pardo. Franco had watched events patiently. In autumn, he acted.

For some time, reports of increasing substance had circulated of a military plot to restore the monarchy, and, in September, a bomb was thrown at the Minister of the Army, General José Varela, well known for his traditionalist, anti-Falangist sympathies. Varela escaped injury, and the crime was attributed to Falangist youths, a number of whom had links with Serrano Suñer.

The situation was hand-made for the Caudillo, and he exploited it with characteristic thoroughness. Both Serrano and Varela were relieved of their Ministries, thus killing two birds with a seemingly impartial stone, and their places taken respectively by the Generals Jordana and Asensio. Since Jordana was sympathetic to America and Britain, while Asensio, though inclined to the Axis, was less emphatically pro-Nazi than his predecessor, the foreign outlook had been modified discreetly in favor of the Allies.

As a final touch, Franco assumed direct charge of the Falange. It was an honor its more ambitious members could have done without.

Count Gomez Jordana was a man of such slight physical stature that when he sat on his office chair his feet hung clear of the ground, but Allied diplomats vouched for the amplitude of his spirit. Ever a good friend of the Anglo-Saxon people, his patriotism, unlike that of Franco, did not lead him to treat foreign affairs purely on the level of expediency.

Jordana was born of aristocratic soldiers. Not only was he of a different mold from the bourgeois dictators of Europe, he had never believed in their ability to suppress the pride and tradition of Britain. In the darkest days of Dunkirk, he had likened that nation to a fighting bull: at its most formidable when wounded.

He arrived at the Spanish Foreign Office in good time to see his views vindicated.

October bode ill for the Axis and, in November, came what historians would look back upon as the turning point of the Second World War. In North Africa, Rommel was on the run before Montgomery; at Stalingrad, von Paulus was losing the decisive battle of the Russian front. Meanwhile, the Americans and the British were planning a combined offensive that was to cut the German retreat in Africa and lead to the overthrow of Mussolini's Italy.

The project was the amphibious invasion of Morocco and Algeria, to which end Gibraltar buzzed with Allied preparations through October. At this manifestly critical moment for all Spaniards, Jordana kept a cool head, maintaining his trust in the intentions of the British and Americans.

"How often," declared Hoare, reflecting on the distinction between the new Minister and his predecessor, "I blessed my good fortune that I was dealing with a wise friend and not an excitable enemy!"

On November 6, secret instructions relating to the proposed Moroccan landing arrived by British code in Madrid. They included the texts of two personal letters: one from Roosevelt to Franco, the other from Churchill to Jordana. Delivery orders were to come later.

"On receipt," ran the instructions, "by either of the [Allied] Ambassadors of the word 'Thunderbird' in cipher, followed by a time, they are to concert together immediately and arrange to make their respective communications at, or as soon as possible after, the time given, which will be the time of the landing in North Africa."

The following day, a Saturday, Hayes received a telegram. It read: THUNDERBIRD. SUNDAY NOVEMBER 8. TWO A.M. SPANISH TIME.

In consultation with Hoare, it was now agreed that their respective arrangements to call on Franco and Jordana should be made at the last possible moment. The Germans already had contingency plans to occupy the Peninsula in a crisis, and it was deemed advisable to minimize the chance of a warning by Axis agents of a special meeting with Franco.

It was decided that Hayes should contact Jordana in the early hours of the coming morning and demand an immediate audience with the Caudillo. When Roosevelt's letter had been delivered, Hoare should present Churchill's to the Foreign Minister. Resolved to "maintain an attitude of unconcern," the British Ambassador spent Saturday afternoon shooting wood pigeons on the estate of a Spanish friend, the Count Velayos.

In the American Embassy there was much bustle. Wisps of smoke rose from the chimneys into a clear autumn sky as the staff busied itself burning confidential documents in the furnaces and grates. Hayes did not intend to be caught unprepared by "the very great possibility that the Germans might make a dash in force over the Pyrénées and down across Spain onto our flank."

That night, after the servants had gone to bed, Hayes sat up with his aides in a small sitting room screened by heavy curtains at the windows. Soon after one o'clock, the Ambassador phoned Jordana at his home. The Foreign Minister was in bed. Hayes said he must see him at once.

Jordana's surprise was muffled by sleepiness. Twenty minutes later, the American was on the Count's doorstep. The diminutive Spaniard appeared in pajamas and bathrobe and, after inquiring in vain the reason for the urgency, agreed to try and rouse El Pardo on the telephone. It took half an hour to get a reply. The Caudillo, it appeared, was away on a hunting party and would not be back until early morning. He would then set an hour to receive the Ambassador.

Again, Jordana pressed for an explanation.

"It was then a little after two," recalled Hayes, "and I knew our landing in North Africa was already under way . . . I decided to take him into our confidence."

Shortly after breakfast, Hayes was ushered into Franco's study at El Pardo, where he handed over the President's letter. The letter ran as follows:

> Dear General Franco,
>
> It is because your nation and mine are friends in the best sense of the word and because you and I are sincerely desirous of the continuation of that friendship for our mutual good that I want very simply to tell you of the compelling reasons that have forced me to send a powerful American military force to the assistance of the French possessions in North Africa.
>
> We have accurate information to the effect that Germany and Italy intend at an early date to occupy with military force French North Africa.
>
> With your wide military experience you will understand clearly that in the interests of the defense of both North America and South America it is essential that action

be taken to prevent an Axis occupation of North Africa without delay.

To provide for America's defense I am sending a powerful army to French possessions and protectorates in North Africa with the sole purpose of preventing occupation by Germany and Italy and with the hope that these areas will not be devastated by the horror of war.

I hope you will accept my full assurance that these moves are in no shape, manner or form directed against the Government or people of Spain or Spanish Morocco or Spanish territories—metropolitan or otherwise. I believe the Spanish Government and the Spanish people wish to maintain neutrality and to remain outside the war. Spain has nothing to fear from the United Nations.

I am, my dear General, your sincere friend,
Franklin D. Roosevelt

At that moment, flanked by the stern-visaged photographs of the Duce and the Fuehrer which still adorned his study, Franco stood at the international crossroads. Acceptance of the landings would underline his first steps toward a new relationship with the Allies and, for the first time, make the enmity of Germany a real threat.

In this situation, it was some reassurance that his defenses were much stronger than they had been in 1940, and he could possibly contemplate holding the Ebro. On the other hand, opposition to the landings would damn him in the sight of the Allies at the very hour the fortunes of war were running for them.

A short time ago, Franco had been shooting rabbits. Now, fate held the gun at his own chest. For all that, his manner was cool and confident. Jordana had warned him of the letter's content, and he had had time to think it over.

"General Franco, when I saw him, was very calm and cordial," Hayes reported. "He showed considerable interest, as a military man, in the landings, and did not conceal his admiration of the strategy involved. He expressed appreciation of the Allied guarantees and said that he accepted them."

This, he later confirmed in a letter to Roosevelt. Not long afterward, diplomatic circles made what they could of a request from the Caudillo for a private screening of the Hollywood film *Gone With the Wind* at El Pardo.

The day had dawned on a prudent changing of the horses.

Though the Falangist press was still firmly pro-Axis and Franco continued to flatter Hitler, the Caudillo now became increasingly ready to do business with the Allies. By leaving his markets open, he cashed-in heavily on the resulting auction in Spanish war goods.

Both America and Great Britain engaged in policies of pre-emptive buying to keep important commodities from the Axis. Spain's ties with Britain's oldest ally, Portugal, strengthened by the forming of a so-called Iberian Bloc, were no longer muffled as they had been in the earlier days of the war, but ostentatiously advertised.

In March 1943 Franco sought to extend his respectability by establishing a nominal Cortes which, though largely appointive, included a considerable number of prominent Monarchists. They were not, however, encouraged to step out of line. When twenty-five members signed a petition requesting the restoration of the monarchy, most of them were deprived of office and either jailed or exiled.

As the year progressed, Franco adjusted warily to the changing fortunes of the belligerents. By midsummer he was propounding, for Allied consumption, a policy based on what he maintained were three separate wars.

The first, he explained, was between Germany and Italy on the one hand and the English-speaking countries on the other. In this, he professed neutrality. The second was the Pacific war, in which his sympathies were with the Americans for he regarded the Japanese as dangerous imperialists and "fundamentally barbarian."

The third was the war against Communism, and in this he was anti-Russian, for if Communist Russia prevailed over the Germans, he insisted, it would eventually dominate all Europe.

By autumn Franco had responded to American and British pressure for the withdrawal of the Spanish division from the Russian front, and was preparing seriously for an Allied victory.

The situation was fraught with menace for the small general whose violently pro-Axis pronouncements of the past could not readily be erased from the public mind. Franco had himself predicted as far back as 1939 that his regime would not survive an Allied victory, and the dismissal in July 1943 of Mussolini, the first dictator to tumble, provided the Spanish despot with a moral setback only partially offset by the fact that he could now forget his large Civil War debt to the Italian.

Though the event was reduced to a few lines in the controlled Spanish press, elated Republicans hailed the news as the beginning of the end of dictatorship everywhere, and a tumult of rejoicing broke out in the prisons.

Disturbed by the sudden rise in morale among the general's enemies, Franco's police hastily denounced a Red Plot, and a flurry of arrests took place in sectors of the populace—both Leftist and Monarchist—officially regarded as harboring latent opposition.

Awareness of such methods, transmitted abroad by exiled Republicans, did nothing to mollify the public indignation roused by Franco's regime in the democratic countries, especially the United States, where the great majority of the people hoped for a speedy resurrection of a Spanish Republic.

Public pressure on the State Department to break off diplomatic and commercial relations with Franco was considerable. As the Caudillo realized, however, so long as defeating

Germany remained the prime objective of the United States government in Europe, that government was unlikely to prejudice its strategic interests by embroiling itself in Spanish politics.

What happened when the war was over would be another matter.

Gomez Jordana had been faced with immense problems in reorientating his Ministry. The whole Franco administration was riddled with German sympathizers and Nazi agents. More than a few of the officials in Jordana's own department were in German pay. Coupled with the customary lethargy of Spanish administration, an almost complete incoherence in ministerial relations and the Buddha-like inaccessibility of Franco himself, the Foreign Minister's task was one which might well have tested a young man's health.

Jordana was sixty-six on coming to office. On top of everything, the Generalissimo, while banking on Count Jordana's efforts, continued to make pro-Axis statements for public consumption while privately exploiting the rivalries of his subordinates for personal security.

It was hardly an environment conducive to effective work. Yet in two years Jordana did much to counter the Germanophilia of the Foreign Ministry and the Spanish press, as well as to oppose the operations of the Gestapo in the Peninsula.

In August 1944 Jordana died with angina, for some time exhausted by his efforts to hack the undemonstrative Franco a path of retreat to the west. Franco showed scant public respect for the death of his Minister. "So far from coming to San Sebastian to show his sympathy with the family," wrote Hoare indignantly, "he proceeded, as if nothing had happened, with a program of celebrations in his own honor in Galicia. He went to a cocktail party on the day of Jordana's death, and did not attend the funeral in Madrid.

"Nor did any adequate and sympathetic notice appear in the Spanish press until a translation was published some days later of a tribute that I sent to *The Times* in London."

Franco was still loath to break with the Germans, yet, disdainfully as he regarded liberal democracy, the course of the war had forced him further and further down Jordana's path.

At the celebrations to mark the most recent "Day of the Caudillo," the Generalissimo had appeared in naval costume instead of the Falangist uniform he had worn in past years. "The hour for changing the guard," he admitted at about the same time, "approaches."

Formally reversing Spain's war status of "nonbelligerency" to "neutrality," he had gone on to withdraw from the Russian front, to evict German agents from Tangiers and to restrict the flow of Spanish supplies to the Nazis.

By July 1944 Franco had removed the large, autographed photographs of Hitler and Mussolini which had adorned his study since 1940, leaving in their place a picture of Pope Pius XII.

For Franco apologists who saw his flirtation with the bigger dictators as simply a deceit to avert occupation, those pictures had always been hard to explain away. They had not been put up for some visitors, taken down for others. They had been flaunted at Allied representatives in the darkest days of democracy.

Said one Spaniard: "Franco wanted the Axis dictators to win not merely because he thought the alternative would finish him, but because he admired and respected them. When he looked at Hitler, he saw a man who had accomplished some of his own fondest ambitions: who had built a powerful army from a demoralized force, who had created order and discipline from chaos, who had raised the morale of a nation by firing its racial prejudice.

"True, he did not relish the prospect of a Europe dominated by Hitler. But he thought that a democratic victory, giving rein to Leftist influences throughout the Continent, would be far worse."

The same summer, with a future Allied victory beyond doubt, he suggested to Ambassador Hayes that the gravest problem at the war's end would be that of civil wars in the various European countries. The solution he advocated was military occupation, coupled with the prohibition of political activities for five years.

With United Nations armies sweeping east toward Germany, Franco's efforts to ingratiate himself with the new favorites reached a level of agility accomplished even among the best of political contortionists.

Suddenly, the man who had hailed Germany as the defender of European civilization and who had promised a million Spanish soldiers to help the German people if Berlin were ever threatened, was offering his congratulations to the conquering generals of the Allies.

On September 11, he described the offensives in France and Belgium to Hayes as "magnificent," enthusing that Generals George Patton and Omar Bradley would go down in history as two of the greatest generals the war had produced. He was very happy, he told the Ambassador, about their success.

Suddenly, the leader of the regime which had congratulated Japan on her attack on Pearl Harbor was eager to emphasize his sympathies with the United States in the Far East.

"He did not like or trust the Japanese and he would be quite prepared at the right moment to rupture diplomatic relations with Japan," he informed Carlton Hayes. "The possibility of a rupture of Spanish relations with Japan was constantly in his mind." In the coming spring, the Caudillo made good the promise.

But diplomatic gymnastics were far from reality. Allied Embassies might brighten at Franco's new friendliness; the ordinary people who had fought the Fascist powers did not. They would have had more respect for the small dictator had he stood by his promises to Hitler. Instead, his turncoat behavior filled them with repugnance. The democratic citizens of America and Europe expected to see Franco dealt with.

By the autumn of 1944, Republican exiles, many of them trained in the French Resistance forces, were arming and assembling on the Pyrenean frontier, awaiting a signal to reenter their country. Toulouse radio predicted the Caudillo's downfall as imminent.

Fearful of mounting opinion in the free world, Franco tried to reassure the United States. His Foreign Minister, José Lequerica, Jordana's successor, informed America that the Caudillo was "giving most serious attention to the problem of effecting an evolution in the existing regime without weakening the state." No, he could not say just how the problem would be solved, but steps would be taken.

Lequerica acknowledged that the Falange "in its current form and trappings" was much disliked in the United States and Britain. Franco, he said, hoped that an evolution could be brought about which would satisfy reasonable public opinion in the English-speaking countries and enable their governments to accept close collaboration with Spain. The central desire in Spain, said Lequerica, was to work closely with the United States.

It seemed a forlorn hope. The American newspapers were virulent in their attacks on the Caudillo. They had even lambasted Winston Churchill for a complimentary remark in Britain's Parliament about Spanish neutrality at the time of Dunkirk and the landing in Morocco. This reference set the Caudillo on a new tack.

Somewhere, he had to find an ally among the World War victors. In desperation, he now turned to the British Prime Minister. Looking ahead, it seemed to Franco that Winston Churchill must emerge from his triumph of wartime leadership as an unassailable force in British politics, a scourge of the

Left whose vision of European developments had never been blinded by popular opinion and sentiments.

Here, perhaps, was the one man to whom the Caudillo could talk turkey, especially since the Englishman, for all his strategic alliance with Stalin, had been as outspoken in his time against Communism as Franco himself.

Accordingly, on October 18, 1944, the harassed Generalissimo dispatched an audacious message to his Ambassador in London, the Duke of Alba, for transmission to the redoubtable British Premier.

In the light of the battle still raging, its theme was frank to the point of impudence.

Having warned the Prime Minister of placing too much value on his present alliances, "history shows the fate of concepts such as eternal peace and disinterested friendship," Franco blandly suggested that Britain would do better to link her future with his own regime than to the United States or Russia.

"Once Germany is destroyed," ran the message, "and Russia has consolidated her preponderant position in Europe and Asia, and once the United States has consolidated her position in the Atlantic and the Pacific, thus becoming the most powerful nation in the universe, European interests will suffer their most serious and dangerous crisis in a shattered Europe.

"I understand quite well that military reasons of an immediate character will not permit Englishmen in positions of responsibility to make any comments on this aspect of the world struggle, but the reality exists and the menace remains.

"After the terrific test Europe has gone through, those who have shown themselves strong and virile among the nations great in population and resources are England, Spain and Germany.

"But once Germany is destroyed, England will have only one country left in Europe towards which she can turn her eyes—Spain. The French and Italian defeats, and the internal decomposition of those countries, will probably not allow anything solid to be built upon them for many years to come . . .

"Spain is a strategically situated country, sound, virile and chivalrous, which has demonstrated her spiritual reserves and wealth of courage and vigor; which has a will to exist, has no vulgar ambitions, loves peace and knows how to keep it.

"She believes that her and England's interests lie in their mutual understanding, and knows the value of British friendship and the worth of her own . . .

"Finally, in view of the attitude of the bad Spaniards abroad who continue to bank on the possibility of internal changes . . . should they succeed in their passionate endeavors to offer an easier understanding with England—a supposition so fantastic that it does not warrant discussion—we must categorically declare that if any change of this sort took place it could serve only Russia's interests."

Churchill's reply was a chilly one.

Having reminded Franco of the Anglo-Soviet treaty of 1942 and the British government's view that Anglo-Russian cooperation would be essential to future world organization, he recalled that German influence in Spain had been "consistently allowed to hinder the war effort of Great Britain and her Allies . . ." He mentioned Spain's seizure of Tangier and Franco's many contemptuous references to Britain and other members of the United Nations in recent years, including his statement that their defeat was desirable.

"Now that the war is coming to an end," he went on, "and plans are being made for the future of Europe and the world, His Majesty's Government cannot overlook the past record of the Spanish Government nor the consistently hostile activity of the Falangist Party, officially recognized as the basis of the present political structure in Spain, nor the fact that the Falange has maintained a close relationship with the Nazi dictatorial party in Germany and with the Italian Fascists.

"I am, however, less interested in the past than the present or the future, and it is my desire to see all the obstacles in the way of cordial Anglo-Spanish relations removed.

"I was genuinely pleased to observe the changes in Spanish policy toward this country which began when General Jordana took office, and I publicly referred to it in the speech I made in the House of Commons on May 24.

"Unfortunately . . . this was not sufficient to remove all the barriers remaining between our two countries. As long as these exist the development of more intimate relations of friendship and cooperation with Spain—desired by His Majesty's Government—will meet with difficulties, and it is out of the question for His Majesty's Government to support Spanish aspirations to participate in the future peace settlements.

"Neither do I think it likely that Spain will be invited to join the future world organization."

The prospects had been spelled out. Franco was alone in a dauntingly hostile environment.

12. The Caudillo Knows How to Wait

Throughout 1945 and 1946 the world waited for Franco's flame to fizzle out. Some countries, notably the Communist States, were in favor of taking steps to douse it; others, resisting intervention, preferred to leave the job to the Spaniards.

Franco faced a friendless future, castigated on all sides.

The Potsdam Declaration had not minced words on the subject of his regime:

"The three governments feel bound . . . to make it clear that they for their part would not favor any application for membership [to the United Nations] put forward by the present Spanish government which, having been founded with the support of the Axis Powers, does not, in view of its origins, its nature, its record and its close associations with the aggressor States, possess the necessary qualifications to justify such membership."

Ernest Bevin, Foreign Secretary of Britain's new Labor government, reflected the sentiments not only of his own cabinet but of the bulk of the democratic West, when he stated in 1946: "His Majesty's Government has on all relevant occasions displayed its dislike of the present regime, which abetted our enemies, and has forcibly enunciated its anxiety that the present regime should, by the activities of the Spanish people themselves, be superseded by a regime properly supported."

Discomforted by such pronouncements, Franco spoke of

"foreign errors," protested his "rule of discretion," Spain's "services to peace and culture," and declared that he had no intention of begging a seat in international conferences. Time, he insisted repeatedly, would prove he was right. "The West needs us in the fight against world Communism."

Meanwhile, early in 1946, incensed among other things by Franco's execution of the Spaniard Cristino Garcia, a former Maquis fighter in France, the government of that nation stopped all trade with Spain, closing the Pyrenean frontier and forbidding traffic between French and Spanish ports. To save face at home, Franco announced the frontier closure as his own initiative. He was spared further embarrassment by the French government's failure to persuade other nations to follow her.

Economic sanctions were thought unlikely to bring the speedy fall of the Caudillo, and a lengthy embargo would undoubtedly have had an adverse effect on the economies of participating countries. Sheepishly, France dropped her policy and reopened trade with her neighbor.

At the end of the year the General Assembly of the United Nations formally barred Franco from membership and attendance of its subsidiary bodies and conferences. Member nations were advised to withdraw their heads of mission from Madrid. Despite warnings, the reality came as a punishing blow to the Caudillo, who promptly called a massive demonstration at home in his favor.

"We Spaniards," he told a vast Falange-organized crowd from the balcony of Madrid's Royal Palace, "must not be surprised at what has happened in the UNO, for a wave of Communist terror is devastating Europe and violations, crimes and persecutions of the kind many of you once suffered or witnessed hang unpunished over the life of twelve nations . . .

"Let us not be surprised that the sons of Giral and La Pasionaria find support among the official representatives of these unfortunate people."

Three-hundred-thousand Spaniards, their pride bruised by the news from the United Nations, applauded the line warmly, chanting "*¡Franco, sí! Comunismo, no!*"

Outside Spain, Franco's obstinate refusal to dematerialize at the wish of UNO aggravated the mounting impatience of his enemies. The Committee of International Socialist Conferences, representing the Democratic Socialist parties of Europe, passed a resolution urging all governments to "treat the removal of the Franco regime as a matter of major urgency for the progress of unity in Europe."

The same year, 1948, advice given by British Foreign Minister Bevin to two Spanish leaders in exile, the Socialist Indalecio Prieto and the democratic Conservative Gil Robles, led to an agreement between their more moderate followers on the basis of leaving the decision between a future Monarchy or Republic in Spain to a plebiscite.

Effectively, however, Franco's would-be successors were as disunited in exile as they had been before he siezed power.

The pure Monarchists counted the agreement as treason to the dynasty while Left-wing Socialists and Communists stormed at Prieto for his compromise. The opposition abroad was getting nowhere. The main hope of the anti-Franco parties remained that the Generalissimo would fall, like dictator Primo de Rivera before him, by his own mismanagement. Soldiering might have taught Franco the art of suppression, but it had taught him nothing, they claimed, of economics.

Despite the benefits of neutrality, Spain had emerged from the World War period on the verge of bankruptcy, to which was added the impediment of a severe draught. While a policy of economic autarchy had produced some benefits in the form of increased industrialization, it also embraced staggering inefficiency, open corruption and widespread suffering among workers, many of whom worked seventy and more hours a week for the barest of livings.

The distribution of wealth was still grotesquely unbalanced. After the best part of a decade of Franco rule, between eighty and ninety percent of the Spanish people accounted for less than a third of the national income. Agricultural production had not improved on that of the early thirties.

Franco could not wait for ever for outside aid. When the Marshall Plan excluded him from its program, his enemies gathered with fresh hope.

While most of Europe looked forward to Franco's demise, the Caudillo cannily refurbished his image to suit the post-war period. He granted an amnesty to many political prisoners, stopped the mass executions and called his dictatorship "organic democracy."

One day, during a shooting party in the Gredos range of mountains in central Spain, Franco's sporting organizer, a man named Max Borrell, becoming aware of an unusual silence in the general's butt, quietly approached the position to find Franco sketching. "Every day I have more and more taste for painting," the Caudillo declared at another time. The results, including seascapes and animal portraits painted with painstaking competence if something of the sentimentality of Bambi-period Disney, were shown demurely to foreign visitors.

Franco's eye for an appealing gloss extended to the principles of his State, which he presented as the defense of "the dignity, integrity and liberty" of all Spaniards, with special regard to the family as a basic institution. There was a nice contradiction, however, between the expansiveness of such sentiments and the detailed laws of the regime.

According to the Charter of Spaniards published on July 17, 1945, the government had the right to suspend several facets of the advertised brochure, most of them concerning the rights of the citizen.

"All Spaniards may freely express their ideas," ran the Charter, "so long as these do not prejudice the fundamental principles of the State."

This State envisaged by Franco was both anti-capitalist and anti-Marxist; a unitary structure in which separatism was a cardinal sin, and in which the gradualness of social evolution in Spain was implicit.

In place of the trades unions appeared the "vertical" syndicate, a Falangist proposal stipulating joint employer-employee representation at all levels. It did not need the Cardinal Primate to point out, as he did, however, that representation of the workers under the system was not authentic. Many Falangists themselves opposed the regime's bias towards the well-to-do and influential at the expense of the working classes.

For traditionalists, there were sweeteners. Catholicism was supported as the official religion, while, as time went on, the idea was allowed to spread that an eventual restoration of the Monarchy was not out of the question. It was a hodge-podge which only a dictator could have made work.

"The Chief of State," as Article 47 of the Statutes of the Falange had it, "answers to God and History." And the Chief of State, though commonly misrepresented as a Fascist, ruled by no political theory save his own innate sense of the expedient. There was a Cortes, but its members were Franco's puppets. A cabinet met regularly under Franco's supervision, but Ministers were entirely dependent on his favor.

Wed to no discernible ideology, responsible to no man, Franco could keep the nation, and indeed the world, guessing. If one policy failed, as his wartime machinations demonstrated, he could replace it by its opposite; whatever else changed, the Caudillo would still be at the helm.

In Germany, Fascism had produced National Socialism, but to Franco, individualist and paternalist, anything suggestive of Socialism was abhorrent. Unlike the old-guard among Spanish aristocrats, he was aware that the mass of people had to be given a fairer share of life's advantages, but he could not admit it as their birth right.

Better standards were something his State aimed to grant them, not something they could demand of their government. One result of the general's insistence on "gradualness" was that while Spain strove for a better living, the rest of the West shot forward at such a pace that Spanish standards, by comparison, seemed to go backward. Yet, if the world at large underestimated his tenacity, nobody in Spain doubted Franco's authority.

In 1940, the first year after the Civil War, he had spent nearly three times as much on his armed services, the nub of his power, as on public works—despite a start to rebuilding in Madrid and a program of road, harbor, and hydraulics construction estimated at 4200 million pesetas.

Not only was the army well paid by Spanish standards, but amidst the confusion of licenses and controls which operated the Spanish economy (there were more than eight hundred bureaucratic departments, most susceptible to bribery and influence) Franco's generals were well-placed to grow fat.

On retirement, senior officers continued to receive full pay and were found government jobs to boost their emoluments. There was little fear of another generals conspiracy. While Franco nurtured and idealized the army which upheld him, he also wooed the administrative bourgeoisie by raising Civil Service salaries, some by as much as forty percent. In return, he expected a high measure of obedience.

The abrupt disappearance at various times from the Caudillo's elbow of his brother, Nicolás, and his brother-in-law Serrano Suñer, among others, had stressed the rigor of his discipline, a feature expressed in the smallest items of protocol and domesticity.

Not even his Ministers of State were allowed to smoke in his presence at El Pardo, and his rare dinner guests noted that

Franco was served first. The austerity and abstemiousness of his private life was remarked widely in a nation where scandal too often attended high office.

If many a Franco supporter had an eye to the perks, nobody could challenge the personal incorruptibility and marital fidelity of this puritanical dictator whose wildest excess was a single glass of wine with his evening meal before settling to read from well-thumbed military histories.

Desire for riches had never been a motive in Franco's life, and his detractors sought in vain for a personal treasure hoard. At one time it was claimed that the Caudillo had a nest egg invested in Mexico, but no one claimed he had made a fortune. For the rest, El Pardo was a normal residence of Spain's Heads of State, who held it on a grace and favor basis, nor were the Rolls-Royces and Mercedes cars in his garage more than status demanded. Indeed, Franco used them less than many of his predecessors.

The only private estate he possessed, El Pazo de Meirás near his home town of El Ferrol, had been given to him after the Civil War as a mark of esteem by supporters in La Coruña. He found fewer moments than he would have liked to enjoy it.

Perhaps the most ostentatious property Franco acquired was the 500-ton yacht, the *Azor*, in which, as the son of a seafaring family, he took particular pleasure. Even so, he preferred the somewhat Spartan activities of deep-sea fishing in the Bay of Biscay or tunney fishing off the south coast to harbor parties and idle sun cruising.

In recreation, as in working life, Franco had few friends, virtually no intimates, confining himself largely to such solitary pastimes as salmon fishing in the mountain streams of Asturias and stalking ibex and red deer in the Cantabrian Alps and the Sierra de Gredos. The man most frequently with him on these trips was his personal doctor, Vicente Gil of Madrid, who was always on short call in case of an accident.

Millions might think Spain better without him. As Franco saw it, the welfare of Spain depended on his good health.

According to Spanish tradition, the *gallego*, the man from Galicia, is austere, inscrutable, and cunning. No one knows what goes on in his head. No one can be sure what he will do next. And when he has done it, it is often hard to tell what has happened.

Above all, the *gallego* "knows how to wait." Like Philip II, he is blessed with a shrewd appreciation of the merits of patience.

Ostracized on all sides, deprived of the funds needed to refloat his economy, verbally flayed from Topeca to Tomsk, Franco pulled into his dour shell and let the wrath of the world break over him. The taciturn *gallego* was under no misapprehension of the danger. He had himself foreseen a democratic victory in the World War as his ruin, and now surmised that his best chance was to stand fast and wait.

Modern military developments had made civilian revolution almost obsolete. So long as the army remained firmly in his own power, and there was no provision to hand over at any time to a constituted body, he could stay where he was for as long as he could bear the discomfort.

Give an inch, however, accept the thin edge of the liberalizing wedges aimed at him from all sides, and nothing could stop the regime cracking asunder. In this realization, though tactically pragmatic and cynical, superficially adjusting to the colors of the international scene, Franco was strategically consistent. He had weathered the pressures of Fascism. As the postwar period progressed, it seemed increasingly possible he could stave off democracy. The world was changing. The personal certainty that would break or save Franco was the knowledge that *he* would not.

By 1947 he had proved beyond doubt the efficacy of his political repression at home. The boasted Republican invasion from France had proved abortive. Though several thousand anti-Franco guerrillas had descended on Spain via the Pyrénées, the popular support they expected had failed them. The dictator's program of executions and imprisonments had removed the core of potential rebellion from the nation and the people wanted no more of the horrors of civil war. When General Yagüe moved against them with units of a reorganized Peninsula army, the bulk of the resistance fighters returned, disillusioned, to France.

In July 1948, the Blockade of Berlin gave Franco the excuse to sound a righteous note. Had he not said that the West would need Spain in its opposition to Bolshevism? The Korean War was less than two years ahead, and many members of the United Nations were doubting the wisdom of the 1946 resolution.

Not only had they underestimated the resilience of General Franco, they had misread the spirit of many ordinary Spaniards, who might not care to be told what to do from within, but cared a great deal less to be told from without.

Wrote United States Secretary of State Dean Acheson in 1950: "The United States has long questioned the wisdom and efficacy of the actions recommended in the 1946 resolution . . . In retrospect, it is now clear that this action has not only failed in its intended purpose but has served to strengthen the position of the present regime . . .

"At the same time," he continued, "it is difficult to envisage Spain as a full member of the free Western community without substantial advances in such directions as increased civil liberties and as religious freedom and the freedom to exercise the elementary right of organized labor."

It was even more difficult to envisage such advances in Franco's Spain. "Spain is destined to be the key and the life of the West," persisted the Caudillo the same year. But he warned: "Our political system is not transitory."

In November, the United Nations revoked the 1946 resolution. From now on the Pentagon was to claim with increasing insistence that bases in Spain, within 2000 miles of the heart of Soviet Russia, were a vital military necessity to the defense of the United States.

Faced with the unenviable choice of seeking a deal with the Spanish dictator, or ignoring the advice of its defense experts, the U.S. government bowed to the authority which President Harry Truman described as "you military men."

Spain's pre-eminent military man was more than ready. Franco had now replaced Foreign Minister Lequerica with a lawyer and journalist of former Christian Democratic connections, Alberto Martin Artajo, who was aptly calculated to smooth the path of negotiations with America.

For her part, America sent Admiral Forrest P. Sherman, U. S. Chief of Naval Operations and an officer with some affection for Spain, to open talks in Madrid. He discovered the Caudillo in bland mood and the principle of cooperation was quickly agreed. Sherman, however, died of a heart attack shortly afterwards, and his successor, General August W. Kissner, found the details of the treaty harder going.

If Franco had failed to bend under the duress of the past six years, he was giving nothing away when at last he sat holding a good hand. Nor were America's allies altogether eager for developments. Britain and France were strongly opposed to a treaty, and much of American opinion itself was outraged.

As the *New York Times* pointed out, one of the results of a deal with Franco would be that the United States would have officially to abandon its critical attitude to the dictatorship. "One of the clear facts that Americans must face is that if we go ahead with this arrangement, we will be helping to perpetuate Franco in power as long as he lives and cares to remain the Dictator of Spain. This will be our responsibility in the face of history." The truth of this prophetic warning was not lost on Franco.

In 1952 he achieved useful publicity through his daughter's visit to the United States. Maria Carmen, a child when the generals had first struck at the Republic, had grown into an attractive young woman with a wide, natural smile, and a vivacious share of her mother's dark-eyed comeliness. Franco, disinclined to attract further politicians to the family, had been grateful to marry her in 1950 to a young Madrid medical specialist, the Marqués de Villaverde. Though Villaverde's acquisition of a motor-scooter concession in Spain led to the wits dubbing him *Vespaverde*, the young couple were hard to dislike and, a generation apart from the strife of their elders, proved a flattering adjunct to the Franco image.

Their visit to America, ostensibly a private one, left General Dwight D. Eisenhower, now President, little choice but to ignore it or extend hospitality. Courtesy and the desire to conclude the negotiations for Spanish bases as rapidly as possible, prompted him to make them State guests for the duration of their stay. Franco had gained a subtle point over his American detractors.

At home, he was working hard against a different form of opposition—the Catholic hierarchy in Spain, which opposed the setting up of American bases on the ground that thousands of Protestants would gain a footing in the country—by seeking a Concordat with the Vatican. So far, the Vatican had procrastinated in the matter, unconvinced since the war's end that the Franco regime was a permanence.

The conviction, however, was gaining way rapidly.

"Thanks to God and the tenacity of Spaniards," proclaimed the Caudillo, "the sun of our hopes begins to shine in the world." Spain, he added tartly, was now "sought after by those who in years past scorned our offer to cooperate against Communism."

That year the Franco regime, already accepted by the World Health Organization and the Economic and Social Council of the United Nations, was admitted to the United

Nations Educational, Scientific and Cultural Organization. Three members, including the celebrated Spanish cellist Pablo Casals, resigned in protest.

Kissner and his team were having a tough job. The more anxious the Pentagon became for its bases, and the harder the U.S. government pressed for an agreement, the sharper became the shrewdly bargaining Franco. Already offered a hundred million dollars in economic aid, he demanded also military assistance of the type granted European democracies.

The demand raised obvious objections. While the free world might accept on humanitarian grounds that economic aid to the Caudillo would raise the living standards of deprived and impoverished Spaniards, it could hardly be argued that the strengthening of Franco's army would bring blessing to the populace. It could serve only to prop the dictatorship.

As one commentator expressed it: "Dining with the devil is bad enough; stoking his fires is intolerable." But the "intolerable" was coming closer. While the Americans haggled, Franco was active. Summer 1952 found him quietly negotiating with a Conservative British government for a quantity of obsolescent military equipment for which the U.K. was seeking a market. In part-payment he held out continuing commercial advantages to Great Britain.

In July, anticipating an American arms deal with Franco, Britain lifted her seven-year-old embargo on military supplies to the dictator and beat the U.S. to the gun. The result was a furore of protest in Socialist and other circles, and a renewed determination in the United States to come to terms with the Spaniard. In December, General J. Lawton Collins, Chief of Staff of the United States Army, was sent to Spain to accelerate matters. There seemed little prospect of doing so except on the *gallego's* terms.

In Rome, the Vatican observers, impressed by Franco's new status among Western nations, were preparing to draft the Concordat that would silence Catholic protests in Spain against a treaty. At the end of August 1953 it was duly signed. The Spanish-American military pact was sealed a month later.

For more than two years the Generalissimo had held out for his own way and, in the end, the American negotiators had given in.

"He has got everything he asked for," said one. "He just tired us out."

Under the terms of the agreement, Franco had allowed the United States the right to use four air bases in Spain and to develop naval facilities in three Spanish harbors. For America, the pact was of great strategic importance. She became, for the first time, a naval power in the Mediterranean, and gained an air strike force in Europe conveniently screened by the Pyrénées. For Franco, the pact was more—it was invaluable.

Apart from $85,000,000 in economic aid, and $141,000,000 in military assistance, already agreed by the United States Congress, his stipulation that Spanish labor and materials should be used in developing the bases insured that hundreds of thousands more dollars would pour into the country.

Not only did Spain retain sovereignty over the bases, Franco shared the right with the U.S. government to terminate the agreement (it was for ten years with two five yearly periods to follow) Spain to retain all installations existing at the time of termination.

Moreover, the use of the bases for war purposes was subject to mutual agreement. Franco's record in the Second World War did not reassure some circles of his eagerness to participate in another one. The dictator had incurred no obligations to NATO and had done nothing to meet American opinion in respect of the lack of civil liberties and other democratic rights in his country.

Ten years later, the International Committee of Jurists would report: The press is completely gagged. Freedom of association is in a similar predicament. Freedom is not granted in the creation of political parties and labor unions, activities which are forbidden and punishable by law." Added the Jurists: "It is scarcely possible to find a single form of opposition activity which is not threatened by legal sanctions."

Meanwhile, Michel Clerc, Madrid correspondent of *Paris Match*, could observe of the pact with America: "Above the four bases, to be constructed by Spanish workmen, will fly the Spanish flag. Spanish officers will be in command. But Franco has done better. The Americans will submit to the customs of the country, pay tax, and not wear uniforms in the street . . . Franco has obtained not merely equality from the Americans. He has obtained deference . . ."

On top of all this, he had provoked Britain into commercial rivalry with the U.S. in the field of military supplies, enabling him to buy British jet fighters and other equipment.

"It was," wrote Herbert L. Matthews of the *New York Times*, "the high-spot of Franco's postwar career. He had defeated his enemies in and out of Spain; he had refused to yield one inch to liberalism; and now his efforts had gained the highest sanction from two of the highest powers in the world, religious and secular—the Vatican and the United States."

13. "We Are a Solution"—Franco

Fifteen years after the Civil War in Spain, journalists and other visitors to a once-quiet valley in the Guadarrama Mountains north of Madrid were stopped by the police who demanded special passes. Those who possessed them were waved forward to witness a most unusual project.

Many people had applauded Franco's hydraulics plants. Foreign experts had admired his irrigation schemes and other aspects of his public works. Few were prepared for what now lay before them. Here, in the so-called Valley of the Dead, gangs of former Republican prisoners had been laboring since the early 1940s to build their conqueror one of the most incredible mausoleums ever constructed. It was designed to hold the remains of scores of thousands of Civil War victims and, in a place of honor, one who was not yet dead—Francisco Franco, the Caudillo himself.

From the granite core of the mountain had been hewn a vast underground cathedral, its 120-feet-high subterranean dome only three feet smaller in diameter than that of St. Peter's, Rome, to be decorated by hundreds of square yards of mosaics in Roman-Byzantine style.

The layout approved by Franco included a crypt and four ossariums with an entrance hall reached through great bronze doors weighing more than eleven tons. Outside, an assembly ground would hold a gathering of 200,000, while a nearby hotel was planned to house posterity's pilgrims.

Above all, reaching five hundred feet toward the sky, was sited a huge white cross, its sections so massive as to accommodate high-speed lifts and separate chapels. Illuminated at night, the cross would be visible from five Spanish provinces.

Beneath it, beside a golden altar, would lie one day the Caudillo, flanked by the legions of the dead. At his feet would be tapestries, stone figures and sixteen smaller, diamond-studded crosses.

"It was as if," declared one impressed visitor, "Franco had come to believe his own publicity; as if his survival in a hostile world truly seemed to him a miracle. What other urge had possessed him to build his own sacred monument?"

Certainly, the planning of such funereal grandeur was strangely at odds with the unostentatious manner of the life of the secluded dictator, but there was more to the structure than vanity. It was also an immediate reminder to his subjects of the awful cost of civil strife, and, by implication, of the contrasted benefits of General Franco's rule.

As the years passed, the cost of the mausoleum, like that of Spain's cost of living, swiftly mounted. In 1954 it was estimated at $7,000,000; by 1959 at more than $27,000,000.

At the same time, Spaniards viewed the project with something less than wonderment. In an attempt to widen its appeal to his countrymen, Franco extended his original plan to make the Valley of the Dead a burial place exclusive to Nationalists, and agreed to allow in the remains of fallen Republicans. Many Spaniards were still far from enamored. Women who through two decades had mourned sons and lovers beside graves in village churchyards wished at least to be left with their privacy. The prospect of transporting their grief to the vast and impersonal tomb in the mountains dismayed them.

Nor were the Generalissimo's supporters always more eager. In 1959, when he ordered the remains of Falange hero José

Antonio Primo de Rivera to be reburied in the mausoleum, many Falangists were furious. Until then, to the chagrin of their rivals the Monarchists, José Antonio had reposed grandly in the Escorial, the burial place of Spain's kings and princes.

His removal to Franco's new tomb in the hillside seemed not only a come-down for their martyr, but a triumph for the Monarchists, who had never wanted the Falange leader to lie amid royalty.

Franco did not deign to attend the reinterment. At the ceremony, slighted Falangists booed his representative, but his instructions were carried out. The Generalissimo no longer feared the Fascists of his movement. His power was as unshakable as the monument.

Like that of Spain's absolute monarchs down the centuries, Franco's Cortes was a mere rubber stamp for his policies. A third of its members were drawn from the only party allowed in the country, a third from the official labor syndicates while the remaining third were either town mayors (trusted Nationalists) or men who had served Franco's Spain well in the past. Even with such guarantees of behavior, the measures prepared required the Caudillo's ratification, and he dismissed or approved them entirely at his pleasure.

That he bothered to maintain the façade of representation at all illustrated a singularly Spanish penchant for legality and protocol, and an instinctively devious nature. Set-piece elections, regular cabinet meetings and so on, helped to weave a web of doubt around his objectives, to persuade many foreign innocents that the dictator was a fundamental democrat.

Among its subtlest strands was the lure of restoration; the frequent hints, especially when his own prestige was at low ebb, that he was about to revive a Constitutional Monarchy. Periodically, from the earliest years of his power, such hints had deceived observers at home and abroad, alternatively rallying the Monarchists when the Falange in its heyday seemed too strong, or placating the traditionalists when they, in turn, grew demanding.

In June 1947, with Spanish Fascism largely a spent force, Franco had pre-empted the rising Monarchist clamor by declaring the nation a Monarchy, though, at the same time, reserving the right to choose a King when and as he wished for himself. The candidate, he made clear in a so-called "Law of Succession to the Headship of the State," would be required to pledge himself to the basic laws and principles of the Franco regime. Royal blood, he warned, would not be enough to uphold the candidacy of those "who lack the necessary capacity to govern," or those who had shown "indifference to the fundamental principles of the State."

When the law was duly "accepted" by national referendum —it was announced that 14,145,163 people had voted for it out of 17,178,812 voters—Franco's much-publicized step toward restoration amounted to little.

There could be no Monarch during Franco's rule unless he ordained it, and then it would be a man of his own choice. Furthermore, since the most likely figures to fill the bill, the pretender Don Juan de Bourbon's son Juan Carlos, hope of the mainstream Monarchists, and the Carlist pretender Don Javier de Bourbon-Parma's son Hugo Carlos, were still children, the entire question was still at best academic. Nevertheless, Franco was too shrewd to let Spain's Monarchists slip into total disillusionment.

In the late summer of 1948, the Generalissimo embarked on the first of a series of discussions with Don Juan, who was living at Estoril, Portugal. The rendezvous was planned on the high seas, the pretender sailing in his yacht the *Saltillo,* Franco in the *Azor,* aboard which the meeting took place.

That the democratically inclined Don Juan should become King was out of the question as Franco saw it. What he hoped for was some sort of an understanding in which the exiled pretender would allow his son, the younger of the two future prospects, to complete his education in Spain: to add an aura of respectability to the regime, which would pass as the patron of the youthful Juan Carlos.

The ensuing dialogue did not accomplish much. Don Juan, an intelligent and liberal-minded man with both the interests of Spain and his own son at heart, upbraided Franco for refusing to move toward constitutional rule and complained of the confiscation of royal properties in Spain and of past abuses against himself in the Franco press.

Franco countered that the future of the line would best be served by Don Juan's acceptance of the "Law of Succession" and by making plans for the education of Juan Carlos in his own country. Future meetings ended in the same apparent stalemate, the pretender demanding freedom and liberalization, Franco remaining patiently unimpressed.

Eventually, in 1960, perhaps conscious that the sixty-seven-year-old dictator could not expect an endless bounty of strong health, Don Juan struck a bargain. If Franco recognized Juan Carlos as Prince of Asturias, a title which would acknowledge him as heir to the throne, the pretender would send his son to Madrid University.

While Don Juan later honored his part of the deal, Franco, having implied agreement, never got round to confirming the title. Perseverance and cunning had once more served his purpose.

Señora Franco greeted the arrival of Juan Carlos in Madrid with a full and gracious courtesy, the controlled press captured the warmth of the welcome and the Caudillo, in a rare mood of magnanimity, bestowed upon the young man the gift of Zarzuela Palace, near the capital.

Characteristically, Franco later offset public reaction with a well-balanced boost for the Carlists. When Monarchist support appeared to be consolidating too firmly around Juan Carlos, he encouraged the Falangist newspaper *Arriba*, normally anti-Monarchist, to publish a tribute to Don Hugo Carlos, son of Don Javier, in which the latter was actually referred to as "His Royal Highness."

Don Javier de Bourbon-Parma, nephew by marriage of the last direct male descendant of the Carlist line, the late Alfonso Carlos, had proclaimed himself Carlist king in 1952. Since he lived largely in France and Austria and had French nationality, Franco could disregard him under a law stipulating that the future King of Spain must be a Spaniard. Indeed, the Caudillo had refused the pretender's kin Spanish nationality.

But this fact had never blighted the ambitions of Hugo Carlos, a determined if somewhat formal young man who had once read economics at Oxford and worked for a West German bank. In 1957, now twenty-seven, he entered Spain secretly and laid low in Bilbao for several months, to emerge amidst exuberant Carlist acclaim for the annual rally of the party at Montejurra.

The following year, Franco attempted, unsuccessfully, to stop the rally. Reluctant to antagonize the Carlists among his own supporters, the Generalissimo imposed his prohibition at half-cock. Enthusiastic devotees of the Monarchist movement dodged police patrols and roadblocks to hold the open-air jamboree as usual.

Meanwhile, Hugo Carlos continued his Spanish activities. In the early sixties, appealingly backed by his four persuasive sisters, he took up regular residence in Madrid where the Caudillo's agents watched him somewhat warily. 1964, in which year he came of age for the succession, saw his marriage to Princess Irene of the Netherlands, an international event which brought him much glamour and which Franco was at pains to minimize in the Spanish press.

The same year, when the young pretender toured Catalonia, Franco forbade the town mayors to receive him, dismissing a number who did so. The dictator was losing patience with the royalists. By the end of 1968, Franco had had enough trouble without Hugo Carlos. Throughout the summer, terrorists had been active in the Basque Provinces, Spanish lawyers had joined intellectuals and priests in protesting at the lack of freedom in the country and the wives of political prisoners had taken to staging sit-ins in churches.

In January 1969, Franco opened the new year by clamping a State of Emergency on the whole of Spain. A few weeks earlier, he expelled Hugo Carlos from the country.

At the same time, the Caudillo had had headaches in other fields. Saved once already from bankruptcy by the West, the Generalissimo's economically faulty use of the dollars extracted from the United States government had led in a frighteningly swift period to runaway inflation. In under a decade, the cost of living in Spain was to soar by fifty percent.

In 1956, one of his most popular Ministers, José Antonio Girón, long-standing Minister of Labor and the architect of many social benefits for the workers, had warned the general that his government faced serious disorders unless he instituted dramatic increases in wages.

That year, with millions of Spaniards still earning less than three dollars a week, Franco increased basic wages by forty percent. The result, an increasingly vicious spiral of inflation, led to the downfall of Girón, last of the old-philosophy Falangists to hold high office, and brought the economically inept dictator once more to the brink of bankruptcy.

By 1958, Spain's gold and hard currency reserves were down to $65,000,000; her foreign trade deficit was almost $400,000,-000. By the summer of the following year, Franco could not have paid for a month's supply of oil from his coffers, and he was crying out for a new loan from the U.S. For the second time since the World War, democratic dollars bailed the dictator out.

The free world responded quickly. Experts from the OEEC and the IMF were sent to Spain to seek a remedy for her financial ills, Franco was forced to renounce his old posture of economic autarchy for one of economic liberalism, and a stabilization plan to halt inflation was announced. Among other things, it involved the devaluation of the peseta and substantial monetary aid from the U.S. government and American commercial banks. Firm restrictions were imposed on wages and government expenditure. Spain became a full member of the OEEC.

When the crisis was over, many things had changed but not Franco. Backed by a well-equipped and cosseted army of 400,000, the Generalissimo had survived his failure and still provided Spain's only government.

With the nation's economic outlook transformed by the cash and expertise of the very political systems he flatly renounced, Franco boasted in 1960: "We can speak proudly of the Spanish miracle . . . Social justice is imposed with love, yet with a firm, hard hand. Not a Spanish home shall be without light, not a Spanish worker without bread."

Among a populace of which eighty-three percent still earned less than ten dollars a week, many Spaniards counted themselves lucky to have as much. The basic attraction for many of the foreign tourists and the flood of foreign investment which now poured into the country, to the Generalissimo's gratification, was the pathetic cheapness of Spanish labor.

As one prominent Falangist, Pedrosa Latas, pointed out: "Our stabilization plan has been paid for by the workers while the banks and big business have augmented their profits."

But such considerations did not prevent Francisco Franco celebrating his twenty-fifth anniversary as dictator in good spirits. At noon on October 1, 1961, amid gun salutes, military music, and the cheers of his supporters, he paid a nostalgic visit to his old Civil War headquarters at Burgos.

A quarter of a century ago to the day, he had been declared Head of State in that city by the aging and apprehensive Cabanellas, now long dead. It was a sobering tribute to his powers of survival that only one member of the military junta which had originally elected him, General Fidel Dávila, was still alive.

The chubby Generalissimo, now balding, his mustache and eyebrows grayer, yet in many ways remarkably unchanged, already held a strong claim to be the world's most persistent dictator. And he showed no signs of giving up in the years ahead. Before a respectful assembly of his senior officers, he hinted that Spain's army should endeavor to acquire nuclear weapons and that her defense agreements with the U.S. would need close reviewing.

His regime, he asserted, had been the "solution" the nation had long awaited. "Neither Capitalism nor Communism," he said, "are solutions. But we are a solution—at least for Spain."

On Christmas Eve, 1961, General Franco was shooting pigeons in the grounds of his Pardo palace when the left barrel of his shotgun exploded as he pulled the trigger. While the Caudillo clutched at a wounded hand, his doctor son-in-law, the Marqués de Villaverde, gave first-aid and hurried him to the nearest hospital, an air force establishment. The injury was diagnosed as "an open fracture of the second metacarpal bone and of the index finger of the left hand."

Thanks to his long-standing dislike of public appearances, and perhaps some of the most rigid security arrangements afforded any Head of State in Western Europe, this unglamorous accident represented the worst injury Franco had suffered in his entire career of dictatorship. But if the Generalissimo felt safe from personal violence, his regime was increasingly beset by the angry rumblings of dissidence.

Two months after the shooting incident, those rumblings erupted into the most significant act of opposition to Franco since the Civil War, tens of thousands of miners, iron workers and other industrial employees coming out on strike in northern Spain in by far the biggest demonstration of civil disobedience the regime had yet witnessed.

Ostensibly, the strike was for higher wages, but behind it—and inseparably linked with the action, since strikes were illegal in Franco's Spain—lay the principle of establishing the right of human protest. When threats that the strikers would lose their jobs, their holiday pay and pension rights, and be liable to arrest for treason, proved futile, the disgruntled Caudillo ordered a State of Emergency in the affected provinces of Asturias, Vizcaya, and Guipúzcoa.

It was May 3. Six million people had been deprived of most of the rights they possessed by the order. Their private mail was liable to interception, they could be detained and held indefinitely without reason, their homes could be searched without warrant and they could be expelled from them and deported by the authorities.

Franco sent thirty thousand troops to the Asturian mining areas and drafted five thousand special police from Madrid to Oviedo. The 1934 Revolution and Franco's repression of that time in Asturias struck a chord in many minds.

In an urgent letter to the Generalissimo, twenty-four prominent Spaniards, including Gil Robles, head of the Right-wing pre-war coalition, Pedro Lain Entralgo, former rector of Madrid University, Ramón Perez de Ayala, former Ambassador to Britain and Menendez Pidal, president of the Academy, protested that the repressive measures in the north were not justified by a strike which would be considered reasonable and legal in any free country.

"The gravity of the situation," ran the letter, "obliges us to insist that the government now introduces something resembling liberty and justice in the country." Franco blamed "Communist agitators" for the protest, but he had to admit that it was well organized.

Since 1950, thousands of Socialists, Christian Democrats, Basque Nationalists, Communists, Anarchists, and others had infiltrated the vertical syndicates to form so-called workers' commissions. In some instances they had succeeded in occupying important posts in the local branches of the syndicates until there was virtually a regional and national leadership operating against the regime.

The Caudillo was not blind to this. He tolerated it, among other reasons, because it diverted efforts to re-establish the big Left-wing unions of the thirties on an underground basis, and because it was useful to create the illusion of budding democracy, especially to impress senators and trade union officials from abroad.

Franco banked on the separatist propensities of the rival opposition parties to neutralize their effectiveness. But the conditions of his regime had wrought a significant change in the power structure of the anti-Francoists.

While the activities of liberal, moderate and democratic elements had inevitably declined with the prohibition of parties, the Communists had made the most of an environment well-suited to the spreading of their gospel. Conspiracy suited them. Franco's economic policies might have been designed for their recruiting purposes while the Generalissimo's habit of crying "Communist" whenever his regime was challenged gave prestige and popularity to their leadership. On top of this, the *Partido Comunista Español* was way ahead of its rivals in foreign support.

While Spain's democratic activists were hamstrung by Western backing for Franco, funds flowing into the Communists from Eastern Europe helped them to maintain many full-time party workers in the field, to produce their own newspaper and to meet other campaigning expenses. Daily broadcasts from the Communist "Radio Free Spain" in Czechoslovakia reached potential proselytes who would never have listened in a land where communications media were freely run.

Many youths, faced with an educational system which had

stagnated under Franco, were tempted with free places in the University of Prague and other Communist centers of learning. In short, the Spanish Communist Party, negligible in pre-Civil War Spain, had become, thanks to the Caudillo himself, the most powerful Leftist organization in the country and the strongest component of the workers' commissions. Its organizing capacity was manifest in the northern strike.

But dissent did not end with the Communists. One particularly aggravating factor for the general was the support given to the strikers by members of the clergy, "misguided and excitable priests," as Franco called them.

"There have been muliplying indications," one observer would write of the dictator's predicament, "that the Church, after the Army Franco's strongest prop, is trying to disengage itself from the regime . . ." Even the Bishops, nominated in Spain by Franco himself, were finding it hard to stay silent about social injustices.

Both the Bishop of Bilbao and the Archbishop of Seville publicly denounced the unjust distribution of wealth which persisted after a quarter of a century of dictatorship. The situation, asserted the Bishop, was more inequitable than that to be found in any other part of Europe.

In the Basque territories and elsewhere, parish priests lent their support to the strikers, some actually speaking at workers' meetings, while Church buildings were thrown open to strike organizers, often Communists.

This incongruous alliance between Marxists and Catholics can scarcely have comforted Franco, who, with the cost of the strike running at something like $300,000,000, finally stopped threatening and lured the men back to work with wage increase promises. It was a rare concession to popular action, but the Caudillo did not let it rest there.

At the same time, his police embarked on one of the largest purges of "trouble-makers" in Spain for a long time. Nearly a hundred strike leaders were jailed; other political opponents

were forcibly exiled to the Canaries or fled to Paris and elsewhere. Throughout the strike, the controlled Spanish press had
been obliged to blame Leftist agitators from Britain and
France.

Attacking the world's press afterward, Franco asserted: "The
case of Spain is a clear example of how people can be deceived. If there were a free press it would belong to a minority
of millionaires . . .

"Freedom of the press has passed into history!"

That summer he brooded lengthily over the disturbances,
then, at the year's end, decided to give the workers a Christmas present to forestall more troubles in the new year.

Accordingly, on New Year's Eve, 1963, Franco announced
that the minimum daily wage would be increased to eighty
pesetas (about a dollar and a quarter) which, he claimed, was
worth a hundred pesetas when sickness and holiday benefits
were added. For some unskilled workers it was a hundred
percent rise.

Though Franco's popularity rose appreciably for a while
among the fraction of the population affected, some eighteen
percent, the implications for dictatorship in Spain were ominous. The complacency of the regime had been shaken. Above
all, the strike had proved that the voice of the people could
still be heard. The army might safeguard the Caudillo from
insurrection, but a new note had been sounded among his
subjects and Franco would enter the closing years of his rule
to a mounting chorus of protest and dissent.

All the rifles and bludgeons in the land could not silence it.

14. Franco and the Future

The year 1966 opened dramatically for Franco's Spain. In January a B52 bomber of the United States Strategic Air Command collided in mid-air with a jet refueling aircraft and dropped four unarmed hydrogen bombs around the small village of Palomares on the arid southeastern coastland.

One bomb landed intact and was quickly recovered. Another plunged into the sea and was salvaged after a long search. The remaining two, falling close to the village, cracked open and spread their frightening contents on the dry earth.

In the multimillion dollar operation which followed, more than a thousand tons of contaminated soil was shipped to South Carolina for disposal at an atomic plant and five thousand more tons were buried in Spain itself. At Palomares, the working life of the farming and fishing community languished while scientists set up detector equipment. When twelve hundred inhabitants learned that medical checks would continue indefinitely, indignation was not confined to the vicinity.

Three years earlier, Franco had renegotiated terms for the American military stations in Spain on the basis of a closer alliance between the two governments. Many Spaniards, while recognizing the benefits for Franco's regime and the Pentagon, took a poor view of such a development.

Spanish resentment of foreign forces on Peninsula soil was historic, justified by the repeated use of Spain as a battle-

ground for conflicting and alien elements in the past. Moreover, after clinging resolutely to neutrality in the last two
European wars, few Spaniards relished becoming involved
in another one. For the majority, the shock of Palomares, disturbing even the complacent, inevitably hardened prejudice
against their rich and apparently dangerous visitors.

Conveniently for Franco, a ready-made diversion for anti-
foreign sentiment existed in the long-standing claim for Spanish rights to Gibraltar, and, as the second half of the sixties
went on, he overshadowed the issue of American bases by
promoting the dispute for the Rock. Gibraltar had passed
originally to the British in the early eighteenth century by the
Treaty of Utrecht, and Spaniards had been trying to recover
it ever since.

Franco had first joined the argument earnestly in the pages
of the Falange daily paper *Arriba*. Writing under the pseudo-
nym of "Macauley," the Caudillo based his case against the
British on three points: (1.) That the transference of Gibraltar
to Britain under the Treaty of Utrecht was illegal, Spain having been unrepresented during the relevant negotiations. (2.)
That George I of England had promised to return the Rock to
Spain a few years later. (3.) That Winston Churchill had
made a similar promise verbally during a luncheon at the
Spanish Embassy in London, 1940, his condition being Spain's
continuing wartime neutrality.

The first two points were of a legality so dated as to seem
distinctly remote in the space age. The third was more immediate. However, since it lacked documentation and was disputed by the British, it seemed unlikely it could ever be
proved either way.

In any case, modern weaponry developments had rendered
the Rock largely obsolete as a strategic stronghold, and the
place was of little other use to one side or the other. Indeed,
the devotion of the Gibraltarians to Great Britain was becoming an embarrassment to both governments.

The real value of Gibraltar to Franco was as an emotional issue on which he could rally the support of most Spaniards. On these grounds, admittedly, its value was considerable, particularly at a time when the Generalissimo's prestige needed bolstering.

Consequently, at intervals in the late sixties, Franco clamped down on border traffic with Gibraltar, prevented planes from its airport from using Spanish airspace and, eventually, enlisted the support of the United Nations—the organization he had once regarded with such disdain.

There was, of course, a limit to the credit to be won from this old cause. Dissatisfaction with the regime, if for the most part suppressed, was too profound to be obliterated by sidetracking tactics.

In January 1967, the Duchess of Medina Sidonia, a member of one of Spain's most illustrious families—a Duke of Medina Sidonia had commanded the Spanish Armada—was arrested for leading a protest on behalf of the welfare of Palomares villagers. The same month, Franco's police made a dawn raid on the offices of the weekly magazine *Actualidad Española*, confiscating 29,000 copies of an edition carrying a reasoned criticism of the lack of political options in the Spanish States. The Caudillo could argue that manifestations of protest in Spain were no greater than antigovernment demonstrations in many democratic countries, but illegality gave them a different significance.

Days after the raid on *Actualidad*, thousands of Madrid factory workers defied the regime to demonstrate for better pay and the establishment of independent unions. Employees streaming from the Barreiros car factory, Standard Eléctrica, the Perkins Hispania diesel works and other factories were charged by police as they chanted: "Union liberty! Union liberty!"

Many workers were arrested. Others fled across fields to escape. Meanwhile, at Madrid University, police were smash-

ing down the doors of the Faculty of Law in their attempts to
break up some eight hundred demonstrating students. A week
later, the students returned to the battle in an effort to obtain the release of their imprisoned compatriots. This time,
pitched battles with the police lasted six hours, the students
rallying to cries of "Freedom!" while Franco's forces responded
with bugle calls.

Already, the powerful surge of radicalism spreading not only
through Europe but in the U.S., especially among the young,
and which was to lead dramatically to General de Gaulle's
crisis of 1968, was beginning to wash around Franco's feet.
Despite the efficiency of its smothering in Franco's Spain, it
continued to disturb the foundations of the police state. Traditionalists were not slow to contribute to the general swell of
protest.

In Navarre that summer, agitation for the preservation of
the ancient and independent rights of the province, the
Fueros, was encouraged by a telegram of support from the
pretender Hugo Carlos.

Feeling reached a peak at the annual fiesta of Pamplona,
famous for the running of the bulls through the streets. Students taunted the central government by parading a miscellany of caricatures of political figures, a source of humor pro-
scribed by the establishment.

In one, the Minister due to open the fiesta by firing a
rocket was shown attached to the rocket by a stout rope. "To
the Moon!" read the caption. So intense was the atmosphere of
dissent that the Minister in question prudently failed to appear
for the ceremony. Instead, the secret police arrived to investigate.

Months later, a series of clashes between the authorities and
Basque Nationalist elements culminated in the murder at his
home in Irun of the chief of San Sebastian's secret police.
Franco, holiday-making at La Coruña, swiftly implemented
repressive measures in the area. Once more in Spain, military

sanctions and jurisdiction were brought to bear on a civilian populace.

Protesting in an outspoken pastoral letter, the Bishop of San Sebastian condemned the methods used by the Spanish police. Citing the examination of archives in religious houses, the arrest of priests and laymen and the "abusive use of force," he claimed that the 1953 Concordat with the Vatican had been violated by the regime.

Reasonably, the Bishop called for a new atmosphere in which all opinions might be expressed with "liberty, sincerity and clearness," and in which governors and governed might seek the most just and beneficial solutions for the community. There could be no doubt that as Franco grew older much of the Church, recognizing the danger of being linked with an unpopular and dying regime, was seeking a stand closer to the Spain of the future.

The pressing question was what, or who, would that future be?

In his seventies, Franco appeared to age suddenly. From the plump, chubby-faced figure of 1963, there had emerged by 1966 a man at last showing in feature and manner the trials and efforts of his long years in office. His face had lost flesh, the skin was sagging. His bald head, rimmed with gray, was hunched closer into his shoulders.

His public appearances, now rarer than ever, revealed a notable inability to maintain concentration. Amidst the private acres of El Pardo and elsewhere, the wild creatures roamed in less peril of his shotgun. The "little major" of his agile, equestrian years, had not ventured to mount a spirited horse for longer than he cared to remember.

Withdrawn, lacking close friends and real contact with the people, the small gray warrior found increasing time for his grandchildren, upon whom he doted, and doubtless for many reminiscences—memories of a remarkably calculated progression which led back to a frail child of fourteen, his hair cropped, his entire worldly possessions in a single bag, arriving at the officers training school in Toledo . . . "no longer a boy," as he put it, "but a man."

Memories of a mother's favorite spurred by his smallness and the bullying he endured at the Alcazar to work like a demon for higher rank. And of his disillusion on passing out with honors only to discover that social graces, drawing-room manners, were more prized in the regimental life of the Peninsula than the military theory and science he had studied so assiduously.

Amidst his subsequent flight into professionalism and action, one traumatic memory lingered in his recollections of later years: the seering nightmare of the road to Anual, where the eastern section of Spain's army in Morocco had been massacred.

Zeluan, Monte Arruit, Dar Drius, carnage everywhere . . . Corpses beheaded, disemboweled and castrated.

"There were," he would write in retrospect, "no tears left . . ."

The hardness, the ruthlessness that overtook Franco then, the brutalizing influences of those cruel wars, would eventually help sign the execution warrants of scores of thousands of prisoners during and after the Civil War. Meanwhile, a shrewd, compulsive young careerist, remembered singlemindedly outpacing his less resolute contemporaries to become the youngest general in Europe—"sniffing at glory as it might be at a flower."

The equal determination with which he pursued the girl of rank and beauty who became his partner, and who, now heavy with the pearls and bangles of her station, was still regal of appearance and comfortingly robust.

Memories of masters, Dictatorial, Monarchical and Republican, each given "Franquito's" allegiance so long as there was room for him to advance.

"I've been waiting. I've had people looking for you . . ."

Echoes of the voice of Diego Hidalgo, one-time Minister of War, as the October Revolution of 1934 burst on a jittery nation, and Franco coolly called in the only troops he could depend on, the Army of Africa, to subdue the Asturian miners.

Visions of at last reforming the outdated, demoralized military ranks of the Peninsula with the small general at their head. Then those fateful elections producing a Popular Front government. Franco's visions smashed.

Memories of a dramatic flight to Morocco, struggling from civilian clothes into uniform as Tetuán came into sight. Craned necks in the shuddering body of the small plane as the general and his companions sought to identify the waiting men on the landing strip. Franco's relieved voice:

"They are friends. It's all right."

A thousand memories of the projected coup d'etat that mushroomed into civil war, of the fortuitous deaths of his rivals for power, his calculating bid for supreme command of the Nationalist State, his flirtation with and ultimate abandonment of the Axis dictators who had aided him and his shrewd exploitation of the "cold war" of the fifties.

Moods shifting and changing: a coy, petulant Franco carping and hedging as Adolf Hitler thumped the table of a grandly furnished railway carriage at Hendaye; a defiant Franco after his rejection by the United Nations.

A bland, unhurried Franco screwing his full price from the United States government in return for air and naval bases in Spain.

No less than three decades of personal dictatorship, of a Spain ruled by the whims and talents of one man with, depending on which view one upheld, a blessed or outrageous flair for survival. And now a tiring Franco, nearing the end of his efforts, but still in the driving seat.

Undoubtedly, the Caudillo looked back with satisfaction. By his own standards, his work for "good" in Spain (i.e. the establishment and maintenance of discipline and traditional values) against "evil" (i.e. the varied efforts of the people to replace some of those values with something better) had been an immense success. Since he had seldom indulged in public promises, and such predictions as he had uttered had been cautiously ambiguous, it was very hard to measure Franco's achievement against his original intent.

Certainly, his attitude had mellowed to some extent. As long ago as 1956 he had granted independence to the Morocco Protectorate. True, he had been pushed toward it by French example, but for one who had staked his earliest claim to recognition by the fervor of his fight to retain Spanish power there, the step was no easy gesture.

In 1963, Franco had finally called a halt to trial by military tribunal for political offenses, though the practice was still imposed in emergencies. The new decade also saw the signing of cultural and trade agreements between Spain and countries in the Communist bloc, at least a nominal sign of new tolerance. "You cannot deny that Russian Communism succeeded in making Russia one of the world's most powerful nations," granted the pragmatic Generalissimo. "There must be some good in it."

Even the most vehement of his detractors had to concede that there had been "some good" in Franco's reign, as well. Parts of the country showed signs of positive prosperity. Encouraged by the peace and security upheld by the Nationalists, an unprecedented army of European tourists was turning the warm Mediterranean coast of Spain into an international playground. If it were a fickle boon in a business of fast-changing fashions, and if it brought with it some of the most tasteless speculative development on the Continent, it could not be denied that it put money in the pockets of a great many Spaniards.

In other aspects of the economy, achievement was less radical. Agricultural and industrial output, though rising, continued in the main to reflect outdated methods. In agriculture especially, modernization posed the problem of heavy unemployment. Planning, therefore, had been based largely on long-term results.

In the reapportioning of land, its sale to peasant farmers on a twenty-year basis and the establishment of industrial training institutes, among other measures, Franco looked to the future. The doubt remained that such progress would keep ahead of rising prices and a growing population.

Meanwhile, despite a spreading and relatively well-to-do middle-class, the mass of people was still inordinately poor by Western standards. Even among the middle-class, many people maintained appearances by doing two jobs.

Franco, depending on the innate endurance-capacity of the ordinary Spaniard, and the horrific memory of civil strife, was alternately sanguine and chastening. "We have created a Spain on her way to higher achievements," he told the nation in 1966.

"It will not be difficult, given our present accomplishments and modern technology, to obtain improved material standards. But do not forget that all things material are superficial, and if we are unable to maintain unity, faith, and solidarity, the process will fall victim of inanity and disorder.

"Let Spaniards remember that each nation is a prey to its particular furies . . . Spain's furies are the anarchical spirit, negative criticism, extremism, and mutual enmity. Any political system which fosters these defects in its bosom will sooner or later—and probably sooner—wreak havoc on all improvements in the lives of our citizens . . .

"Abstract political formulas mean little, and have no value until reflected in the personality of the citizen. Every nation must find the formula most adequate to the needs of its temperament."

For thirty years Franco had pursued his own formula: the philosophy of the practical militarist and patriot, unfettered by ideology, discussion, or argument. His insignia, the yoke-and-arrow symbol of the Catholic Sovereigns, purported to underline its pedigree, and certainly the regime had reflected at least the despotism of the old kings. To a turbulent and divided Spain, it had brought a remarkably long spell of public peace.

But how deep was that peace; how real the "unity, faith and solidarity"? How adequate to modern needs was the Caudillo's long-term social program and his insistence on the inevitability of gradualness? Most urgent of all questions—that which had bedeviled Spain and her absolutist systems so often—what would happen when the one man above all men was gone?

It was a problem at which even Franco gibed. "Providence will provide for Spain when I go," the Caudillo had once declared.

Again, slyly: "I have never bothered with politics."

It is a considerable paradox that the Spanish, who prize above most people the idea of personal independence, have suffered the rule of despots for so many centuries that they have had little chance to learn to live responsibly in political freedom. On the few occasions when they have found themselves with a free choice of government, the very intoxication of the situation has resulted in a confusion of separatist factions, plagued by what Franco called the "furies" of fanaticism and uncompromising enmity.

"The greatest requirement for democratic freedom in Spain," asserted one historian, "is a fair chance to practice—to practice, that is, without the inevitable mistakes bringing down an avalanche of revolution from the Right or the Left."

Or from both. The brave, if unpracticed, Republican experiment of the thirties was betrayed by the inexcusable impatience of the Socialists, who took arms in the Revolution of 1934, *and* by the generals in 1936, whose rebellion had even more horrific consequences.

But it had all happened before. Every time Spain, seeking to emulate the great eighteenth-century liberation movements of France and North America, began to ferment with ideas of liberty and civil freedom, some reactionary had appeared to put the cork, as it were, on the bottle.

By a fateful whim of history, when ordinary Spaniards made their splendid bid for freedom at the beginning of the following century, a spontaneous rising through the length of the Peninsula, it was of necessity directed against the intruder Napoleon and not their own decadent monarchs. Scarcely had the exhausted partisans time to hail a people's victory when Ferdinand VII, the unscrupulous son of the family which had sold the country to the emperor, returned from comfortable retreat to plunge the stopper on their hard-won liberty.

Henceforward, through the strong-arm tactics of Narváez and his fellow generals of the eighteenth century, through the manipulations of Canovas and the complaisant opposition of Sagasta, to the dictator Primo de Rivera, and finally Franco, political evolution in Spain had been retarded by a series of corking operations.

Like many dictators, General Franco not excluded, Spain's strong men had been patriotic and well-intentioned. Such men believed that by enforcing law and order at gunpoint it would become habitual, and that by suppressing dissent it would wither and die. Then, from the turbulence of the nation would emerge a general's dream: the true State of contentment, unity and discipline.

"What Franco and his forerunners failed to appreciate," according to one Spanish liberal, "is that enduring order is not born in frustration; that suppression must make eventually for eruption."

Each time a Narváez or a Franco came to power, Spaniards of intellect, vision and moderation began to opt out of politics, seeking more fertile fields for their talents. At the same time, the more committed elements of opposition, denied legal activity and emotional outlet, grew increasingly fanatical. Each emergence from a period of dictatorship found them less adaptable to constitutional government.

The dictators claimed they were gaining time for moderation and reason to develop. History, some impartial observers pointed out, suggested they were creating conditions for the very opposite. Certainly, thirty years of Franco's rule had erased neither separatism nor latent revolt from the country. Basque Nationalism was so virulent that martial law had had to be declared in the north. Workers were increasingly defying the law by striking and demonstrating. Communism was more organized in Spain than ever before the Civil War, while the Anarchists, if less numerous than at one time, were still active. All this regardless of the fact that hundreds of thousands of Franco's enemies had been killed in the Civil War and its aftermath.

Nor could the Generalissimo hope that better standards of living would bring relief from the protests. The poorest of Spaniards were too busy surviving to make trouble. Ironically, it was those better treated by Franco's system, the relatively well-paid industrial workers and the student sons of comfortable people, who demonstrated and rioted. There looked like some heavy work ahead for the police.

In September 1968, when Portugal's aging chieftain Antonio de Oliveira Salazar had a stroke and his place was taken by his close associate Marcello Caetano, Franco became both Europe's longest-ruling dictator and the next natural candidate for the exit. Unlike Salazar he had no obvious successor. So cautiously had the Caudillo shuffled his Ministers and balanced the strengths of the interests which supported him that an heir apparent had had no chance to emerge from his subjects.

Theoretically, a Regency Council would be established when Franco passed, but the likelihood of a Monarch appearing with Franco's capacities for ruling was improbable.

Among large sections of the populace, the appeal of the Monarchy had eroded, while the days when the Falange might have dominated the government had long passed.

Since then, a new force, *Opus Dei,* had attracted increasing attention throughout Spain, its members gaining some significant technical offices. An influential Right-wing religious order for laymen, *Opus Dei* had played an important part in effecting the stabilization plan of 1959 and in making the new economy work.

With the sixties, Franco had brought into his government such *Opus Dei* stalwarts as Minister of Commerce Ullastres Calvo, Minister of Finance Navarro Rubio, Minister of Industry Bravo de Castro and Commissioner of the Four Year Plan López Rodó. People talked of a powerful new caucus. As servants of government, *Opus Dei* members had the merit of being efficient and honest. There was, however, no evidence of a future Franco among them.

Indeed, at precisely the time Franco appointed his *Opus Dei* Ministers, he elevated an old military trusty, General Muñoz Grandes, to the post of Vice-Premier, and gave important government positions to two other conservative officers, Vice-Admiral Nieto Antúñez and Vice-Admiral Carrero Blanco.

When all was said and done, the armed forces were still there, the one unchallengeable power Franco would bequeath to the nation.

If it wished, the Spanish Army could undoubtedly force any government of its choosing upon the people of the country, just as it had forced Spain to accept General Franco. Yet the army, while traditionally political, was not an ideology. It had hailed Franco as a leader who had perhaps done more for its morale and welfare than any man in a century, but that did not guarantee its behavior when he had gone. In the past two hundred years it had produced radicals and reactionaries with remarkable fickleness.

Only one thing was certain. Sooner or later, the Spanish

people would assert the yearning of all people to be rid of despotic government. If, when that happened, they moved peacefully and fraternally to political liberty, Franco's era of paternalism might seem justified in the eyes of history.

If, on the other hand, the decades of frustration and denied responsibility left them no better able to control their destiny than in the days before he seized power, the small general would have failed Spain—as so many before him.

Selected Bibliography

The following list of works on Franco, his times and the historical background, is suggested to the general English-language reader sufficiently interested by this book to read further.

The first requirement for a better understanding of the Franco era in Spain is some over-all appreciation of Spanish history. Alan Lloyd's narrative history of Spain, *The Spanish Centuries*, New York, Doubleday, 1968, was specially written for those seeking a simple orientation in the complex drama of Spain's past, her outstanding personalities and national character. The book contains a wide-ranging bibliography of works in English, Spanish, and other languages.

Among other handy, single-volume Spanish histories, W. C. Atkinson's *History of Spain and Portugal*, London, Penguin, 1960, is lucid and concise, while *A History of Spain* by Rafael Altamira, translated by Muna Lee, provides a short history by a Spanish-born writer.

Moving from broader history to the modern scene, a number of works serve as excellent introductions to the period which produced the Civil War and the regime of General Franco. *Spain* by Salvador de Madariaga, New York, Scribners, and London, Jonathan Cape (2nd edition), 1942, has both the urbanity and commitment of one who is not only an eminent liberal historian but probably the most readable of all Spanish writers on the subject.

Again, *The Spanish Labyrinth* by Gerald Brenan, New York, Macmillan, and London, Cambridge, 1943, provides a perceptive view of an indeed labyrinthine situation by a Spanish-domiciled writer with a deep feeling for Spain and her people, while *Spain 1808–1939* by Raymond Carr, Oxford, O.U.P., 1966, contributes a scholarly survey of Spain from the year of the great popular revolt against Napoleon.

The best general history of the Civil War is *The Spanish Civil War* by Hugh Thomas, New York, Harper, and London, Eyre and Spottiswood, 1961, an exciting and thorough reconstruction of the whole episode by one who writes with both objectivity and heart. This book may be usefully supplemented by Brian Crozier's *Franco: a Biographical History*, New York, Little, Brown, and London, Eyre and Spottiswood, 1967—equally scholarly and interesting as a compilation of data for Franco's period by a discriminating writer with a sympathetic spot for the Generalissimo.

With some such brief introduction behind him, the reader new to modern Spanish history can move with a measure of awareness among the ubiquitous pitfalls of prejudice and partisanship which characterize the bulk of memoirs, commentaries and eyewitness accounts of the Franco period.

The short selection which follows includes many shades of political opinion, from the uninhibited pro-Republic sympathies of such as Claude G. Bowers, U. S. Ambassador to Spain at the outbreak of the Civil War, to the trenchant Nationalist viewpoint of such as Luis Bolin, one-time official Press officer to Franco.

ALTAMIRA, RAFAEL. *History of Spain.* trans. Muna Lee. New York: Van Nostrand, 1949.

ALVAREZ DEL VAYO, J. *Freedom's Battle.* New York: Knopf, and London: Heinemann, 1940.

ARRARÁS, JOAQUÍN. *Franco.* London: Geoffrey Bles, 1938.

ATKINSON, W. C. *History of Spain and Portugal.* London: Penguin, 1960.

BAHAMONDE, ANTONIO. *Memoirs of a Spanish Nationalist.* London: United Editorial, 1939.

BAREA, ARTURO. *The Clash.* London: Faber, 1946.

BOLIN, LUIS. *Spain: the Vital Years.* London: Cassel, 1967.

BOLLOTEN, B. *The Grand Camouflage.* London: Hollis and Carter, 1961.

BORKENAU, FRANZ. *The Spanish Cockpit*. London: Faber, 1937.

BOWERS, CLAUDE G. *My Mission to Spain*. New York: Simon and Schuster, and London: Gollancz, 1954.

BRANDT, J. A. *Toward the New Spain*. Chicago: University of Chicago Press, 1933.

BRENAN, GERALD. *The Spanish Labyrinth*. New York: Macmillan, and London: Cambridge, 1943.

BRERETON, G. *Inside Spain*. London: Quality Press, 1938.

BUCKLEY, H. *Life and Death of the Spanish Republic*. London: Hamish Hamilton, 1940.

CARR, RAYMOND. *Spain 1808–1939*. Oxford: O.U.P., 1966.

CASADO, SEGISMUNDO. *The Last Days of Madrid*. trans. R. Croft-Cooke. London: Peter Davies, 1939.

CASTILLEJO, J. *Wars of Ideas in Spain*. London, John Murray, 1937.

CATTELL, D. T. *Communism and the Spanish Civil War*. Berkeley: California University Press, 1955.

COCKBURN, CLAUD. *Discord of Trumpets: an Autobiography*. New York: Simon and Schuster, and London: Hart-Davis (under title *In Time of Trouble*), 1956.

COLES, S. F. A. *Franco of Spain*. London: Neville Spearman, 1955.

CROZIER, BRIAN. *Franco, a Biographical History*. New York: Little, Brown, and London: Eyre and Spottiswood, 1967.

DUNDAS, L. *Behind the Spanish Mask*. New York: Transatlantic, and London: Hale, 1943.

ESPINOZA, A. M. *The Second Spanish Republic and the Causes of the Counter Revolution*. San Francisco: Spanish Relief Committee, 1937.

FARMBOROUGH, F. *Life and People in Nationalist Spain*. London: Sheed and Ward, 1938.

FEIS, H. *The Spanish Story*. New York: Knopf, 1948.

FOLTZ, CHARLES. *The Masquerade in Spain*. Boston: Houghton Mifflin, 1948.

FONTERIZ, L. DE. *The Red Terror in Madrid*. London: Longmans, Green, 1937.

HAYES, CARLTON J. H. *Wartime Mission in Spain*. New York: Macmillan, 1945.

HOARE, S. J. G. (Viscount Templewood). *Ambassador on Special Mission.* London: Collins, 1946.

HODGSON, SIR ROBERT. *Spain Resurgent.* London, Hutchinson, 1953.

HUGHES, E. *Report from Spain.* New York: Holt, and London: Latimer House, 1947.

HULL, CORDELL. *Memoirs.* New York: Macmillan, and London: Hodder, 1948.

KNICKERBOCKER, H. R. *The Siege of the Alcazar.* New York: McKay, 1936, and London: Hutchinson, 1938.

KNOBLAUGH, H. E. *Correspondent in Spain.* London: Sheed and Ward, 1937.

KOESTLER, ARTHUR. *Spanish Testament.* London: Gollancz, 1937.

LAST, J. *The Spanish Tragedy.* London: Routledge, 1939.

LLOYD, ALAN. *The Spanish Centuries.* New York: Doubleday, 1968.

MADARIAGA, SALVADOR DE. *Spain.* New York: Scribners, and London: Jonathan Cape (2nd edition), 1942.

MATTHEWS, HERBERT L. *The Yoke and the Arrows.* New York: George Braziller, Inc., and London: Heinemann, 1958.

MCCULLAGH, F. *In Franco's Spain.* London: Burns, Oates and Washbourne, 1937.

MCKEE, SEUMAS. *I Was a Franco Soldier.* London: United Editorial, 1938.

MORA, CONSTANCIÂ DE LA. *In Place of Splendour.* London: Michael Joseph, 1940.

ORWELL, GEORGE. *Homage to Catalonia.* London: Secker and Warburg, 1938.

PAYNE, ROBERT. *The Civil War in Spain.* London: Secker and Warburg, 1962.

PAYNE, S. G. *Falange.* California: Stanford University Press, 1961, and London: O.U.P., 1962.

PEERS, A. E. *The Spanish Dilemma.* London: Methuen, 1940.

"PITCAIRN, FRANK." (Claud Cockburn) *Reporter in Spain.* London: Lawrence and Wishart, 1940.

RAMOS OLIVEIRA, A. *Politics, Economics and Men of Modern Spain.* London: Gollancz, 1946.

ROLFE, EDWIN. *The Lincoln Battalion.* New York: Random House, 1939.

RUIZ VILLEPLANA, A. *Burgos Justice.* trans. W. Horsfall-Carter. New York: Knopf, and London: Constable, 1938.

SENDER, RAYMOND J. *The War in Spain.* trans. Sir P. C. Mitchell. London: Faber, 1937.

SMITH, R. M. *The Day of the Liberals in Spain.* Philadelphia: University of Pennsylvania, 1938.

———— *Spain.* Michigan: University of Michigan Press, 1965.

THOMAS, HUGH. *The Spanish Civil War.* New York: Harper, and London: Eyre and Spottiswood, 1961.

THOMPSON, SIR GEORGE. *Front Line Diplomat.* London: Hutchinson, 1959.

TREND, J. B. *The Origins of Modern Spain.* New York: Macmillan, 1934.

WELLES, BENJAMIN. *Spain: the Gentle Anarchy.* New York: Praeger, and London: Pall Mall, 1965.

WORSLEY, T. C. *Behind the Battle.* London: Hale, 1939.

Index

Printed in the United States
by Baker & Taylor Publisher Services